Thirty Years in Deep Freeze

Thirty Years in Deep Freeze

My Life in Communist China

Ching-chih Yi-ling Wong

FITHIAN PRESS, S∕

Published by Fithian Press
A division of Daniel and Daniel, Publishers, Inc.
Post Office Box 1525
Santa Barbara, CA 93102
www.danielpublishing.com

LIBRARY OF CONGRESS CATALOGING-IN-PUBLICATION DATA
Wong, Ching-chih Yi-ling, 1933–
  Thirty years in deep freeze : my life in communist China / by Ching-chih Yi-ling
Wong.
    p.; cm.
Includes index.
ISBN 1-56474-333-0
1. Wong, Ching-chih Yi-ling, 1933– 2. China—Biography. 3. China—History—
1949—Biography.   I. Title.
CT1828.W66 A3 2000
951.05'092—dc21   99-050457
[B]

Dedicated to the

"great, glorious and infallible"

Chinese Communist Party,

without whose long-term

love, concern, education, protection

and persecution the production of this book

would have been impossible

Contents

Preface

Today it is June 15, 1999.

I was born on June 15, 1933.

But I consider myself thirty-six.

All these three statements are true as steel, because I vow to tell you the truth, nothing else but the truth.

If asked, "1999 minus 1933 is sixty-six, not thirty-six. Why the thirty years difference?" I would like to tell you that as far as I am concerned, the thirty years between 1949 and 1979 do not count. Here's why.

When the Nationalist Kuomintang (KMT) government of China retreated to Taiwan and the Communists took over, or, as they were fond of phrasing it, "liberated" the mainland on which I was staying, I was only a teenager. I had no choice but to involuntarily accept the baptism of liberation. I spent thirty years of my life in the "socialist heaven" until I finally left China in 1979 for good.

It was very inappropriate for me to live under a totalitarian regime. Although I was never an anti-Communist or a counterrevolutionary, I felt totally incompatible with that environment in every aspect of my life over those thirty years.

There is a half-truth in one of the folk songs popular in mainland China which goes like this:

Just as fish cannot leave water and
Flowers cannot be separated from their seedlings,
So the revolutionary masses should always be one
with the Communist Party.

However, it ignores the other half-truth. What about some of the masses who dislike and do not want revolution at all?

Take myself. I hated rebellion and despised the stirring and "heroic" undertakings of a great revolution. All I wanted was to live in a stable society with certain rules and laws. Communists claim that all societies other than that of socialism are under the system of exploitation. If that is the case, I do not even mind being exploited, as long as I have the freedom to speak, to write, and to express myself. I am not a fish, but a bird. In water, I may be suffocated; I desperately need air and like to fly above the earth across the expanse of the sky. I do not want to be a flower and care much less about seedlings. I want desperately the freedom of self-expression. I have never been able to keep in line with the Communists.

Forcing me to live under the rule of communism not only made me suffer, the Communists suffered, too. They knew very well that I was never their man, though it always appeared that I was a youth with plasticity. On the other hand, I deliberately refrained from any confrontation with Communists in order to keep my viability under their regime. I wasted thirty years trying to survive, while the Communists wasted their time and energy trying to remold me ideologically.

Thank God, I was finally able to leave. But I should also thank the Communist Party for its "open policy." By taking advantage of it, I finally jostled out of the so-called socialist heaven in 1979. To the Communist Party, my departure must have been a sort of relief from a burden; for me, all I was deprived of was no more than invisible fetters and shackles. Therefore, my departure benefited both sides. What is regrettable is that it came too late, after thirty years. How many thirty years does one have in one's lifetime?

Worst of all, when I reached this mundane world from the "secluded heaven," I discovered that almost every one of my peers who had never had the "luck" of baking under the Red sun had received ample education and had made outstanding achievements. Compared to them, I found myself inadequate. In our competitive society, time is money and youth is gold. I did feel inferior, but I mustered the courage to catch up to them.

Then how should I deal with the lost thirty years?

The "freezer" provided me an inspiration. The metabolic process of foods can be prolonged by storing them in the freezer. By analogy, the thirty years that were wasted in the "socialist heaven" could be counted as a freezing period, or as a period during which I was nonexistent. That would be fair. With this new insight, I engraved a seal for myself as my proclamation, on which ran the Chinese characters: "Thirty years in deep freeze count naught."

Though the thirty years should not constitute part of my age, they should be faithfully recounted as part of human history. Hence this book.

Ching-chih Yi-ling Wong
California

Acknowledgments

It is almost impossible to thank one by one all the people who have helped with the writing of this book. I owe the idea of writing it to a friend who was later to become my supervisor. At the end of our first meeting in January 1980, just after I first I set foot on American soil, he suggested that I write down my past experiences so that they would not sink into oblivion. It was a good idea. Since then, I have contributed articles to various newspapers and magazines as a free-lance writer.

Dr. Marcus Konick, professor of English emeritus of Lock Haven University in Pennsylvania, read my whole manuscript and offered many valuable opinions and constant encouragement. I benefited enormously from his scholarly comments on the earlier version of this book, but I am not sure whether the present version will meet his standards.

I am especially indebted to Shirley E. Stephenson, oral historian, archivist, editor emeritus at California State University, Fullerton, who meticulously edited this book.

While acknowledging the above-said valuable contributions, I must take the blame for any inaccuracies or mistakes I have made.

Thirty Years in Deep Freeze

CHAPTER I

Debate on the Eve of Doomsday

TIME AND TIDE COME AND GO. Numerous waves in the long, long river of life disappeared amid incessant torrents as though nothing had happened. Few things in one's life carve deep into memory as vivid and fresh as right at this moment. However, one thing will never be erased from my memory, no matter how many years pass by. This was the soul-stirring debate in my family on the eve of judgment. Actually, it was not a debate. It was only a familial get-together and a casual, informal exchange of views among family members. No red faces. No heated arguments. At that time I did not find it very impressive and I never intentionally memorized it, but it has never faded from my memory over the last few decades.

It happened at the turn of 1948 in Shanghai. That was an extraordinarily cold winter. People were irritable not only because of cold, but out of trepidation and panic as well. As a teenager, blessed with my elders' protection, I never had to worry about food, clothing, and other mundane matters. Besides the daily routine and attending school, I enjoyed practicing calligraphy and carving seals. These were all I cared for. Enclosing myself in an ivory tower, I had very little interest in politics and worldly affairs. But even such a child was not immune to anxiety about the calamity that was to befall our entire society. Turbulence could be inhaled in my little ivory tower.

That was the period of internecine duel between the Nationalists and the Communists right after the victory of the Resistance War against Japan. The clamor of the fireworks celebrating the triumph over Japan was almost connected with that of the gunfire of the civil struggle, while the public hilarity of envisioning piping times of peace and prosperity gave way to their fear and anxiety about the oncoming tremendous change.

China, still under Nationalist rule at that time, was torn by what General George C. Marshall called "embezzlement, corruption and ineffectiveness." Unbridled and rampant inflation made life difficult for almost everybody. Complaints about daily life and apprehension about what was going to happen could be heard all the time among my elders. These lively discussions seemed to lead to one common conclusion: the Nationalists were losing the civil war and the Communists were going to come to power. There was no doubt about this situation. But on how to deal with this inevitability, there were differences of opinion. Rumors emerged endlessly. The Nationalists always labeled the Communists a group of devils sharing all the property and each other's wives. On the other hand, many intellectuals, especially the so-called progressive figures or patriotic personages—terms very cleverly concocted by the Communist propagandists to prettify those intellectuals—followed the Communist way of depicting the Chinese Communist Party as the only hope for China, and Marxism as the ultimate truth. They saw the Communist takeover as a process of liberation. Hence, so-called "liberated areas" were areas occupied by the Communists. A popular song in vogue at that time said, "The sky in liberated areas is always bright; people in the liberated areas are always happy." Most of the middle class, who had totally lost faith in the Nationalists, did not trust Communists either. They were very much puzzled about their future, just like criminals awaiting a verdict.

Conversations among the elders in my family, from both my paternal and maternal sides, during this period were often concentrated on the topic of leaving or staying put. But it seemed that no matter how many times they discussed this topic, they were as uncertain as ever.

In the society as a whole, there were people longing for liberation and expecting the arrival of the Communist regime. But among my paternal and maternal kin, only Uncle Hung, my mother's younger half-brother, had this opinion. Being just three years older than I, he treated me as his small playmate while my family lived in my maternal grandfather's house. Uncle Hung was one of the brightest students in his elementary and junior high schools. But he had liked politics even when he was a young kid. The heroes he was crazy about were invariably the men of the hour. First he adored Generalissimo Chiang Kai-shek. My maternal grandfather, as an adamant political opponent to Chiang, used to make bitter remarks against Chiang, and Uncle Hung, though still a small child, always contradicted him.

Later, in the high days of World War II, he added to his list of icons Hideki Tojo and Adolph Hitler. As other children played games of dollhouse as usual, we, under the leadership of Uncle Hung, played games of powerhouse, and I was instructed to hail him with the Nazi salute. At the end of World War II, he still did exceedingly well in his studies at school and managed to enter the best senior high school in Shanghai. But before long, he fell prey to the so-called progressive influence and underwent a tremendously extreme change in ideology. He devoted himself to the Communist revolution and cared less and less about studying. He quit the first-class high school and enrolled instead in several lower-grade schools with loose discipline. He became a professional student, a euphemism for those underground Communists camouflaged as students.

When Uncle Hung joined the task force to pull down what they called the "Chiang Dynasty" and erect a "new China," he went so far as to attempt to put me to death. It came about like this: My mother's father, though a famous lawyer, was a poor manager in matters of money and died almost penniless in 1947 when quite a few of his children, including Uncle Hung, were still underage. Thanks to the long-term friendship between my maternal grandfather and paternal grandfather, the latter worked out a foundation for the former's children's tuition fees and living allowances, and Uncle Hung was one of the beneficiaries. My mother, as these beneficiaries' elder half-sister, had the obligation to execute the foundation and direct them onto the right path. It was only natural that my paternal grandfather and my parents vehemently objected to Uncle Hung's neglect of his serious studies at school. But Uncle Hung firmly resisted their objection and, before he finally went underground, declared, "One day, when we liberate Shanghai, the first thing I want to do is to sentence all the Wongs to death."

On the other hand, among all my relatives, few resolved or prepared to flee China before the Communist takeover. Strictly speaking, only Auntie Doreen, my father's sister, and her husband did. Before them, Uncle Paul, my mother's brother, and his wife, Auntie Margaret, had gone to the United States, but that was due to Uncle Paul being offered a job there as an alumnus of the Massachusetts Institute of Technology. In this sense they did not really flee China. Still earlier, Uncle Sunyuan, my father's younger brother, had gone to study in the United States.

It would be more accurate to say that the majority of my relatives on both paternal and maternal sides stayed put and accepted the baptism of liberation, having no alternative. This kind of feeling might be represented by my grandfather. Then in his late sixties, Grandfather was determined to stay put. As a retired director of the official Bank of Communications and a member of the elite who had intimate connections with the leaders of the Nationalists, he had easy access to the re-treaters to Taiwan. But he refused to go there. For one thing, he was very disappointed with the unsuccessful rule of the Nationalists. During that period I often heard him say with a sigh, "I am expecting the Communists' arrival in a mood of putting some arsenic into my body to be swallowed by the tiger." Unlike those Chinese elders who used to favor several generations living under one roof, my grandfather believed in small family systems and had all his sons and daughters live independently with their spouses and children. However, he derived much pleasure from frequent visits from his children and grandchildren. I heard his above-quoted remarks again and again during this period. My parents took the same attitude. "What else can we choose, since the Nationalist regime is so corrupt?" Not impressed by the cheap slogans of progressive students, they were struck by the news being spread by the underground Communists that the Communist Party was going to implement the New Democratic Policy, whereby the urban capitalist status quo would be respected and remain unchanged. While half believing and half doubting, they were inclined to stay put.

It was at this time and in this atmosphere that Uncle Ramsey,

Left to right: my grandfather and two of his best friends, the famous painter T'ang Ting-chih and the famous writer Chen Tao-yi.

My mother (left) and my Auntie Doreen (right).

another brother of my mother, arrived in Shanghai from the newly "liberated" Peking. He was then in his thirties, and had served as a senior clerk in the Bureau of Postal Reservation in Peking for several years. Now, at the end of 1948, he had given up his job and left Peking after one month's experience of Communist rule. He and his wife were always very close to my mother. So when they arrived in Shanghai, they stayed with us. At that time, my mother was a housewife and my father Deputy Director of the Shanghai branch of the Bank of Communications. As a comparatively well-off household, our house had been packed with guests almost every evening for several years, and now it was even more crowded because of the arrival of Uncle Ramsey and Auntie Kay, his wife. But not bustling with fun and excitement as before, our house was now permeated with an atmosphere of anxiety. Relatives and friends tried to seek first-hand information about Communist rule from someone they knew, hoping to hear something other than propaganda.

Outside, the bitterly cold wind chilled us to the bone. Inside, we all sat around the dining table by the side of the fireplace. Sipping some wine and immersed in happy reunion with relatives and friends, Uncle

Ramsey was in an exalted mood with a zest for talk. He answered all the questions and even talked without being asked. The first thing each of us was eager to know was how the Communists managed in their territory. For example, people inquired about the rumor of "Communists sharing all the property and each other's wives." To this question, Uncle Ramsey's answer somewhat astonished us all, "No such thing. It may have happened in some backward rural areas once upon a time. I can't tell when. So far as I know, they are not doing this kind of thing now. On the contrary, they are pursuing a policy that protects private property. The Communist soldiers are strictly disciplined, and I have never seen or heard of any rape or pillage done by the Liberation Army. If they borrow something from you, they are sure to return it."

It seemed incredible. The propaganda at that time about the Communists sharing property and each other's wives was abundant and incessant. Now we knew from someone we could trust that all this propaganda was nonsense. To say the least, I was rather confused and angry at having been deceived by those propagandists.

Someone asked about inflation, a major nightmare in Shanghai during those days when prices not only skyrocketed but fluctuated every day, even every hour. People rushed to the market immediately after they got their salaries to purchase some commodities, because a few hours' delay would make the money they earned shrink tremendously. The Nationalist government had tried all its means, reforming its currency again and again, with only disastrous results for the common people. There was some hope when Chiang Ching-kuo had a close relative of his step-mother arrested, who had been engaged in unscrupulous smuggling and embezzlement. But when Chiang Ching-kuo's campaign, impeded by his step-mother, Chiang Soong Mei-ling, ended in a fiasco, prices ran wild. Thus, Uncle Ramsey's words exploded in our ears, "I believe the Communists can surely control inflation."

"Are you saying that prices are stable in Peking now?"

"When I left there, prices were still moving upward. But this is a legacy of former inflation. I have the feeling that the Communists have already brought it under control, and I am pretty sure that they will be able to stop inflation quite soon." Uncle Ramsey spoke with curt finality like a specialist. Having majored in economics in London, he seemed confident.

When asked about the personnel of the old regime who were kept on after liberation—Uncle Ramsey himself fell into this category—he just answered by relating his own experience.

"It is the Communists' policy that all the personnel of the old institutions should remain in office. I was not an exception, and was given the same position with the same grade on the wage scale. But I had nothing to do. Fortunately, the foreign library in our neighborhood was still open. I borrowed books from that library every day, and read two books a day. The French librarian was astonished at the speed of my reading."

"How come the Communists put up with you reading books all day without doing any job, while getting your salary as usual?" someone asked.

"It's not I who did not want to work," replied Uncle Ramsey, "it's they who did not have anything for me to do. So they not only put up with my reading, but were very polite to me."

At this point someone mentioned that it had been widely said that the Communist officials were fierce as devils. Uncle Ramsey said, "I have never encountered fiend-like officials. Communist officials have a common peculiarity: they are good at talking about principles and theories. At least outwardly, they pose as reasonable people. Of course, I did not have too much contact with them, and never offended them. And, as I observed, the Communists are more patient with the young people." Then Uncle Ramsey turned to me, "Kids like Yi-ling who had no relationship with the old regime and whose personal histories appear to be pure and clean to the Communists don't have to worry too much about their behavior in the presence of Communist officials. Even if you strike the table before them, they might still be tolerant toward you."

Uncle David, the eldest brother of my mother and Uncle Ramsey, asked bluntly, "I am really puzzled by your leaving them for good. Since, according to what you said, the Communists have the ability to control prices and maintain strict discipline, and most important of all, they let you keep your original job and did nothing to hurt you and even were very polite to you, why didn't you continue to stay there? What made you quit the job and flee?"

Uncle Ramsey was not offended, nor was he able to explain

explicitly. Opening wide his prominent myopic eyes, with contact lenses which he had acquired in Germany at the end of the 1930s, he replied forcefully and complacently to his eldest brother, "Well, first of all, what I have talked about was all happening right during this period. Who knows what will develop later? Secondly, I just feel the Communists are not human beings, at least they are not human beings in the usual sense."

"Well, if only they can run our country well, what's wrong with that?" Uncle David objected.

"I am not arguing about right or wrong. Be they right or wrong, they are not human beings," retorted Uncle Ramsey.

Apparently not satisfied with Uncle Ramsey's reply, Uncle David challenged, "Do you really put your faith in the Nationalists, who you think would be able to change things?"

"That's none of my business. I couldn't care less," Uncle Ramsey declared. "There is only one point which is clear enough to me, and is that living in a place under the rule of the Communists is just unbearable for a human being."

Uncle David retorted, "Come on. All you have told us about the Communist rule and your own experience under it does not reveal anything unpleasant. What on earth made it unbearable to you? I really can't understand why you left there."

Uncle Ramsey made a last effort to explain. "All I have just told you are facts. But are these conditions sufficient for human beings to live a decent life? No. Let me tell you another anecdote which is also true. After I left Peking, I could not go directly to Shanghai. I had to take a route to a place under the control of the Nationalists, where I came across a newspaper published by this side. It was the first time in a month of seclusion in the Communist area that I had the chance to read it. I suddenly felt this kind of newspaper meant so much to me that I read the paper word for word and could not put it down, just as when one gets a glass of juice after a long, desperate thirst."

These remarks stunned almost all the audience, including me. At that time, ordinary people had a general aversion to the pro-Nationalist news media, which was untrustworthy. For example, it was a well-known fact in those days that the Nationalist army was suffering a crushing defeat under the fierce offensive of the Communists, but the pro-Nationalist media did not dare to tell the truth and coined a new and incomprehensible terminology using "shift-proceed" in place of some clear and plain terms such as "retreat," "disperse," and "escape." By using the newly coined term "shift-proceed," they tried to convey an impression that the Nationalists were still advancing. This was really misleading. It was unimaginable that this kind of newspaper could capture Uncle Ramsey's trust.

Uncle Ramsey might have discerned our doubts. Shaking his head slightly, he said with a sigh, "It's impossible for you to understand at this point. Formerly, I, myself, was also suspicious of these newspapers. It was only after a full month of seclusion in the Communist area without any access to these papers that I began to feel how precious they were. You might well have sufficient reason to be dissatisfied with these papers now, but I am sure you will miss them later when you are fed solely with Communist papers. These two kinds of newspapers are totally different and beyond comparison."

As this was but a gathering among close relatives, of course, no conclusion or resolution was needed. It is hard to tell whether or not Uncle Ramsey convinced anybody at that time, but it was certain that he had not been persuaded to stay. Several days later, he and Auntie Kay took their newborn son, waved farewell to the land where they had been born and brought up, and bade goodbye to all the relatives who were reluctant to give up their temporarily passable life. At the moment of their departure, neither he nor any of the relatives could have predicted that the separation would be almost lifelong.

During the decades of our separation, whenever I felt suffocated in an abyss of misery, the words that Uncle Ramsey uttered on the eve of his leaving the country came to mind. I admired the keenness of Uncle Ramsey's observation about the inhumanity of the Communists. However, Uncle Ramsey had also made another statement to the effect that "kids like Yi-ling who had no relationship with the old regime and whose personal histories appear to be pure and clean to the Communists don't have to worry too much about their behavior in the presence of Communist officials. Even if you strike the table before them, they might still be tolerant toward you." This also lingered in my memory and made me relax my vigilance against the Communists. At first I really thought that as long as I did nothing against the law, the

Communists would not raise difficulties. But the stark fact was that before haughtiness developed to the extent that I would strike the table, I had already been labeled a rightist—a political opponent. This made me live in humiliation from then on.

It was thirty years later that I was able to emigrate to the United States. Another eight years later, my parents made a trip to the United States, and they especially wanted to go to New York to get together with Uncle Ramsey and Auntie Kay. Uncle Ramsey and Auntie Kay had had a difficult period after they left China and struggled in foreign countries. But their determination and diligence were rewarded by their current life with ample food and clothing, and, most important of all, by a sense of stability and security. Uncle Ramsey is now a retired professor with academic fame.

When my parents toured the States in 1987, Uncle Ramsey and Auntie Kay asked them to stay with them for a time in their spacious apartment by the Hudson River. They chatted and chatted about endless topics. They looked back together on the past with many sweet and bitter recollections. Naturally, Uncle Ramsey inquired about Uncle David, his eldest brother, who had failed to prevail on him to stay put. Needless to say, Uncle David stayed to welcome the "liberation."

Uncle David had studied in London in his youth. His education had been Western, but his aspiration was for socialism. In reality he knew nothing about Marxism and socialism. He just regarded socialism as synonymous with fairness, righteousness, and progressiveness. After liberation, he applied to enter the Communist-run Revolutionary University for brainwashing. There, he volunteered to be dispatched to Korea when the war broke out. Thanks probably to his fluency in English, he was assigned to deal with the war prisoners, and this might have contributed to his safe return without a scar on his body. On the other hand, his service in the army did not provide him with any political capital, and he remained a small potato.

After demobilization, he got a job as translator in some trade institution. Fortunately, Uncle David had the sincere desire to "serve the people" wholeheartedly as Chairman Mao taught. He did not care very much for high position, and was satisfied with the arrangement. A taciturn person, he quietly immersed himself in hard work. He seemed to be immune to being the target of any political movement. But at last, sometime around the "Great Proletarian Cultural Revolution," he still could not escape the destiny shared by all intellectuals. His bad luck was triggered accidentally and somewhat amusingly. At a meeting of mass criticism, the target of which was someone else, he was forced to say something like everybody else, because reticence could label one as the target's sympathizer or even accomplice. Because Uncle David was not good at talking, and especially weak in criticizing others, all he could do was chime in with other participants. So he said, "That's right, such-and-such. How are you going to account for this? You should honestly confess and make a clean breast of your crimes. Since they are now asking you about this, why don't you just answer? You shouldn't shut your mouth. You should answer what they ask."

A terrible mistake! Now they got hold of Uncle David, who had inadvertently diverted attention to himself. "What! What were you saying? You used 'they' instead of 'we'! This means that deep in your mind you are not in the same boat with us. This reveals your true feeling and real political standpoint." After that Uncle David suffered as an alien element for a period of time. Of course, like most of the sufferers during the movement, he finally was rehabilitated. Years later he died of cancer. Therefore, Uncle Ramsey's discussion with Uncle David forty years ago turned out to be the last one between them.

Uncle Hung was another person whose whereabouts Uncle Ramsey wanted to know. Uncle Ramsey had liked this younger half-brother when the latter was in his childhood. He especially appreciated Uncle Hung's diligence in studying. During a summer vacation, Uncle Ramsey even taught Uncle Hung some Chinese classics in his leisure time. When he left Peking and returned to Shanghai forty years before, Uncle Hung had already been an underground revolutionary and never showed up in his home. Uncle Ramsey felt regret and was very disappointed. In the following decades abroad, Uncle Ramsey still missed his half-brother. But he always assumed that this half-brother must have been doing well in the Communist camp. Actually, the assumption was wrong. Uncle Hung did not communicate with his family for years after the liberation. A few years before the Cultural Revolution, he suddenly appeared in Shanghai. It was only then that we were aware that he was not doing very well in his big revolutionary family, because of his family background and class origin. He had not been able to climb to any high perch. Worse than that, he had never had the chance to get married, so all the relatives tried very hard to introduce girlfriends to him. Regrettably no longer a child prodigy, as he had been, he was now a somewhat weird and whimsical person. Almost all the girls introduced to him declined the next date. Then came the Cultural Revolution and Uncle Hung disappeared again, maybe forever this time.

Uncle Ramsey was not the only person who sighed with emotion when looking back on the past. While staying with him in the United States, my parents paid a visit to my father's alma mater. I drove them from New York to Philadelphia. My father had entered the Wharton School of the University of Pennsylvania sixty years before, in 1927, and studied there for four consecutive years until he got his doctoral degree in 1931. Away from the campus for over half a century, he could still recognize some familiar spots. After having toured the corridors of today's Wharton School, which was not located at the same address as the one he had attended, he stood quietly on the terrace in front of the gate of the school, watching the students coming and going. He stood and watched, for a long, long while without uttering a word.

The PROVOST VICE-PROVOSTS and PROFESSORS of the
UNIVERSITY OF PENNSYLVANIA
To all to whom thefe prefents may come GREETING

WHEREAS it is the ancient right and cuftom of univerfities to reward meritorious attainments in Letters Sciences and Philofophy as well as notable achievements in behalf of the Public Weal by admiffion to appropriate academic degrees:

NOW therefore We under the authority of a mandate from the Truftees of this Univerfity have with due form admitted   Yun Yuan Wong who has honorably fulfilled the requirements impofed by the ftatutes to the degree of   Master of Business Administration granting therewith all the rights honors and privileges thereunto appertaining.

Given under our hands and the Seal of the Truftees at PHILADELPHIA on this 20th day of June in the year of our Lord 1928 and of this Univerfity the 188th

Secretary

Provost

Dean

My father's master's degree from the University of Pennsylvania.

CHAPTER 2

A New Life

S INCE THE EARLY POST-LIBERATION DAYS, the Communists liked to call their takeover "liberation" and precede everything they did with the epithet "new"—a new society, a new nation, a new social system. Therefore, the life the people began to live under their rule was, of course, a "new life." As for myself, I really entered a new life after the Communist takeover, a new life not in its usual sense.

It was near the end of May 1949 that Shanghai, the city where I was staying, was liberated. I was then in the last semester of high school. The school was close to my residence, both of them being in the same district—Ching-an District. My impression is that I went to school as usual in those days. I have no recollection of any suspension of classes. Even if there was, it must have been just for a couple of days; otherwise I should be able to remember it. Ever since the Communist troops started crossing the Yangtze River, the last natural barrier for the Nationalist regime, the change of situation had become dramatic. The Nationalist Party was suffering such a crushing defeat that the irresistible Communist forces advanced triumphantly like a knife cutting through hot butter. It was said that sometime and somewhere the retreat was precipitated in such a way that the pursuing troops were unable to catch up. It is hard to tell whether this observation was an exaggeration or just propaganda, but anyway, by the turn of the month of May, the fields of struggle had already moved to the outskirts of Shanghai and liberation had become something that could happen any minute. Shanghai residents were like terminal patients in the intensive care unit, helplessly and submissively waiting for the verdict of their fate. However, when the liberation did happen, it turned out to be more like a drumbeat than an earthquake.

As for my family, the so-called liberation at first brought about no discernible change at all. My mother continued as a housewife, while my father kept for a while his original job as Deputy Director of the Shanghai branch of the Bank of Communications. There were only tiny modifications, if any, in our life. For example, my father, on the advice of the new Communist leader in charge of the Bank of Communications, had to give up the privilege of the small car originally allocated for his use. But this minor alteration could hardly be seen as something significant. As an extremely punctilious and overcautious person, my father had never allowed any of his family members, including my mother, to use the car, which he himself used mainly for work. Therefore, having or not having a car did not affect our family life at all.

Not very long after the liberation the Communists began to make rearrangements for the personnel taken over from the old establishments. Father was sent to Northwest China as a railway specialist and participated in the construction of the Tianshui–Lanchow Railway. Although reluctant to work so far away from home, he was happy that he was eventually able to apply what he had learned in the University of Pennsylvania for the first time since he had returned to China twenty years before. His doctoral thesis was on railway management. But his happiness was transient. It did not take too long for him to find out that those so-called Soviet experts who were supposed to work side by side with their Chinese counterparts were actually overlords thinking of themselves as supervisors. Father could not stand their insufferable arrogance, so he later resigned and came back to Shanghai. This happened later than the period I am now recounting.

Right at the time of the Communist takeover, I had some immediate benefits from the liberation, without which I might never have graduated from high school. I was a child of preschool age when my mother pressed a writing brush into my tiny hand and guided it through the

OMNIBUS et fingulis has Litteras lecturis SALUTEM

QUUM ACADEMIÆ ubique gentium inftitutæ viros Philofophia Scientiis Litterifve Humanioribus excultos aut de Republica bene meritos titulo jufto et congruente folitæ fint condecorare:

Nos igitur PRÆFECTUS VICE-PRÆFECTI Ceterique PROFESSORES UNIVERSITATIS PENNSYLVANIENSIS auctoritate Curatorum spectatiffimorum perlitteras mandatorias nobis commiffa   Yun Yuan Wong bona indole præditum omnibus muneribus atque officiis quæ hujus Academiæ legibus ei impofita sunt conftanter et fideliter expletis ad gradum   Doctoris in Philosophia   rite admifimus eique omnia jura honores privilegia ad hunc gradum pertinentia libenter conceffimus:

Cujus rei teftimonio huic diplomati nomina noftra die Menfis Juniixvii anno Salutismcmxxxi et Univerfitatis conditæ cxci Philadelphiæ subfcripfimus et quo major sit fides auctoritafque Curatores confentientes Academiæ noftræ sigillum apponi jufferunt.

Sigilli Cuftos

Præfectus

Decanus

My father's doctoral diploma from the University of Pennsylvania.

first strokes. Later on, my parents always urged me to keep on practicing Chinese calligraphy, though they did not intend to make a professional calligrapher of me. Likewise, they never wanted me to be a man of letters when they hired scholars to give me private lessons in Chinese classics. They did so because they were concerned that the Western-style education I received at school might cause me to neglect my own culture.

Living up to their expectation through incessant drilling and practicing, I gradually developed a kind of ascetic interest in calligraphy and compelled myself to keep going without the need of anyone else's push. After I met Mr. Chen Chu-lai, a master seal engraver, and became his student in seal engraving, an art closely related to calligraphy, my enthusiasm for calligraphy became greater and greater. I set for myself the daily task of practicing different sizes and styles of characters, prior to everything else, including the school's homework. The rest of my leisure time I used to spend in Master Chen's house, watching him engrave and listening to him talk about various interesting topics. Thus, I simply did not have much time and energy left for the science classes, in which I was becoming less and less interested. In the end, when I entered high school, I entirely lost interest in such subjects as physics, chemistry, and mathematics. I failed almost every test.

The reason that I never failed to move up to the next grade was because my high marks in literature courses helped raise the total average. But putting all my energy and time into literature and history, which I liked, and paying no attention at all to natural sciences, which I hated, unintentionally annoyed the chemistry teacher, who had a very high prestige and powerful position in that school. He was so vexed that he tried to bring pressure on the principal in the summer of 1948, the summer before I went up to senior-grade, to issue a formal notice to my parents demanding that I quit that school and be transferred to another. According to the common practice of that period, no decent high school would accept any senior-grade transfer student. So this attempt, once successful, would mean no less than a dismissal. Fortunately, the history teacher, who had the highest seniority in that school, stepped up and spoke on my behalf, advising the principal against this attempt, which he said was unfair to me since I had never committed any offense.

Under pressure from opposite directions, the principal eventually complied with the latter's advice, and agreed to my promotion to senior grade on condition that I could not graduate if I failed to pass all the courses. Without any other option, I had to accept this condition, which was, in fact, quite lenient and reasonable, and I stayed on. However, there was no way whatsoever for me to achieve this reasonable goal. Owing to my extremely weak foundation in all the science courses, it seemed almost impossible for me to pass the graduation examinations in physics, chemistry, and mathematics, and thus my prospect for graduation was very gloomy indeed. But I should be thankful to the so-called liberation of Shanghai, which took place just about a month before my last semester in the high school. To me it was an event that happened in the right place at the right time. The school administration, eager to get rid of all the old files and anxious to let as many senior students as possible go away, drew up a new regulation stipulating that the passing grade required for graduates should not be calculated on a course-to-course basis, but on an average. My high grades in literature and history made up for the low ones in natural sciences, and thus I graduated. For this I had to shout "Long live the Communist Party!" three times.

After my graduation, I faced the challenge of entering a university. As the Communists had just seized power and had a number of other priorities to take care of, they had no time to interfere in education, and so they let the education system take its natural course. That is to say, the procedures of both applying for admission to a university and taking entrance examinations remained unchanged; they should be completed in the same summer. As before, all the national universities administered one unified examination. Applicants had only to take one examination and then wait to be selected by the various universities according to their individual results. As for the private universities, each held its own entrance examinations.

Knowing very well that I was not competent enough, I took almost all the entrance examinations available. I spent that whole summer filing registrations and writing examinations. The subject I applied to study was law. That was because, from my childhood, my life model had been my maternal grandfather, who was one of China's famous lawyers and was chancellor of China's first modern university known for its law curricula at the turn of this century. Unfortunately, I was turned down by the law school of Soochow University, to which I had applied, and this put an end to my dream of being a lawyer. In retrospect, I should say that I was fortunate not to be accepted by Soochow University because only a couple of years later all the judges and lawyers in the new society were compelled to change their jobs or undergo ideological transformation. Even if I had been accepted, I still could not have become a lawyer, and the only possible result would have been a waste of time.

My participation in the unified entrance examination of the national universities was simply doing something for the occasion. I never expected it to be a success. However, beyond expectation—I still don't know why and how I passed the examination by the national universities' admissions committee—I was enrolled in the business administration department of the very famous Jiao-tung University in Shanghai. Instead of being overjoyed, I was weighed down with anxiety. I lacked no enthusiasm for this prestigious university in China, but I also lacked no wisdom regarding my own limitations. With my poor foundation in

My maternal grandfather, Wang Yu-ling.

natural sciences and most of all my disinterest in figures, how could I keep up with the business administration classes? I resolved to give up the opportunity of entering a national university and pinned my hopes on several private universities.

Soon I was accepted by St. John's University, which was one of the few missionary colleges in China that the Communists had not yet had time to abolish. I applied to study in the department of journalism, and my application was approved. I was particularly happy to be admitted into St. John's University because it was well known for its use of English as the medium of instruction, and also because at the back of my mind I still cherished the desire to study abroad. Ever since my childhood I had regarded studying abroad as the natural course in one's life, something taken for granted. New China had been liberated, but I still indulged in wishful thinking that the Communist regime would not last long and that all I had to do was to prepare myself for further graduate studies abroad during my undergraduate years.

I entered St. John's University in the fall of 1949. The period immediately following the liberation seemed to be a hibernation. For St. John's, it was the first time since its founding over half a century ago that it had been under the control of an atheist regime. Although it was a missionary-operated school, no religious atmosphere could be felt any longer at that time. The school never compelled students to go to church; however, I started contacting various foreign missionaries outside of the campus during that period. I went to the Inland Mission regularly and attended the Bible class at the residence of Dr. Frank Price, an American missionary, until all foreign missionaries were evicted a year or so later.

On the other hand, although it was the post-liberation period, I could not feel the strong control of the Communists. The Communist regime had just started to rule a vast, unified mainland and founded a new country, called the People's Republic of China. The Communists were in no hurry to tighten their control. At first, they seemed to assume a laissez-faire attitude and allow the school to go its own way. The school was widely known, at that time, to be traditionally very liberal. The university administration was allowed to follow its tradition in almost every aspect. The library on campus opened and closed as usual, seemingly unaffected by the Communist liberation, even having such anti-Communist books as *I Choose Freedom* in its collection.

A few foreigners on the faculty had departed, but some lingered. Nearly all of the Chinese faculty members had studied abroad and

My student card from St. John's University.

most of them had connections with the mission. Generally speaking, the faculty were in a fidgety mood, worrying about their future. With this uncertainty, they could not be very serious and strict in tutoring. Furthermore, St. John's University traditionally had a liberal ethos wherein the teachers were not supposed to push the students too hard, except to encourage their individual research efforts. During this period, such an ethos provided the teachers with an excuse for taking an even more laissez-faire attitude. In the journalism department, almost all the professors were American trained. They were sensible enough to refrain from uttering anything that could affront the new regime.

Under this circumstance, how much progress a student could make depended solely upon his own initiative. If you worked hard, you could learn a great deal. But if you did not, you still could pass. Many of my schoolmates took advantage of the best professors available and especially the rich collection of the library and acquired a lot of knowledge. But there were also quite a few students who, instead of devoting their time and energy to study, were involved in political activities, since by then the Communist Party organization had just emerged from underground and a new Youth League branch had been organized. Students with political aspirations, either because of their naïve enthusiasm or career ambitions, naturally rallied around the Party and posed as leftists. Taking advantage of this noninterference, I pursued my own way of life, which was identical neither with that of those industrious individuals nor those hanky-panky groups. I was so liberal-minded that I attended only those classes I liked and stayed absent from those I disliked.

An anecdote sounds somewhat absurd but is true. In the first term after liberation, a compulsory course in "Chinese Revolution" was offered. It was taught in a big class with several hundred students in the Social Hall, and roll-calling was just impossible. Because of this, a lot of students were absent from each class and I was one of them. The only difference between us was that I overdid it—I never attended that course. But I did take its final examination which, in St. John's tradition, took place in a large hall with examinees of different courses seated alternately. I arrived there late, and all the examinees were writing on their papers while several examiners were supervising and promenading. I did not recognize the instructor of the course I was supposed to take, but fortunately I remembered his name. So I approached the examiner standing at the gate and asked, "Where is Mr. So-and-so?" "It's me," he replied. I was in too much of a hurry to express any embarrassment, and said, "I have come for the exam in your course." He may have been too embarrassed to refuse and just handed the exam paper to me without uttering a word. As I expected, I passed the exam and got the required credit.

In private, I continued my practice in the arts of Chinese calligraphy and seal engraving, and had become very close to Master Chen Chu-lai, who had tutored me since I was a little kid. He was a diehard anti-Communist, had many connections with the Nationalist officialdom, and ever since the Communist takeover had kept saying that the Nationalists would come back soon. At first this kind of statement did not impress me very much, because I was in a certain degree keeping aloof from politics.

The first indelible imprint that the Communists made on my mind occurred during the "Suppress Counterrevolutionaries" movement. One day toward the end of April 1950, just as every other institution across the nation did, St. John's University held a general meeting attended by all the personnel on the campus at which it was announced that four students were going to be arrested on the spot. Of course, their crimes were also made public at the same time. I did not have too much aversion to this kind of action, as these seemed normal in the turmoil of political struggle. But shortly after that, another meeting was held at which a student gave a speech recounting how his father had been executed by the government in this movement and how he himself fully supported the execution of his counterrevolutionary father. I felt disgusted. Personally, I did not know this student or his father. No matter what kind of person his father really was, I could never be reconciled with the performance of this student. I gnashed my teeth in hatred and said to myself, "He is much worse than a beast. If this kind of person can be termed a human being, I would rather not be called a man." The Communists who created and extolled this model should really not be deemed human beings either. From then on, I thoroughly broke with the Communist regime, at least in ideology, though not in action. I could not identify myself with this kind of organization. Deep in my mind I did not believe that the Communist regime could last long and was awaiting a drastic change day by day. I failed to realize that my physical growth was faster than the decline of the Communist regime and that I would have to waste my youthful vigor under its rule.

There was one person who often disagreed with me, and it was my grandfather. Grandpa lived in a large townhouse with my step-grandmother, because he had long been of the opinion that each of his children should live independently with his or her own family. But all the children were allowed to visit him occasionally. For a long period after the outbreak of the Korean War, I kept on dining with Grandpa almost every day for the purpose of listening to the Voice of America. At that time, it was not easy to receive the broadcast of the Voice of America over an ordinary radio, probably because of too much interference. Grandfather owned a radio of the best quality then available. Too, his big house with a garden fenced with thick, tall walls gave a sense of security, since listening to the Voice of America was an act of high risk, though there was no explicit prohibition. Grandfather listened with me, also intently and expectantly. But he was far more realistic than I.

In the yard of my grandfather's townhouse.
Left to right: my father, stepgrandmother, grandfather,
brother, mother, and second auntie.

He kept urging me to give up the hope of a quick Nationalist come-back, saying, "You'd better make friends with the Communists. Be well prepared, for you may have to live under their rule for quite a long while, maybe for a lifetime. The Communists will finally fail, there's no doubt about it, but that won't happen very soon. Even a cruel dynasty like that established by the First Emperor of Ch'in lasted almost two decades. So did the Rebellion of Long Hair, the Taiping Heavenly King-dom." The way he uttered these words while sitting on the sofa right next to the radio with a cigar in his hand has always been vivid and fresh in my memory.

Later, during the movements of Three Anti's and Five Anti's,* some of Grandfather's friends in financial circles committed suicide by jump-ing from tall buildings. Grandfather was very dejected and despondent. However, he kept saying to me by way of warning, "You are so young. You have a long way to go. You've got to be prepared for living in the reality of Communist control." Grandfather also taught me, "In deal-ing with them, you have to suspend your conscience temporarily. Do whatever they order you to do. If they want you to denounce me as a capitalist, exploiter, bloodsucker, robber, bandit, or whatever, just go ahead and comply with their orders. Don't take it seriously. Never irri-tate them so as to get yourself into trouble. It's not worthwhile to argue with them. Deep in my mind, it is very clear that if the Communists can be called human beings, then I definitely refuse to acknowledge myself a human being. Be confident of yourself and flexible in dealing with devils." These words I took seriously, and less than twenty years later, when my grandpa was too old to remember his own principles in deal-ing with the Red Guards and revolutionary rebels, it was I who repeat-edly reminded him of what he had said to help tide him over the diffi-culties.

With this kind of sentiment, it was only natural that I increasingly alienated myself from the Party members, Youth League members, and other leftists on campus. I was very stubborn. Sometimes I did not com-promise. For instance, the regulations concerning the centralized place-

---

*Both the "Three-Anti's Movement" and "Five-Anti's Movement" were waged in 1952. The former one was against embezzlement, while the latter was against private businessmen.

ment of college graduates nationwide were announced when I still had several semesters to go. The centralized placement meant eliminating unemployment among college graduates on the one hand and depriving one of the freedom to seek a job he liked on the other. The stiff practice by which every graduate should unconditionally accept the placement caused deep concern among a portion of the students. Suddenly, I came up with an idea: since they had already counted on me as part of their labor power, why should I continue to pay my tuition fees? So for the remaining semesters, I refused to pay anything. When the registrar asked me about the payment, I replied with perfect assurance that I was not going to pay and waited for any penalty. "If you want to dismiss me, please go ahead." Of course, they did not dismiss me. They referred this matter to the Students' Union. The official of the Students' Union came to me and said, "If you have difficulty paying tuition fees, you can apply to our organization for financial assistance." I answered, "No. I don't have any financial difficulty. I just don't want to pay. As a matter of fact, my parents already gave me the money, but I have spent it. So now I am awaiting the penalty." They did not know how to handle this case and simply employed the most effective means, that of procrastination. The case was left unsettled and, later, when I graduated and the university was closing down, no one bothered to pay attention to it any longer.

It was inconceivable that an ideologically "backward" person like me should have been appreciated by the Communists more than some of the students who strove very hard to follow them. I transferred from the journalism department to the English department in the second year of my stay at St. John's, and one of my classmates, Morley, was Uncle David's stepdaughter. Active and popular, she never missed any meeting called by the Communists or accessible to her and took the floor whenever a chance arose. She would tell the audience how she adored the revolution or how she admired the heroic acts that the Communists were propagandizing. At the same time, she worked terribly hard. Because she spoke beautiful Mandarin, she was assigned to set up a broadcasting network on campus for the use of the Communist and youth organizations. She did it almost single-handedly. Then she moved into the school dormitory so that she could get up early in the morning and stay late in the evening. It was said that she was the person who got up earliest in the morning, since she was given the task of turning on the microphone to wake everybody for the sitting-up exercises performed to radio music. She also volunteered to work as a full-time broadcaster, and every now and then would announce some notice from the authorities. It was incredible that such an activist should be disliked by the Communists. Their dislike was borne out by the fact that her application to join the Youth League was repeatedly turned down. It was further borne out by their discrimination against her when assigning the students to various "revolutionary duties" and putting her in the group of the politically untrustworthy.

At the beginning of my third year in the university, the Communist regime finally decided that missionary institutions should no longer be allowed to exist in this atheist country and that all the missionary-operated universities should be disbanded by the end of that academic year and merged into the state-controlled universities. To facilitate the course of incorporation, it was required that students in junior classes of these missionary universities enroll for more credits so that they could graduate along with seniors. Thus we became the last graduates of St. John's. Later, the campaign for closing down all the missionary schools in China was launched together with the Thought Reformation movement in 1952 at St. John's. All the students "voluntarily" had to do a "revolutionary" job on campus. Those whom the Communists considered not so trustworthy were assigned to help make an inventory of all the collections in the library. Morley belonged to this group. Those who were deemed reliable were entrusted with the work of checking and sorting out the university's several decades old administrative files. I was assigned to this group, but I did not appreciate it at all. The gossip that I was trusted by the leadership did not have much appeal to me. I did not care a whit whether I was trusted or not, and as far as my personal interest was concerned, I would have been much happier to deal with books than with files. But, anyway, I accepted the assignment, without any premonition that it would give rise to the first romance in my life.

CHAPTER 3

A Revolutionary Romance

I N THE EARLY YEARS OF ST. JOHN'S UNIVERSITY, which was situated
in the rear of a big public park and flanked on either side by the
Soochow River, most of the foreign faculty, including the presidents, lived on campus. They resided in detached houses scattered
among the trees and surrounded by a beautiful lawn which then could
claim to rank first in the Far East. Now, during the last days of the missionary schools, these residences were almost empty, as nearly all the
unwelcome foreigners had been driven out of the Chinese mainland.
Temporarily, I enjoyed the privilege of working in these pretty houses,
for they were now used as offices for the file-sorting group.

For the first time in my life, I had to observe labor discipline, which
required that every member of the group be punctual for office hours.
Following is the way we did our job: Several persons were grouped as
a team and seated around a table in a room; we read, discussed, and
made judgments while searching through the old files, for the purpose
of finding evidence of imperialist aggression in China. This effort was
directed toward the establishment of proof of imperialist crimes which
were to be displayed in an exhibition. The assumption was clear
enough: foreign missionaries were equivalent to imperialists, especially
Americans. Vigilance against the enemy had already been heightened to

such a degree that the thought of working in these once foreigner-occupied houses made people nervous. There was a member who seemed to be ever on the alert. He proposed that we pay special attention and make sure that no weapons or bombs were concealed in some dark corners, as though those foreign missionaries and professors had been so wise and farsighted as to be able to foretell the coming of the Communists and, therefore, had bothered to hatch plots years before. Who would have thought that such a stupid suggestion would win serious applause? At one time we did play Sherlock Holmes, searching all the corners of those houses gingerly.

Probably we may be said to have been the harbingers of the Red Guards who were to stalk through the land of the Cultural Revolution some twenty-five years later. But my generation, not as audacious as our successors, was somewhat more conservative and, by then, had not developed the skill of planting or fabricating a charge against someone. We were still quite innocent in a sense and pursuing something genuine in substance, although we might accept or interpret the substantial materials in a different or a sometimes far-fetched manner. For example, we discovered some stars-and-stripes flags and dozens of pamphlets on the United States Constitution. They were real. The Communists attached great importance to this matter and exhibited them as an ironclad proof of U.S. imperialist aggression in China. Of course, no one would refute this accusation and question why the United States flags and the pamphlets on the U.S. Constitution should be regarded as weapons and bombs. To those who walked through the exhibition, as well as to those who were responsible for the exhibition, this seemed to be a self-evident truth.

I could never cultivate a keen interest in the work of file sorting and found it boring in comparison with reading in the library. However, my regret did not last; for, before long, a girl who was later to become my wife for some thirty years came into my life.

Jane was a quiet, obedient, and well-behaved student both in high school and in college. Her father being a clerk in Nationalist China but lacking any connections with the Nationalist ruling clique, she had a relatively good family record in the eyes of the Communists. In contrast, the majority of the students of St. John's had bad family backgrounds. Under this circumstance, it was only natural that she was recruited into the New Democratic Youth League at the time it was founded. Now she was already a veteran member of three years' standing. Most of the members who joined the League at the same time as she did had already climbed higher and become Party members or League secretaries. But owing to her weakness, timidity, reticence, and particularly her reluctance to speak at meetings, she was deprived of the opportunity for meteoric rise like her comrades. Besides, she herself lacked the desire to climb that ladder. Nevertheless, the organization, as the political bosses in China used to be called at that time, did not overlook her, and selected her as the leader of the small League group to which she herself belonged. At the same time, she was appointed head of the file-sorting group to which I belonged and given the task of uniting with and educating me, by instilling the advanced revolutionary ideas into my stubborn "backward" head. To everybody's surprise, including hers and mine, through working together and frequent conversations, we fell deeply in love, for the first time in both our lives.

No one except God knows how we fell in love. I myself cannot give an exact date when all this happened. You could say it came gradually or you could say it came all of a sudden.

Although Jane and I had been schoolmates for years and in the same class at St. John's, we had never talked to each other. From the very beginning of our acquaintance, we were in a rather romantic environment. From morning to evening, we were together in the detached house surrounded by verdant lawns. We read and chatted together, and with other boys and girls on our team. I used to joke with our fellow members, saying something funny to cheer them up or make them laugh. But most of the time Jane would cleverly affect casual unconcern when I made some careless remark transgressing a certain permissible political boundary. It was in this way that she helped gloss over some of my "mistakes." When the team dispersed after office hours, we still could not bear to part. We would take a stroll on the lawn or sit under the shade of a big tree. It was perfectly justifiable for Jane to have private talks with me, since her organization entrusted her with the task of helping me "make progress." When two young persons of opposite sex talk to each other heart to heart for any length of time, they are apt to feel admiration for each other. This was our case.

By the time Jane's comrades and political bosses found out what was going on between us, she already loved me determinedly and unswerv-ingly. When asked, she never hesitated to acknowledge that she loved me. I, too, was ready to do the same, and did it even more frankly and unambiguously. It was now too late for the organizations of the Party and the League to interfere in our affair. Since I was not a formal mem-ber of either of the two organizations, what could they do with me?

So they began to bring pressure to bear on Jane. The political boss-es talked to her in person or enlisted her best girlfriends to dissuade her from talking about love with me. They admonished her not to let me lead her by the nose since it was her duty to remold me ideological-ly and bring me to the revolutionary ranks. "Your love affair will lead nowhere. You are a League member and Wong is such a backward guy, never applying to join the League. How can you expect your or-ganization to approve your marriage with him?" They also pointed out to her clearly that with her educational level and political status she would have a very bright future if she married a Communist mem-ber instead of me. "Your ready-made, promising future will surely be damaged if you marry him. It would really be a pity." In a way these words were no exaggeration. Most of the League members or alternate members who were in the same group with Jane at that time advanced rapidly in their careers. Some of them later became diplomats, such as chargés d'affaires or spokesmen for the Foreign Ministry of Commu-nist China. Had Jane not married me, she might have acquired a simi-lar position.

Usually very gentle and weak, Jane was adamant on this point, not-withstanding all these pressures. She defended herself against her lead-ers and comrades tactfully and tactically, being neither supercilious nor obsequious. "It's true that Wong is stubborn and reluctant to advance at the moment, as you analyzed," Jane argued, "but was it not just be-cause he is backward that I was given the responsibility to help him?" She then expressed confidence in finally winning me over to the revolu-tionary ranks. Furthermore, she challenged them, using the orthodox Communist theory of looking at a person with an eye on the course of his development, and asked them, "On what ground should you have such a rigid opinion of Wong?" I did believe and still do believe that she had no intention to offend her bosses and comrades by this kind of contradiction. At the bottom of her heart at that time, she might really have believed that I would be likely to be influenced by her and move forward along the so-called progressive line. She was mistaken. However, she should not have been blamed for her naïvete, because she was not alone. In later years, I encountered quite a few shrewd old bureaucrats who were versed in the ways of the world but thought that it would be easy and natural for a young man like me, who had had no deep involvement with the old society, to toe the Communist line. Few could imagine my incorrigible obstinacy.

At that time, we were under tremendous pressure. Love needs pressure; the weight of pressure is in direct proportion to the depth of love. Setbacks may be much more helpful to the consolidation of love than is matchmaking. There were many couples on the campus, in addition to Jane and me, and their love affairs had various outcomes. Without such a setback, our love affair would, at best, have been as good as theirs, especially when I had already regarded studying abroad as the priority of my life and had no intention of entering a permanent relationship with any girl in China. Thanks to the adversity bestowed upon us by the Party and League organizations, we became a couple of tested lovers. Trials and tribulations only strengthened our resolve to go through thick and thin together.

With our determination to love each other, toward the end of the last semester our relationship was eventually recognized by all, willingly or unwillingly. Nobody who knew us would imagine that we could be separated by force. The leftists must have fully understood this. I still do not know how and when the leaders changed their attitude toward us, but definitely there was some important change. Maybe the Party and the League organizations had too many tasks on hand at that time. One of them involved the campaign for the centralized placement of college graduates.

Our graduation was due in September 1952, when the campus was scheduled to close down. For several months before the "Doomsday," all the graduates had been excitedly engaged in the political study sessions where they studied the Party's policy regarding job assignments. Everybody had to take, at least in words if not in deeds, a firm stand and express a willingness to accept whatever job our kind and great Party was going to assign to us. Each student was required to declare at the meeting how greatly impressed he was with the past revolutionary experiences propagandized in the campaign and how ready he now was to be relocated to economically backward areas. What the Communist party called for was "unconditional obedience to the centralized placement of graduates." All in all, numerous and various high-sounding words were heard during this period.

It was tough for both the leaders and the participants in the campaign. On the one hand, the leaders had to try very hard to obtain the graduates' full compliance with the Party's policy. Any noncompliance with it could mark down the success of the leaders' job; therefore, they employed both hard and soft tactics to deal with those difficult participants, one by one. On the other hand, the graduates were very worried. Some of them I knew very well were extremely nervous. They were apprehensive of being sent outside of metropolises, especially of leaving Shanghai, a city considered the most glamorous and comfortable in China. They feared being assigned to an unsatisfactory job. But the thing they were most afraid of was making those insincere, high-sounding statements, which, as was widely known, were deemed a sort of criterion for one's progressiveness and, therefore, the prerequisite for getting an ideal job assignment. Under this circumstance, the students feared that if they failed to put up the lofty stance that the Party called for, they might lose the chance of obtaining a decent job, but that if they ostensibly took a magnanimous attitude such as the Party required, they might be caught in a trap from which they would have no way to free themselves once offered an undesirable post. To be or not to be—it was a gamble.

Very few students had the guts to deal with the Communists by playing tricks. Among my classmates, there was a guy who was so "backward" as to make cynical remarks all the time. With the launching of the campaign of placement, he was aware that it would be impossible for him to get a good assignment. To avoid this fate, he shifted his ground overnight. "I am determined to go to the most difficult areas and contribute all my energy and intelligence to them," he shouted. Not content with this sudden shift, he further declared that he wanted to go nowhere but to the battlefield of Korea. Being the direct victim of the cultural aggression of U.S. imperialism, as he claimed, he wanted to fight it out with U.S. aggressors, with bayonets, and did not hesitate to sacrifice himself for the sacred struggle against imperialism.

He spoke with such feeling, excitement, and sincerity, that tears streamed down his cheeks and some in the audience were really moved. At last, he had his wish fulfilled when the Party announced the results of placement and approved his request.

First of all, he would have to stop at Peking which, as it was well known, was the assembling place for all the personnel to be dispatched to Korea. He left the Shanghai railway station as a hero, wearing large red flowers on his chest. Then, all of a sudden, when he arrived in Peking and reported at the Personnel Ministry, which was responsible for the centralized placement and final assignment of college graduates, he stated explicitly that he was not going anyplace else, certainly not to Korea. He said that all he wanted was to get a job in Peking.

It was 1952, many years before the clarion calls such as "Never forget class struggle" and "Never forget proletarian dictatorship" were raised, and the Communists were still stressing the importance of straightening out the people's thinking in the manner of, so to speak, a gentle breeze and a mild rain. This student took advantage of this situation and used his patience to outwit the old officials of the Personnel Ministry. Whenever the latter came to persuade him to go to Korea, he asserted that this was not a problem of ideology but a practical one. It was nothing but, according to what he said himself, "I am a coward and fear death." No matter what the old officials talked about— thought, spirit, honor, or future career—he retorted only with one terse sentence, "I am afraid of death."

In the end, he showed his hand, saying that the sole purpose of his application for going to Korea was to be able to come to Peking. "As you can see, I did not take my cotton-padded trousers with me when I left Shanghai," he remarked frankly. "This means I had no intention at all to go further north. Peking is my destination. Period." For several months he was engaged in protracted warfare with these old officials. Room and board taken care of by the Ministry, he had nothing to worry about. Finally, it was the Party that gave in, and he was sent back to Shanghai and assigned to work there. This was just what he wished for.

This incident happened after I had already left Shanghai. Jane and I had been dispatched for assignments long before the end of the campaign; therefore, the whole story was told to me by the "hero" when we met in Shanghai again afterward.

Fortunately, I was head over heels in love at that time and had no mind or energy for this kind of revolutionary gamble. Just as the Communists were unshakable in their determination to carry out their plan for the centralized placement of graduates, Jane and I were unshakable in our determination to love each other. Perhaps it was due to my concentration on love or maybe to my fallacious belief in the transitoriness of Communist rule that I was not at all heavyhearted like most of my classmates. I did not care where I would be relocated or to what job I would be assigned. All I cared about was that Jane and I should be together. This stand was firm and simple.

At that time, I really had no idea what a hard life and arduous work were like. Further, I thought, even if the job or location happened to be unsatisfactory, the situation would not last longer than the authorities who had sent me there, and who, I expected, could not last long. Why should I worry? I did not want to be separated from Jane even for a short period; so I made it clear to everybody that if Jane and I were assigned to different places I would definitely reject it, no matter what the consequences. To explicitly express such a determination might cause trouble. It was true that there existed a policy of "taking the relationship of lovers into consideration," but it was also true that this was at the mercy of the organization. Each of the graduates was supposed to express his attitude of unconditional obedience. My explicit statement might be held against me. But just as newborn calves are not afraid of tigers, as a Chinese proverb goes, so I did not care a whit if I should be used as a typical negative example. Fortunately, it did not happen. They not only exempted me from being criticized, but even dispatched us ahead of schedule.

To my surprise, one day toward the end of July 1952, when the "centralized placement study sessions" were just starting to reach their climax, Jane rushed excitedly into my home early in the morning. There must be something extraordinary because never before had she come to my home so early. I was still in bed. She could hardly wait until I got up. She walked into my room shouting with excitement, "I was just informed by our organization that we have been assigned to work in Peking—we, together." Taking it for granted that I would certainly be happy with the assignment, she added, "the organization has already made arrangements. We are going to leave by train at midnight tomorrow." "What?" I could hardly believe my ears, but Jane never lied. So I rose and listened to her explain in detail.

"The leaders of our organization got an urgent telegram from Peking to the effect that 'Owing to the need of the preparation of the Asia and Pacific Peace Conference to be held in Peking, please send as many foreign language workers as you can.' Our university has been ordered to send four graduates to Peking immediately. Both of us have been chosen. The other two are Chai and Chang." Chai and Chang were also a couple of serious lovers. We were not familiar with them, as they both had been transferred to St. John's from some other college about a year before. But it was known to all that they were lovers as soon as they stepped onto the campus. As neither of them belonged to any organization and both of them were commonplace, reticent, inactive persons who did not attract attention, their relationship as lovers seemed never to have caused any problems and had always been recognized by the organization. So it was quite relevant that they had also been assigned to work in Peking as a couple. Years later, they got married and were permitted to emigrate to Europe.

We had only thirty-six hours to make preparations. I was so excited that I would have finished packing within three hours. Not only did the assignment fulfill my wish of being together with Jane, but I was extremely pleased with the locale. At the same time, I was attracted by the preparatory work for an international conference. Most of all, I had longed to visit Peking, a city with so many historic sights, a city I had read so much about but had never seen.

Happily and hurriedly I finished making preparations within two days. My father had by then resigned from Si'an, and was now working as a free-lance translator of scientific and technological literature. My mother, who had been a housewife for years, was applying for a job by way of a friendly gesture, because the new regime called on every able person to work, and working meant joining the revolutionary ranks. She was participating in the pre-job vocational study program. My parents had no objection to my acceptance of the job. I took a couple of hours to call on my grandfather and say goodbye to him, as the journey from Shanghai to Peking was said to be quite a long one. Grandfather's stand remained the same as before. He said, "Be sure to stay with the Communists. You might have to spend your whole life in that camp."

The next night Jane and I were aboard a train heading for Peking for the long trip of one day and two nights. The other couple, Chai and Chang, traveled on the same train, but were in a separate car; so we did not communicate with one another very much. In accordance with the then-prevailing regulations, we were not eligible to take the sleeping car with soft berths but could only sit on the "hard seats" known as third class. At that time I was not as strong as I am now, and could not stay up all night without feeling very tired. No serious problem arose during the first night, because the excitement from the new and fresh experience propped me up against the fatigue from sleeplessness.

When morning came, I enjoyed watching the scenery along the way, and the view of the wilderness outside kept me in high spirits. Trouble came with the second nightfall. At first, I just felt ill and worn-out. Later, I could not help lying down, and I fainted. I did not awake until the sky turned bright, and I discovered that Jane was standing by her seat, which I had taken by lying on it. She was weeping, partly because she was very worried about me and partly because she was almost exhausted since she had not slept a wink for several nights. She told me that I looked ghastly pale during the night and that she was terrified and felt helpless.

By that time the train was approaching Peking. When it slowly pulled up at the railway station early in the morning, we were greeted by an official from the Ministry of Personnel. We were sent to different dormitories and asked to contact the Ministry of Personnel directly as soon as we put away our luggage. My speculation was that we should be assigned to work immediately since we had been required to come in such a hurry. Not at all!

The first time Jane and I went to the Ministry of Personnel, the woman officer who received us seemed to know nothing about the Asia and Pacific Peace Conference at all. "Please stay in your dormitory and have a good rest. As soon as we locate the jobs for you, you will be notified." That was all we ever heard from her. I was brave enough to make it clear to her that I would not accept any job that was to separate us from each other. She was not offended, however, and instead replied mysteriously, "We will take this into consideration."

As neither of our two couples was married, it was only natural that we were accommodated in four separate rooms. From then on we never met Chai and Chang again. Jane and I saw each other every day and were together from morning till evening, sightseeing around Peking. We visited almost all the well-known spots. We spent most of our time in Beihai Park. The green hills and the big lake in the park dotted with white pagodas and red walls provided us, as it were, with a daytime resident villa. Such a romantic environment helped to further consolidate the knot of love between us just as much as the pressure brought on us by the St. John's Party and League organizations.

But this romantic environment was not ideal in every respect. The uncertainty of our job positions made us ill at ease. It was prolonged for nearly two months. Worst of all, we did not know how long we would have to wait during this period. Had we known the exact length of time, we might have felt less restless. We were held in limbo for almost two months, being told to be patient each time we went to the Ministry.

When we went there on one day, we would be told to come back the next day, and when we were there the next day, we would be advised to come on the third day. The game was played over and over until we were totally frustrated. It was by no means a vacation, but a period of anxiety. This was certainly not ideal for romance.

Our uneasiness was aggravated by still another episode. In one of our numerous routine visits to the Personnel Ministry, we unintentionally overheard a conversation between the woman official and some other graduates waiting to be assigned like us. Apparently they had been waiting for a longer time than we. They had been assigned to work in the Central Military Committee. They refused, in spite of the forceful persuasion from the Personnel Ministry. Their discussion with the woman official eventually developed into a heated argument. Their dialogue was as follows:

OFFICIAL: For what reason don't you want to go to the Central Military Committee? It is one of the most important departments in our Party's Central Committee.

GRADUATES: We simply don't want to enter names on the army roll as required for anyone who serves in the Military Committee.

OFFICIAL: Why? What's wrong with entering names on the army roll? It's an honor for you.

GRADUATES: Thanks. Who cares about honor? We want to get married, and in line with the military regulations, those who join the army won't be allowed to marry in the first few years. We don't want our youth to be wasted.

OFFICIAL: This is the need of our Party and the need of the revolution. To get married is a matter of individual choice. But the Party's need is a matter of revolution. Don't you understand the basic truth that one's personal interests must be subordinated to those of the Revolution?

GRADUATES: We are not going to live up to these principles. All we are interested in is to get married. It is simple as that.

OFFICIAL: Your marriage is irrelevant to the topic of our discussion. I am in charge of your placement. We understand that while participating in the campaign at college, you pledged to accept unconditionally any assignments given to you by the Party. Now you are subject to the test of the sincerity of your pledge. I should tell you, at the moment, only the Central Military Committee has job openings available for you. This is the only place you can go to, whether you accept it or not.

GRADUATES: No. We are not going.

OFFICIAL: You should not reject any jobs that the Party offers to you. You must take the responsibility for refusing to go.

At this point, these graduates left abruptly. Apparently, the matter was not ended. It was impossible for us to know its ending. Neither was it possible for us to understand why this woman official, who seemed to be so easygoing in talking with us, should have been so rude and adamant in dealing with them.

Credit must be given to Jane. For unlike me, who was apt to enter into confrontation with those officials, Jane had the power of winning their sympathy; therefore, it was always she who made inquiries at the Ministry of Personnel. She not only never argued with that woman official who was in charge of placement, but gradually a kind of understanding developed between them and she left a good impression on her. However, after this episode, Jane felt very uneasy and was terribly annoyed by the prospect that we might also be asked to join the army. From what we had heard during the argument in the Ministry of

Personnel, it seemed that the Military Committee was in urgent need of foreign language workers. We had some serious discussions as to how we should respond in the event that we were asked to work in the Military Committee. Our views diverged on this question. I intended to accept the offer as long as we were together. But Jane was reluctant. Thus we argued endlessly in beautiful scenic places like Beihai Park, but to no avail. This unhappy episode was like a wet blanket thrown over our romance.

Later, facts proved that our worries were uncalled for, because we were not asked to have anything to do with the military. Our anxieties and worries ceased with the end of August. The die was cast when we went to the Personnel Ministry as usual and met this woman official, who received us with a smile, "I have located a place perfectly suitable for both of you. There you can apply what you learned at college. You can go report at the Hsin Hua News Agency. Go there right now."

However, I had some doubt. I did major in journalism during my first two years in St. John's, so the proposed job could be called relevant to what I had learned. But since Jane's major had always been English, how could you say the job was relevant to what she had learned at college? Before I had a chance to voice my doubt, Jane had already accepted the appointments with a profusion of thanks. Jane was wild with excitement as soon as the announcement was made and overjoyed at not being assigned to work in the Military Committee. Bye-bye Personnel Ministry!

The Hsin Hua News Agency was then located at 26 Congress Avenue, inside the Hsuan Wu Gate, occupying a complex of several buildings surrounded by yards and squares. As the sole news medium in Red China at that time, it was the official organ of the Communist Party and its regime, equivalent to a governmental ministry. Jane and I were sent to work in the Foreign Language Broadcasting Department. Then I realized that the words of the woman official in the Personnel Ministry were true.

Being the grass-roots unit of our organization, the Foreign Language Broadcasting Department assumed full responsibility to make arrangements for our work and daily life. Jane was assigned to the data center, taking care of the collection of materials for reference use. I worked in the editing section. My job was proofreading the English broadcasting articles while checking the validity of the factual data in those articles.

My identification card from Hsin Hua News Agency.

In Red China, whoever worked for the bureaucratic institutions was a member of the revolutionary ranks. Therefore, the so-called organization was also responsible for accommodating us. For the first few days, we were put in separate dormitories for singles. At that time, whether in the male or female dormitory, a room was usually shared by several people. A few days later, the head of our department approached us and said that if we went to the district government and registered for marriage, the organization would allot a room to us as our nuptial chamber. Our love affair had been strictly conservative and no emergency called for immediate marriage, but at that time we just gladly accepted the kindness. What made us take the favor from our organization and get married with their blessing was not just a single room for ourselves.

On my part, although I never gave up the hope of studying abroad in the near future, I could not resist the same feelings that Adam had had for Eve and, therefore, reason gave way to emotion. On Jane's part, before we left Shanghai, her father had suggested we be engaged. But my parents objected to the idea. They had no objection to our being close friends, nor any personal aversion to Jane; however, they thought that I was too young. In their view, the ideal age for a marriage would be one's late twenties, when one is more mature. Following the traditional moral code, I did not want to disobey my parents, so we left Shanghai without holding an engagement ceremony. However, the days we had spent

A holiday in Peking, autumn 1952.
A colleague on my right and a classmate on Jane's left.

together in Peking had enhanced our relationship to such an extent that we longed for a union. The willingness of the organization to play the role of the sponsor of our marriage provided me with a good occasion to explain my intention to my parents. By the time the letter in which I broke the news to my parents arrived in Shanghai, we had already been pronounced husband and wife by the Party "ministers."

To celebrate our marriage, a party was held in the Foreign Language Broadcasting Department. Although far from pompous and ostentatious, given the situation of that time it could be said to have been a grand ceremony. Probably it was because this department consisted chiefly of bilingual intellectuals. Its leading members spoke English very well. This department was provided with some foreign experts sent by the British Communist Party to assist in the Chinese Communist revolution; therefore, it had an atmosphere unlike the rest of the country which was permeated, so to speak, with rusticity.

The organization also sponsored our wedding party. Tea and pastries were served. Dancing began after the department head made a

My marriage photo with Jane.

speech in which he, besides conveying his congratulations on our wed-
lock, emphasized the happiness derived from living in the big revolutionary family and encouraged us to settle down in this place and serve
the people wholeheartedly. In the evening, following the Chinese custom, we were subjected to the trial of "cracking jokes in a nuptial
chamber," which meant that every guest of that evening, regardless of
the seniority in the family or clan and the closeness of the relationship,
could make almost any kind of jokes with the newlyweds in their nuptial chamber. Our nuptial chamber was a single windowless room with
no bath or toilet; however, I was quite satisfied with it. It was a private
room with no connection with others.

It was very regrettable that Jane became pregnant right away. Several days after the nuptials, she went to the hospital and was informed
that she was expecting. The news was a blow to me. I feared that the
birth of my baby might dim my prospect of studying abroad. But worse
still was my conviction that the so-called heavenly socialist society we
were living in had already forsaken all the values of human morality
and that it would be absolutely senseless to produce any more human

beings for it. The belief was so deeply rooted in my mind that no soon-er had Jane excitedly brought home the news of her pregnancy than I asked coldly, "Can we request an abortion?" This question sent Jane into a terrible rage and it was the first time we had a quarrel. As a mat-ter of fact, my demand could hardly be met, for during this period, Mao Tse-tung was obsessed with his theory that it was good to have a big population and the bigger the better, and throughout the land a campaign was being launched vehemently against Thomas Robert Malthus and all those Chinese scholars who dared to advocate birth control. All across the country, abortion was strictly prohibited and neither contraceptives nor condoms were available.

Extraordinarily strong was Jane's physiologic reaction to pregnancy. She could neither eat nor drink, and vomited from time to time. She was very ill. Too, she was more homesick than ever and missed Shang-hai very much. Unlike me, who loved Peking, she disliked Peking the moment we got there. At that time, Peking was far less prosperous and modern than Shanghai. However, this was not the main reason that Jane disliked it. As she looks very much like a Hindu, people on the streets in Peking used to surround her, stare at her, and mistake her for a foreigner. This upset her very much. Now, since she was so ill, the physician wrote out a sick-leave certificate allowing her quite a long pe-riod of rest. Under that social system, those who were employed by state institutions or state-operated businesses enjoyed free medical care. Each work unit, *dan-wei*, had one certain hospital to take care of its personnel. No one could go on sick leave unless he or she got permis-sion from one of the physicians in that hospital. Jane was now fully entitled to take a long rest and was free to go to Shanghai. However, she was a little scared of the one-day-and-two-night train trip and des-perately wanted me to accompany her. In order to comply with her pleading, I managed to obtain a sick-leave certificate.

There is a long story to tell about my sick leave, and I would like to go back to what happened in my childhood. Dr. Christy T'iao, a well-known St. John's and University of Philadelphia trained lung specialist in Shanghai, was both my father's schoolmate and the husband of one of my father's sisters. As such, he was very trusted by my father. In my childhood, my parents used to take me to Uncle Christy's clinic for a reg-ular X-ray checkup. Once, Uncle Christy discovered a dark spot on the

X-ray negative and concluded that I had contracted tuberculosis. He prescribed Ramifon and confinement to bed, but I held out against the prescription. I felt very well and had little faith in modern science; therefore, I totally distrusted his diagnosis. I refused to take any medication or lie in bed, and declared that I would not go for X-ray checks anymore. My parents worshipped Uncle Christy as if he were God; thus, a great war between two generations broke out in my family. As a compromise, they rescinded the order of long rest, while I took Ramifon as prescribed and promised to continue the regular checkups. After a certain period, Uncle Christy claimed that I might have been cured, but he was not quite sure of it until several months later, when he was able to compare the X-ray negatives taken before and after. He said that only through the comparison could the stability of my disease be confirmed. I did not care very much about his judgments about me. I believed only in myself and was sure that I was not ill at all.

Now, as I needed a sick-leave certificate, the precious dark spot on my chest suddenly came to my mind. I went to the hospital that took care of the Hsin Hua News Agency employees' health and claimed I had some common symptoms of tuberculosis, such as coughing and perspiring in my sleep. They immediately gave me an X-ray checkup, and the doctor said I had contracted tuberculosis. He prescribed sick leave and also hospitalization. Oh, my God! How could I agree to be hospitalized! But the problem was that the certificate for sick leave could not be separated from the notice of hospitalization. There was no way that I could pick one and ignore the other. I had no choice but to follow the nurse who was asked by the doctor to escort me to the ward, but as soon as the nurse left the ward, I went home. I packed up some clothing and took the train back to Shanghai with Jane. Thank God! This took place in December of 1952.

After we had got to Shanghai, our so-called organization repeatedly wrote us trying to persuade us to go back to Peking. Although we both had certificates for sick leave and, therefore, were not guilty of absenteeism, they still severely criticized me for fleeing the hospital without the doctor's consent. This, they said, demonstrated how serious my anarchist ideology and behavior were and also showed a typical bourgeois individualism. Their charges strengthened my determination not to return to Peking, for it was crystal clear that if I returned there, I would certainly be used by them as a negative example. My sick leave was long and Jane's gestational reaction lasted until childbirth, so we stayed in Shanghai for the whole period. After her parturition in July 1953, we started writing to the Hsin Hua News Agency to request resignation.

Frankly speaking, I had no aversion whatsoever to the job in the Foreign Language Broadcasting Department, where I had ample opportunity to learn and practice English and, most of all, had access to the dispatches of Reuters and the Associated Press. It was true that the conditions of room and board were not as good as in Shanghai, but I could easily accommodate myself to them. What I could never become accustomed to was the political ambience of this government agency. In spite of the fact that it had some foreign atmosphere around it, it bore the trademark of communism. One thing which Communists of all persuasions have in common is regimentation or what they call collectivism. No individual inclination is tolerated. The atmosphere of collectivism in the Foreign Language Broadcasting Department was never diluted.

This was what I once experienced. During that period, ballroom dances were quite popular within the Communist Party. Dancing parties were often held in the Hsin Hua News Agency, but at that time I was not as interested in dancing as I had been in Shanghai, and Jane and I often excused ourselves from these parties. But to go it alone in such a highly disciplined camp involves some danger. It seemed wrong that this newly wedded couple never showed up for the dancing parties while others did. Later, I heard some gossip that we refused to dance because of our feudalistic and conservative ideologies. Although I did not mind how people thought of us, I could no longer put up with such a strong collectivist situation. That was the main reason I decided to quit the job.

But it was not easy to resign. Quitting a job meant quitting the revolution. The organization took it seriously and took a long time to study it. So it was not until September 1953 that we got approval of our resignation through the mail. The organization advised us that we no longer belonged to the Hsin Hua News Agency on the grounds of automatically leaving office. In the meantime, Jane's relationship with the Youth League was also automatically terminated. I could not be happier with that, for from the first day the Party and League organizations of St. John's forced Jane to part from me, I was so indignant that

I vowed, "Not only shall I defeat your attempt to either entice me into your camp or stop my relationship with Jane, but I am also determined to draw Jane away from your League. We'll wait and see." Now I felt elated by the fact that Jane had married me and also that she had withdrawn from the Youth League. That meant that in the tug-of-war with the Party and the League organizations, I had won. But something that was indiscernible then was going to happen later. I had won this game, but I was to lose the next, a bigger one. The game I won became the stake for the next game I lost.

Five years later, during the Anti-Rightist movement, my resignation from the Hsin Hua News Agency and my insistence that Jane give up her membership in the Youth League were cited by the revolutionary critics as proofs of my antagonism against the Communist Party.

CHAPTER 4

A Counterrevolutionary Rendezvous

J ANE AND I RETURNED TO SHANGHAI FROM PEKING at the end of 1952. From then on, I was determined not only to leave the Hsin Hua News Agency for good, but also never to enter any other official institution. Knowing that it would be impossible for me, a liberal, to become a Party follower, I decided to pick up a job as a free-lance translator.

At that time, there existed three types of publishing houses: state-operated, state-private, and private. The state-operated publishing houses were actually bureaucratic organizations, accessible only to big shots. Translators, other than big shots, relied primarily on private and state-private publishers, which were much more active in inviting contributors. Royalties, calculated on the basis of the number of characters, were sufficient to provide a decent living, much better than that of government employees. The nationally known writers got somewhat confused and disoriented at the time of liberation and were not to publish anything; thus, there were not very many literary works on the market during that period. But people need nourishment for their minds. Once creative works were not available, translations flourished. There was a shortcut for the selection of materials to be translated. During the period of one-sided reliance on the Soviet Union, mainland

China followed its example in almost every respect. Publishing was no exception. For the selection of translation materials, all the translators had to do was keep an eye on the literary commentaries in *Pravda*, *Izvestya*, and some English periodicals published in Russia. Whoever was praised by the Soviet critics was suitable for translation and publication. Just like a hungry person who was not so choosy about his food, the Chinese readers were not particular about the available publications at that time.

Two years earlier, while I was still a student at St. John's University, I used some of my leisure time to translate Erskine Caldwell's novel *All Night Long* into Chinese. This novel, which I had borrowed from my professor of English and American literature, tells the story of Soviet guerrillas penetrating into German-occupied areas and fighting with German enemies. I thought this kind of content would surely come into vogue, so I finished the translation in one breath and tried to have it published. At first, a certain publisher did consider publishing it, because another novel of Caldwell's, *Tobacco Road*, had already been rendered into Russian and published in Russia. The good comments it received in the USSR were like a green light in China. But unexpectedly, right in the middle of negotiating about the publication of my Chinese version of *All Night Long*, some reports from Russia said that Howard Fast, the pet of the Soviets in America then, had written and invited Caldwell to participate in the activities of the World Peace Council, a tool of the Soviet Union's united front in the international arena. Caldwell simply disregarded the invitation. This was viewed as an act of unprogressiveness or deviation from the proletarian revolution. His name was expunged from the list of revolutionaries and his works taken off the revolutionary bookshelves. The publication of *All Night Long* was, of course, banned in Red China as well as in the Soviet Union.

At that moment, two of my best classmates, Hugo and Antique, happened to have problems with the centralized placement and were out of employment simultaneously. We lived in the same neighborhood and saw one another very often. We entered into partnership for translation. Our purpose was to publish, so we tried hard to cater to the political taste of the proletariat in selecting materials. At that time there was only one state-operated foreign-language bookstore in Shanghai.

We bought a book written by a British worker whose name was so obscure that I forgot it long ago; however, I still remember that the name of the book was *Not Like This*. The book was so bizzare that even after we had finished the translation, we still did not know what it really meant, and what the author liked or disliked.

It was neither fiction nor nonfiction nor autobiography. Though as dry as dust, it sold. Maybe it was the quality of translation that sold, who knows? It was published by a very small publishing house, an enterprise run by only one man who acted both as boss and as servicing boy. His name was Hsu. He was a little bit clumsy even though he had an air of haughtiness about him. He was quite shrewd in business but knew very little about literature. He contracted all the editing chores to a person who, during the 1940s, had been in Shanghai as an advertising expert for the cinema industry and a translator specialized in rendering the names of American films into Chinese. As copywriting was no longer needed in mainland China, he changed his job and became a contract editor.

In the wake of the publication of our first translated work, we started undertaking another project. We translated *Brother Bill Mackie*, a book by an American author who was also a worker. Unlike our first attempt, in which we submitted our translation to the publisher after its completion, our second one followed the general practice of the time, that is, before we started the translation, we obtained Hsu's consent to publish it and acquired a contract with him. The benefit of signing a contract was that the authors or translators, as was the case with us, were entitled to draw a tiny portion of the royalties in advance and be compensated in case the publisher failed to publish the work after the translation was completed. Nevertheless, sometime later it happened that one of us somehow offended the contract editor. So when we finished the translation of *Brother Bill Mackie*, he told the boss, Hsu, that this book might find no market and lose money. Thus, Hsu refused to carry out his obligation to publish it.

Young people are likely to be impatient. We had assumed that contracts should be honored by everybody under any condition; therefore, we sued Hsu in court. A court session was opened one day. We three innocent youths put on our best clothes and for the first time in our lives took the sacred contract to the court. But, to our surprise, it was not the court that we knew or could imagine. No wig, no robe, no seat for the plaintiff, no seat for the defendant, and no seats for the observers. As a matter of fact, there was no courtroom at all. All of us just sat in a row in front of some classroom desks in a schoolroom-like hall. The judge, dressed in the ordinary Maoist uniform, said nothing about law. Maybe there was no law to be discussed. Having cross-examined the plaintiffs and the defendant, he seemed to begin to have a clearer idea of the case. After setting Hsu free, he tried to help us three young men straighten out our wrong or muddled thinking: "You are youths. Youths should follow our Party. To follow the Party, you should participate in the revolutionary work and not choose a free-lance job like yours. You can gain nothing from a free-lance job and, most of all, there is no future in working for private businessmen like Hsu." From his tone and attitude we could discern his good will and, maybe, some real kindness. But what did this have to do with our lawsuit? Since we wanted to win the case, we were very cautious not to do anything to offend the judge and, therefore, just listened to him and said nothing.

A few days later, we received a written court decision. Hsu was supposed to pay us a certain amount of money as compensation, in addition to the cash we had drawn earlier. What the amount was I have forgotten. All I can remember is that it was very small, obviously meant to be a token of consolation. The court verdict did not mention our contract at all, nor how the amount was calculated. But even this tiny amount Hsu refused to pay. We called him by phone, but no one answered. We went to see him in person, but no one answered the door. We wrote him, but no reply came. After some period of procrastination, Hsu was arrested because of some other case which, it was said, was related to Hu Feng, a literary critic personally persecuted by Mao Tse-tung, and whom, for safety's sake, nobody wanted to have any contact with at that time. As we did not want to get into trouble by letting people know that we had had any contact with Hsu, our case was finally settled by leaving it unsettled.

I came to realize that it was not easy to earn a living by freelancing. Intellectuals were apt to jostle with one another, and the translation workers were no exception. Moreover, to translate fiction, one had to watch the new literary trends in the Soviet Union closely, rush to the Foreign Languages Bookstore to purchase the books which the Soviets were praising, and fight to be the first to submit the plan for the translation and publication of these books to the authorities for censorship. The swiftest won the race. We, the young people, not being familiar with the literary circles, were far from competitive.

Fortuitously, I became a teacher. Some alumni of St. John's had run a school of continuing education for a number of years called Johanean Continuation School, and at this time they were short a teacher and needed someone to teach on a temporary basis. Hugo, one of my translation collaborators, got this information and introduced me to them. It was spring 1954. As the school was privately owned, it retained the right to hire people. Nevertheless, the owners were trying very hard to have this school turned over to the state, so that they could "eat from the big iron bowl." Accordingly, they took the initiative in courting the Bureau of Education by reporting all important things to it from time to time. This was a period when the whole society was under the strong influence of the policy of "leaning to one side," in other words, leaning toward the Soviet big brother only. The teaching methods used in the USSR were adopted in all parts of China and carried to the point of ludicrousness. Every teacher was required to prepare his or her lecture notes for each lesson, which were called the teaching plan. The course I taught was Chinese. The contents of the textbook were indiscriminately chosen articles of cheap propaganda, full of dogma and slogans. But I was still required to write a teaching plan for each lesson. For the sake of eeking out a livelihood, I muddled along for a semester.

Fortunately, in the following summer the Johanean Continuation School was accepted by the Bureau of Education as a state-operated, regular junior high school. As the school was going to increase its classes, more teachers were needed. Thus I became a regular teacher when the summer vacation was over. Taking advantage of this opportunity, I requested that I teach history instead of Chinese. The request was granted; thenceforth, I was in my element. On the one hand, I was familiar with numerous historical stories and, in order to make my classes more interesting to the students, used to employ the techniques of those storytellers who really fascinated their audience. On the other hand, I not only learned by rote all those names and years that would be mentioned in class, but I could always step into the classroom without bringing the textbook with me and could always insert such sentences amid my storytelling as "Now please turn to page such-and-such and look at line such-and-such and you will find such-and-such words." Students were stunned. They found my classes interesting and the teacher erudite. Even the most disorderly class in the school was quiet and concentrated on my history lessons.

I was so proud of my achievements that I became overbearing enough to refuse to participate in any collective teaching preparation, which was also one of the things required of all teachers by the Soviet educational system. As to the teaching plan, I did not bother to write it at all. The principal was aware of my popularity with the students attending my course, so he turned a blind eye to my self-exemption from the teaching plan. When some of the other history teachers ventured to ask about my teaching plan, they simply got a reply from me such as, "It's here," while I pointed to my brain. All they could do was complain to the principal, and all the principal could do was advise me to restrain my arrogance.

That semester saw the fast growth of my prestige among the students. As a result, I became known to other schools in the district. One middle school nearby invited me to teach history part-time there. So the extra and full-time jobs together resulted in a very tight schedule for me. I had to shout for five or six hours in a row almost every weekday. But I managed it very well, for I was young and vigorous, and the two schools used the same textbook.

As the school had just been turned over to the state, its salary system remained unchanged; that is, pay was counted on an hour-to-hour basis. Therefore, during that period my monthly income exceeded a hundred *yuan* in RMB (*renminbi*) while the official salary for a college graduate was forty *yuan* per month. That is to say, I made one and a half times as much as what I had earned in the Hsin Hua News Agency. The principal had no objection to my concurrent jobs, because he felt honored that another school was seeking help from his faculty. He was very nice to me and he helped Jane to land a teaching job in another middle school. At first I had had the intention of having Jane work in the same school with me, but the principal thought otherwise. He confided to me that he had been much annoyed by the situation where this school had already had too many family ties. Among the existing colleagues, there were two pairs of husbands and wives, two pairs of brothers, and one pair of sisters. He did not want to make the situation more complicated. I fully understood his predicament and was happy enough that Jane had been offered a teacher's job at the school nearby.

The atmosphere of this school had in fact been fouled by these complicated relations. Various factions had been formed. Although I did not belong to any of them, it was inevitable that I should have contact with my colleagues, and this led to different degrees of closeness. Those to whom I was relatively close did not count me as their man because I never gave the kind of allegiance they required of me. Those toward whom I was relatively distant took me for a sort of dissident. For example, the two pairs of brothers—one a deputy principal and history teacher, and the other a Chinese language teacher and the teachers' union branch leader—were antagonistic to each other and they both took me as their foe. They always spoke ill of me behind my back to the principal, whom they half-jokingly criticized as my shield. Their enemies told me all these things with the intention of further sowing discord between us. But I would dismiss it with a laugh because I did not care very much about what people said about me. The principal, out of good will, repeatedly warned me in private to be careful in airing my views, but I did not pay enough heed to his warnings.

Personally, I hated playing games with others but loved watching others playing games. Sometimes I could not hold back from making some humorous, sarcastic remarks, which would set the whole room rocking with laughter. I never anticipated that some of my colleagues, who had laughed at my jokes so heartily, would later use them as a tool against me. For example, I still remember the day when we were required to talk at the group meeting about what each of us had learned from a Soviet movie which we had just seen and which was said to be a model movie at that time. It was about two Soviet soldiers demobilized after World War II who discovered that they had married one and the same woman, but solved the problem with courtesy and thoughtfulness. The official media then praised this movie to the skies and held that it represented the moral standards of communism. When it was my turn, I said, "Now I understand that the superiority of communism lies in its inconceivable system of 'two husbands partitioning one wife,'" and this caused a roaring laugh. Present at the meeting was my best friend, Hugo, who by that time had also joined the faculty of this school. He was a cool-headed young man. He sensed some danger that might lie ahead of me, so he gave me some earnest warnings. He was right. Before long, some of my other friends in Shanghai attended a seminar at which the director of the Bureau of Education made a speech. He cited without mentioning my name the above joke as an example of the current anticommunist trend of thought. Apparently my sarcastic comment had been reported to the Bureau of Education. It was fortunate for me, however, that there was no political movement going on at that time; otherwise, my joke would have caused immediate disaster to me. But those who took malicious pleasure in my bad luck were pleased to have made a breach.

Originally a school of extension studies, this school had quite a number of older-than-average students. In the classes I was teaching many students were older than I, and the others approached my age. Among them, one beautiful and sexy girl, two years younger than I, entered into my life unexpectedly. At first, my awareness of her existence was due to some gossip. Both at faculty meetings and in private talks, quite a few teachers liked to choose this girl as their topic. It seemed that she had done nothing wrong, and the sole reason that they criticized her was that she had had too many romances and too many boyfriends. I thought that she was a good girl, because she was very attentive and quiet in class, and that she was treated unfairly. I began to sympathize with her. Of course, my doubts about this rumor might have been groundless, as one's academic performance is not necessarily a criterion of one's behavior. I neither argued nor joined with my colleagues in gossiping about her. However, whether my judgment about her was right or not, I kept aloof from other people's criticisms about her, and there was no doubt that my attitude toward her was somewhat different from that of other teachers. For one thing, she was never antagonistic toward me, as she was toward other teachers. Only in my class was she attentive and hardworking just like any good student, a sharp contrast with her ordinary attitude of acting recklessly and writing herself off as hopeless.

At that time, I used to walk to and from work, as it was only a half-hour walk for a single trip. This girl, Eva, lived far away and usually took the same route that I did after getting off the bus on her way to school. Sometimes we met en route and greeted each other and walked the rest of the distance together. She was friendly to me and willing to confide her complaints that some people had made malicious criticisms of her. I offered some advice and said that everyone should treasure his or her reputation. I made it clear that I held the strong opinion that one should mind his or her own business and not interfere with others, nor should he or she care what others talked about. She also made no secret of her having had boyfriends when she was still underage and having made love with one of the boys, who was later jailed for other offenses. Since she was now a grown-up, she said, she was eager to learn. At this point she had no boyfriends at all; therefore, she was very annoyed by the rumors and gossip about her and especially upset by the discrimination other teachers had shown. She acknowledged that among all the faculty members, only I did not alienate her, so she felt admiration as well as appreciation for me.

Confucius was right: Male and female should keep a certain distance from each other, for intimacy can lead to attraction and attraction to courtship. The relationship between Eva and me developed in this way. At first we walked together by chance, and later by intentionally going in a roundabout way, sometimes under the moon and stars. Fortunately, or unfortunately, we did not have any physical relationship, not because we did not want to, but because we did not have time. Before we could start any intimacies, we suffered a destructive blow.

Since she became one of my students, her peculiar attentiveness in my class had given rise to other teachers' and students' suspicion and gossip, such as "Why is she so obedient and diligent in Wong's class while so obstinate and unruly in other classes?" Without any real evidence, they could only talk about it in private. When we started to meet en route to school occasionally, neither of us had the intention of evading others' eyes and ears because we did not have any guilty conscience. At that time we, at least I, did not know that some busybodies had been keeping an eye on us. Neither were we aware that someone had been spying on us in the dark. The next morning, after we had walked together into the small hours, I was summoned to the principal's office soon after I reached school.

"You don't have to go to class today," the principal said to me, "someone will substitute for you."

Before I had time to ask why, I was interrogated by a group of three or four, including the principal and the union leader. They asked me to make a clean breast of my relationship with Eva. They repeatedly proclaimed to me the well-known policy of the Communist Party, "Leniency to those who confess their crimes and severity to those who refuse to." By so doing, they implied that this was a criminal case.

"I've committed no crimes," was my only answer.

Then they made some retreat outwardly, "Okay, we are not talking about crimes. Just tell us what's going on between you and Eva."

I did not intend to hide anything from anybody, whether what I had done was right or wrong. I did what I did. No secrecy. That was my natural disposition. But at this point, when some girl's reputation was at stake, I flatly denied any extraordinary relationship between Eva and me. Then they tried hard to extort a confession from me. They repeated over and over again the well-known slogan, "We will not withdraw our forces till complete victory." This helped to prepare my mind for a protracted war against them. That first day they got nothing out of me, in spite of incessant interrogation from morning to evening.

Before they allowed me to go home, they issued an order to me, "Don't try to say anything to Eva, not a word. Don't even think about arranging to give the same story. We can tell you frankly that we have already spread a dragnet and kept a lookout for your every single activity." On the safe side, I carried out their order to the letter without questioning their truthfulness.

The next day, they continued interrogating me and I continued denying their accusation. They attempted to force me to admit our sexual relations. I denied not only this charge, but any other alleged erroneous relationships existing between Eva and me. After I had been at loggerheads with them for several days, they finally showed their false cards.

When they heard me say with curt finality that no erroneous relations had ever existed between Eva and me, they tried to cow me into submission, "Not to mince matters, this is not something you did alone. Even if it was done by you alone, there is no way anything could escape the discerning eyes of the mass of the people, let alone something done between two people. Almost every criminal hopes to obtain leniency. If you do not, how can you be sure that your accomplice does not? Now, we can tell you frankly, Eva, through the education of the school and her parents, has undergone drastic changes in ideology over the last few days. She has acknowledged that she was formerly deceived by you and fell in love with you. Now she has a clearer understanding of your ugly features and hates you. She has exposed your hideous behavior of bewitching her and raping her."

Without hesitation, I refuted this accusation and said, "No such thing. Neither did I deceive her, nor rape her."

"How stubborn you are! Okay, let's give you a little bit of a hint. At such-and-such an hour on such-and-such a day, you two were promenading along such-and-such a road and had a long hug and kiss. Was that not something erroneous?"

I was somehow stunned then. This was really something between her and me. How could they know if she had not confessed it? It seemed that Eva had succumbed to their pressure. Since she had acknowledged it, it did not make any sense for me to deny it. So I said that was true. Instantly they pulled out pen and paper and asked me to put it in writing. That I did. "No," they said, "that's not enough. We want every detail. Rewrite it."

I complied with their order. "No," again they said, "We don't need your day-to-day account. Our ultimate goal is to transform you by changing your thoughts and attitude. You should confess not only what you did but also what you thought."

It seemed that they needed a lengthy article. This I complied with, too.

"No," again they said, "that's not what we want. You have to tell in detail the whole story of your romance, from beginning to end."

"I have already told it," I retorted.

"Not at all," they said, "you only talked about trivial things. Your confession was far from thoroughgoing. Even these things were not told voluntarily. Of course, it's better to confess involuntarily than not to confess at all. But why don't you confess all you did from now on? That would be far better for you. We will give you one more chance."

"I have no more to confess."

"You don't? We have something." They said, intimidatingly, "What we hinted to you was just one percent or even zero-point-one percent of the information we have. Just because you are a young man, we are trying as hard as we can to redeem you. This is our Party's policy of protecting youth. Even if you are so stubborn as to try to bring ruin upon yourself, we still want to make every effort to pull you back from the blind alley. That's why we are allowing some leeway for you. We will not tell you all that we know about you. When the time comes to let you know all the information we have about you, your case will be handled as an example of refusal to confess and will be dealt with severely. Right now the authorities concerned are just waiting. A car will come and pick you up whenever we give them a call."

The message was very clear. They were going to put me in jail. I was concerned about the possibility that Eva had been compelled to add color to her confession because of their pressure. If that was the case, how could I keep up with it? Even if I consented to add some sensational details to the story, I still could not make my account tally with her fabrication, and they would certainly use the inconsistent parts as a new weapon for further extortion. It would be a vicious circle. I decided to refuse to make any fabrication, despite the fact that they repeatedly put psychological pressure on me. Some of these self-appointed judges urged me to make a clean breast of it, while others played the role of friends for the same purpose of luring me into confessing the "serious crimes" I had never committed. Once they pointed to some people in police uniforms outside the office, saying, "The police car is waiting outside. Are you really intending to receive the severest punishment by stubbornly refusing to confess?" I was so naïve that several times I did prepare my mind for being put into the police car and tasting life in jail, but somehow those uniformed persons always disappeared later and the police car never showed up. In retrospect, the police car, at that time, gave much better service than does the taxi these days; it was available whenever it was sent for and never minded making fruitless trips.

Finally, at my firm declaration of no more to confess, they resorted to bluffing in order to get me to play into their hands. The principal, who was formerly known to be too friendly toward me, now tried to talk to me in a friendly tone, "You probably are not aware that this case actually is not handled by us." Pointing to the others, he said, "The parents of Eva have already submitted their petition to the police. As we consider that you are still young and that it is not good for a young man to have a record with the police, we took the initiative to shoulder the responsibility of helping you. We did our best to protect you from being taken into custody by the police. But, as you know well, we all are very busy with our work, either administrative or teaching. We really don't have much time. And, also, we haven't had this kind of experience. So in this case we have been guided by the police all the time. Just think about this: can you imagine that the police would be helpless in dealing with cases like yours?"

During that period, the literature market was flooded with counterspy fiction and movies in which the Communist policemen were depicted as omnipotent and infinitely resourceful, and I was more or less influenced by them. The principal continued, "To tell you the truth, at first Eva did not confess having had any sex with you. It was only after she had had a physical checkup under the authorization of the police and her hymen was discovered to be broken that she acknowledged that you were the one who had taken away her virginity. Her confession was taken as a voluntary one, though it was made under the pressure of evidence. She got leniency in accordance with the Party's policy. Now it is up to you. Whether you will deserve leniency or severity is not under our jurisdiction or that of the police. You can make your own choice. But there isn't too much time left. This is really your last chance. I would like to show my hand to you. If you make a confession right now, I guarantee that you will receive leniency. Please don't wait until we put Eva's written materials in front of you or have Eva confront you. Then you'll lose all chance of getting lenient treatment. Even if you yourself don't care about it, you have to think about your family. You have just had your second son, and your wife is still on maternity leave. If you should be put in jail, how would your parents, your wife, and your sons feel? It is still not too late to make a confession right now. We promise to take it as your voluntary confession and keep the secret for you."

His intimate words and sincere attitude, backed by his fierce facial expression, subdued me. As a matter of fact, this scandal had already created a sensation; therefore, how could he talk about keeping a secret? Excessively nice words usually connote something untrue and insincere. But at that time it did not occur to me to make such an analysis. I did not, as I should have, even question the story he told me about Eva's being compelled to make a charge against me only after her hymen had been proven to be broken, for it totally contradicted what they had said earlier—she had thoroughly exposed my crimes because she had broken away from me in ideology. Failing to make such an analysis, I took his words as true, because Eva herself had once told me that she was not a virgin. The reason might be that she had been so disheartened by the physical checkup that she just wanted to make light of this matter by shifting the responsibility onto me. It sounded rather logical, and I would not blame her.

While these thoughts were flashing through my mind, I considered some countermeasures: Since the checkup had proven her to be no longer a virgin, someone had to be responsible for it. And since she had accused me of having sex with her, that meant that she had been under huge pressure and cajolery from the school leadership and also that she had been reluctant to mention her ex-boyfriend. I might go and reveal the truth, but then I might be countered with another question, "How do you know it was her ex-boyfriend who did it?" And if I said that she herself had told me about it, then they would retort, "If there exists no extraordinary relationship between you, why did she confide such a secret to you?" I was caught in a dilemma. Under such circumstances, I would rather take the responsibility, so that things might be easier for both of us. But how could I fabricate a story of having had sex with her, when in reality I had not?

These investigators were all alumni of St. John's University who had graduated several years earlier than I, and all of them had grown up in pre-liberation Shanghai, a "paradise" for adventurers. They were very worldly-wise and could tell what one thought just by one's facial expression. When they discerned some traces of my vacillation, they changed their tone and sounded as if they were placing themselves in my position. "We have no intention of deliberately making things difficult for you. On the contrary, we just want a justifiable account for this case. Now, it is an undeniable fact that she is not a virgin. We have to make further references to it. Of course, we should look at the problem from all sides. As you are both adults, each of you has his or her own responsibility, although you as a teacher should shoulder more responsibility than the student. However, it is the Party's policy that the final conclusion depends more upon the attitude than on the mistake itself. If you make a confession now, we guarantee that you will be considered to have had a good attitude. All you have to do is write an apologetic letter, acknowledging your mistake, but we do not need any details of your lovemaking, because we are not interested in any sex stories. But you need to admit that you did make love with her and then make a self-criticism and self-analysis using the moral standards of communism. That's all. We sincerely hope to put an end to this case as quickly as possible. We have many other things to do and can't afford to waste any more time on this matter."

It seemed to me at the time that they were placing full confidence in me. I trusted them, so I wrote my self-criticism right away as instructed. I just touched upon the fact that we had had sex and then made a lengthy analysis of the seriousness of the mistake from the revolutionary point of view. I put the blame on my feudalistic and capitalistic outlooks on life, and felt ashamed when comparing myself with the numerous Communist martyrs and warriors. I also apologized for letting down the leaders of this school, since they had been so kind and magnanimous to me. I wrote more than ten pages at one stroke. It eventually came to a finale. They made it clear to me that the administrative disciplinary penalty would be meted out by the Bureau of Education. But, until that happened, I could continue to teach as usual. They also informed me that the woman student had already been transferred to some other school on the insistence of the Bureau of Education, but exempted from any punishment.

With the resumption of my teaching work, I thought the crisis was half over. Especially Eva's exemption from punishment made me feel good for her as well as for myself. Even if they said that the teacher should take more responsibility than the student, I might at worst have some warning or an error put on record. However, beyond my expectation, just a few days later the disciplinary penalty was announced. On this kind of thing, there was no procrastination, no bureaucracy. The principal informed me that the Bureau of Education had made the decision to clear me from the ranks of teachers. That was an order of dismissal. The principal made some final remarks, and I have never been able to tell if they were honest or hypocritical: "I have never anticipated that our friendship would terminate like this. I hope to meet you again sometime in the future. And I also hope that you, in your introspection, can be strict with yourself and broad-minded toward others." Without further conversation, I departed.

Peril from the outside is always helpful in relieving one of internal disturbance. During the period in which I was not allowed to teach and put under investigation, the news inevitably spread to my wife. Naturally, it upset Jane a great deal and caused a lot of trouble in my family. In a certain period and to a certain extent, Jane did the same as the school administration, that is, tried to find out the facts and criticized my mistake. I was attacked from both within and without. The dismissal directly affected the economy of my family. This shocked Jane even more. But the shock helped to end our estrangement, just as a wall, which has first been damaged by a car, has the traces of its original damage eliminated by an earthquake that follows. Jane was no less upset than I at such a severe punishment. Together we went to the Bureau of Education.

There we were received by an official from the Personnel Department, who looked very much like one of the two pairs of brothers in the school where I had taught. And even the name he signed on our "exit certificate" was almost the same as that of the pair of brothers, except for one character. I did not know whether they belonged to the same family or not. When we went there for the first time, I did not complain about the disciplinary penalty or demand its redress, because I was fully aware that the Communists would not listen to any grievances. They could never be wrong. So I just stressed the fact that I was a young man and should participate in revolutionary work. This official, at the sight of my wife and me, revealed a trace of surprise, but soon returned to normal. Having listened to what I had said, he made no direct comment, but remarked, "Your attitude was bad while in that school, so you deserved such a severe penalty. If you want a job now, you should write a profound self-criticism. This is the initial step." I took him at his word. I returned home and wrote another lengthy self-criticism. I put such labels on myself, as "feudalistic literate," "old diehard," "hooligan in a metropolis," "immoral intellectual," and "dirty soul." A number of other derogatory terms was employed. Anyway, I acknowledged that I had committed a serious blunder.

I delivered my self-criticism in person. The official accepted it and promised to study my case soon. But for a long time there was no news at all. Jane and I went there again. Jane, in her position as my wife, came straight to the point that the punishment was much too severe. She spoke mildly and tactfully, but firmly. She implored him to give me a new job. However, this official went back on his word and evaded the subject by pointing to my written self-criticism. "Could you say his mistake was not serious enough? Look at what he wrote. He himself acknowledged his mistake was most serious."

I did write "my mistake was most serious," but I never expected that he would use my self-criticism as a weapon to oppose me. He added, "Our Party has a style of work, that is, making decisions based on the situation. For instance, during the movements of Three-Anti's and Five-Anti's, some Party members were executed for some petty offenses of graft and embezzlement. Can you say the punishments they received were much too severe? Wong, both as a 'teacher of the people' and as a married man, seduced and raped a woman student. This was a crime deserving imprisonment. Dismissal is far from severe."

At this, I began to think about totally reversing the original verdict by denying that I had had any sexual relationship with the woman student at all, but instead of waiting for my response, he made some further remarks which astonished me even more.

"You never treated your teaching job seriously," he said, "nor did you attend the collective preparation. You could never produce any lecture notes. Politically, your thoughts are reactionary. You slandered the Soviet Union and the Communist system. We have a reliable record of all your offenses." Then he turned to Jane, "I hold a very different opinion from yours. I think the punishment was too light."

Now it seemed clear that the case was not simply a romance between teacher and student. Somebody must have played some underhanded tricks and stabbed me in the back, informing against me on every joke I had made about the Communists. My romance offered them a pretext for attacking and punishing me. Evidently, this official in the Bureau of Education was singing the same tune as those who had been plotting against me. It would be a waste of time to implore for kind deliberation, so we left and never went there again. It was a nightmare to go there. Each time we had to spend a lot of time and energy. The information desk was itself a bureaucratic organization, and always gave visitors a hard time. We were at their mercy. We were not allowed to go in unless they were "kind" enough to call to inform the officials inside the building of our arrival. Even if the official in charge agreed to see us, we still had to wait for a long while before he stepped out to meet us. Sometimes he just refused to see us without giving any reason. Then, could we make an appointment with him for sometime later? No way. We could come back and try our luck if we wished, but we still had to go through the same procedures.

One day, sometime after I was fired from that school, I went out and on the corner of the block to which my house belonged, I encountered a woman student from my former class. She was Eva's neighbor and for a time had shared the desk with Eva. Though she had been one of my students, I had seldom talked with her, as she was rather reserved. This time she rushed to me the moment she saw me, and handed a letter to me, saying, "Eva asked me to deliver this to you." I was stunned for a while, and she took the time to tell me that while I was under investigation, Eva had several times stood on the street near my house for a couple of hours hoping to meet me. But each time she failed to run into me and, therefore, had not been able to disclose to me what had been happening. Now she had heard of my dismissal and was very angry. She wrote this letter, but had not been able to find a way to deliver it to me. It was not safe to post it by mail, and she did not dare to be seen walking around in this area because it was on condition of no longer keeping in touch with me that she had been exempted from punishment. So Eva had implored her for help. Moved by Eva's sincerity, she agreed to play the role of courier. She had already stood on this street that day for several hours when she met me. It was totally beyond expectation, and all I did was say, "Thanks," and urge her to leave instantly. I did not want to have any further trouble, but I still accepted the letter and took it home.

In this letter, besides expressing her regret for my predicament, Eva described in some detail what had happened during the process of investigation. The following is a summary of her letter.

> I was also investigated at the same time you were, but in another office. They wanted me to confess. But from the very beginning, they made it clear that I should have nothing to worry about. They said that as you were a teacher and I was a student, the

entire responsibility would rest upon you and I would be under their protection. Moreover, they said, you have a bureaucratic and capitalistic family background, while I come from a peasant-worker family, so it had to be you who corrupted me. My awareness that they were deliberately plotting against you made me careful not to give them any way to harm you. Therefore I kept saying that it was I who loved you even though I knew you were married and that I took the initiative. That was what I told them. I also said that just because I knew you were married, we had never developed any relationship beyond the boundary of normal friendship. At first, they wanted me to fabricate a story of your seducing and raping me. They were utterly disappointed at hearing these words. They were so furious that they tried to intimidate me by pointing out that I had committed the crime of wrecking a legal family since I had known you are a married man and I still loved you. They told me that one might be sentenced to prison for committing this kind of crime. I retorted that I only loved you but had never entered into any sexual relation with you, so it was unfair to say I had wrecked your family. During that period, they repeatedly told me that, as you were endeavoring to obtain leniency, you had already made a confession and that if I still resisted exposing you, it would be I, not you, who would get a serious punishment. I never trusted one single word they said. Furthermore, I was very calm at the bottom of my heart, because I had prepared for the worst. Therefore all their intimidation meant nothing to me. Finally, as a last resort, they decided to send me to the hospital for a physical checkup. This made me worry. I was afraid that its result would cause you trouble, as they would blame you as the one who had taken my virginity. I was compelled to let out my top secret, which had never been confided to anyone except you, that I had had sex with that former boyfriend. I thought that even if they should send me to the hospital, the result would have no use for them. Evidently they suspected that I had told the story simply for the purpose of extricating you. They made detailed inquiries about this former relation, which I had long since buried deep in the past and was very reluctant even to think about anymore. But they insisted on saying that it was merely a fabrication and that its purpose was to protect you. Under their pressure, I had no choice but to forsake my privacy and reveal every detail about it. Having questioned me about my former affairs, they stopped mentioning the proposed hospital checkup anymore. It never occurred to me that just at the moment I felt the ordeal was over, they told me that you had acknowledged having seduced me and having made love with me. They wanted me to confirm what you had confessed. At first, I flatly refused to do so, as I did not believe what they had said. Then they produced your written "confession," the sight of which almost made me faint. I could never have dreamt that you would make such a confession, which rendered fruitless all the efforts I had made. But please do not think that I am now writing to accuse you. Neither am I vindicating you. I am pretty sure that the pressure they exerted on you was a dozen times what they put on me. Furthermore, I was not punished, but you were dismissed. I could only feel sorry for you. I assume that the best consolation I can give you now would be revealing to you all that happened. So please don't take my explanation as an accusation of you. I fully understand that you need no consolation, because I know how strong you are. You are not the type of person who is struck to the ground and lies there for long. I am praying that you will stand up very soon. Ahead you have a long way to go, so don't lose confidence. As for myself, this incident has made me stronger, and I can face this cruelty with composure. After I have written this letter and you have read it, any contact between us is no longer needed. I shall not meet you again, and I am not going to miss you either. Please forgive me and forget about me. God bless you and your family.

Having read this letter, I could not have felt worse. How could I have given in to pressure and overlooked all the efforts Eva had made to protect me? What made me feel even more remorseful was that I had damaged her reputation. From then on, we never met again. What was the good of meeting again? I have always felt guilty with regard to my wife, and no less guilty with regard to Eva.

CHAPTER 5

Reemployment

I T WAS A SULLEN, COLD, WINTER MORNING in 1955. A queue of people lined up in a piercing wind on the sports ground of the middle school near my home. I was among them. Nearly all the people seemed insensitive to the cold wind and showed warmth in their facial expressions, some cherishing ardent expectations and others prematurely reveling in rosy dreams.

It was only a few months after my dismissal by the Bureau of Education. Hope and chance came to my rescue before I had fully tasted the experience of being unemployed. At that time, the great Chinese Communist Party just started to raise the clarion calls, "March on, science and technology," and "Give full credit to intellectuals' professional knowledge." The intelligentsia was eulogized by the media, which were then invariably the mouthpieces of the Party. Across the country, each city and town was authorized to investigate and keep on file names of all those hitherto unemployed intellectuals. The sports ground was used as the makeshift registration site for the district where I lived.

Had I not been present on this scene, I could never have known that China was so rich in its human resource. In only one district of Shanghai, there were so many unemployed intellectuals that they formed a long line. They were eagerly standing in line, waiting patiently in the icy cold. No complaints. As officialdom stated publicly, and some people were inclined to think, only the elite were eligible to stand in that line.

The administration was effective in this matter. For instance, not long after the registration I got a response from a steelworks in Inner Mongolia, which was recruiting in Shanghai, saying that they were willing to offer me a job there. As I still reveled in the pipe dream that Communist rule could not last long, whatever job I took in this society seemed only a temporary affair. Therefore, although it would be a terrible hardship to live in a border area considered poor and backward, I thought it was a good chance to make a free trip and see the vast grassland of Inner Mongolia. Just when I was going to fill out and sign the form accepting the offer, a much better offer came from Lu Hsiao-man, who asked my cooperation with her in translation.

Lu Hsiao-man was the widow of the late famous poet Hsu Tsemou. After Hsu Tsemou's accidental death in 1931 she had become an opium addict. In the initial years of liberation, she lived in straitened circumstances until one day when Chen Yi, then vice premier, heard someone talk about the late poet Hsu Tsemou. By chance Chen Yi asked someone about Lu Hsiao-man, was told about Lu's hard life, and instructed that Lu be treated as a typical "object of the unified front."* Thus, Lu became a member of the Culture and History Council, where she did not have to show up regularly but received a salary each month. However, the salary was barely sufficient for her daily necessities. She needed some extra money and, in that situation, the only source of extra money seemed to be doing translations. With her fame in literary circles and her "unified front" position, the state-operated publishing houses, as official organizations sharing the responsibility of uniting the

---

*The "unified front" was a special term coined by the Communist Party which used to classify people into categories of left, middle, and right. Communists engaged themselves in endless struggles with "enemies," and in order to isolate the "enemies" they had to flirt with those whom they actually disliked but who either were no longer or had not yet been hostile to the Communists. The name "unified front" was both a slogan and a particular department for handling the flirtation. Those who had the luck of being pursued by the Communists as darlings were called "objects of the unified front" and were entitled to enjoy various levels of special treatment.

Lu Hsiao-man.

"unified front objects," were willing to make contracts with Lu Hsiao-man and advance her royalties. Lu desperately needed these, but lacked the energy to do the required job. She was in such poor health that she could hardly sit down to write. As I had the energy but had no access to this kind of contract from the publishing bureaucrats, she proposed our cooperation. I was more than happy to accept this proposal. She got the contracts, and I did the work. The remuneration for me, though only half the royalties, was much higher than the salary I would have received if I had taken the post in Inner Mongolia.

During the early years of the Republic of China, Lu Hsiao-man's father and my maternal grandfather were in the same political circle.

She and my mother had known each other when they were young, but I had never met her before. By chance, we met in a house of a master of martial arts. Since 1955, I had studied shadowboxing with Yue Huan-chih. Though a master of martial arts, Yue was originally a scholar. Prior to the so-called liberation, he had been a professor and, later, president of a university. During the fierce struggle between the Nationalists and the Communists, on the eve of liberation, he declined all public jobs and began to enjoy a very private life by coaching students in martial arts. In my impression, he never even once wore a Maoist uniform, but was always attired in the traditional Chinese fashion. It seemed that the traditional Chinese moral code still prevailed in his house. His pupils, including me, revered and served him as ancient Chinese pupils had their masters. We made tea for him and his guests, fanned him during hot seasons, and waited aside for his orders. He never addressed anyone as "comrade," as was the custom with the society at large then, but always called his guests Miss, Mrs., or Mr. So-and-so. His *kung-fu* was not only good for attack and defense, but effective at curing diseases. He never rejected any request. Those who asked for his treatment had only to drop in on the fixed dates of his martial arts classes and could get his help free of charge.

Lu Hsiao-man was one of these patients. She suffered heavily from pulmonary emphysema. Her incessant coughing could only be stopped by taking codeine. Codeine was to her what chewing gum is to young Americans. However, her access to codeine was increasingly limited as she could find fewer and fewer physicians willing to prescribe it. On the other hand, even if she acquired some through pleading, the effect of codeine on her became weaker and weaker. To her, the most effective and easiest way was to resort to Master Yue. Each time she came into the martial arts room coughing incessantly, Master Yue put one hand on her back while talking with other guests or instructing his exercising pupils. Several minutes later, Lu would stop coughing and come to life again, talking and laughing cheerfully and humorously as though nothing had happened a couple of minutes before.

Our cooperation brought me into close relationship with Lu, who, childless herself, treated and trusted me as her own child. Whatever happened, she would consult me and ask for my opinion. For example, when one of the so-called democratic parties—actually political fronts—offered her membership because she was treated as a "unified front object" by the Communist Party, she inclined to reject it, as she had no interest in politics. But when she asked me for advice, I suggested, "Although membership in this kind of party is meaningless politically, it can be very helpful to your daily life. For example, you will be eligible for the hospital that gives treatment exclusively to high-ranking people, and the physicians there will not hesitate to prescribe codeine." She was moved by my words. Beyond my expectation, she said, "All right, I'll follow your advice. But please write the application letter for me." Then she gave me a brief description of her personal history, which was to be included in the application. When I had finished the draft, I asked her to review it. If she approved it, she should copy it herself, as it was the social custom for the applicant to handwrite this kind of application. She said, "How do I have such patience and energy? I trust you. Please send it by mail. That's it." I implored her to read it over, and this she refused too. Finally, at my insistence and by putting a pen in her hand, she signed the three characters of her name herself.

But this was not too ridiculous in comparison with what was to happen two years later when, after the Anti-Rightist Movement, in which I was labeled as a rightist, all the intellectuals were called on to "lay their hearts bare" to the Party. As she was also called on to do so, she once again requested my service. This time it was a sort of full service, for she did not even bother to tell me how to "lay her heart bare." I just wrote for her a "laying-one's-heart-bare report to the Party," concocting all the thoughts that were supposed to be self-criticism. Later, as she told me, her leaders even praised her by saying, "Your report is very sincere, very good." This happened in 1957. Now I will go back to 1955 and 1956.

Our cooperation lasted until the Anti-Rightist Movement. But before that movement had begun I got a regular job, concurrent with my translation for Lu Hsiao-man. The state-operated New Literature Publishing House, which had been then devoted merely to the publication of Chinese translations of foreign works, started to publish Chinese classics on a small scale. I got some inspiration when I noticed that some elder scholars had made contracts with the publishing house to work on some anthologies. As I had always loved mountains and rivers and was fond of reading travel notes, I approached the publishing house with a proposal for editing an anthology of ancient Chinese travels. The proposal was accepted after I, at the editor's request, handed in two annotated travel notes as samples. A contract was signed. So I had to work on both translation of foreign literary works and the selection and annotation of Chinese classics at the same time. I worked at my desk over ten hours a day, but was happy and full of satisfaction.

A huge party on June 1, 1956, turned out to be a turning point in my life. It was held in the so-called Cultural Club, formerly the French Club of the semi-colonial days, frequented by the Communist elite after liberation, but, of course, inaccessible to the common people. I took advantage of an invitation from the publishing house which I was dealing with and which had rented this club to celebrate the third anniversary of its establishment. The head of this publishing house was a high-ranking old Communist official, who was influential enough to make arrangements for the publishing house to use the whole space of this club for a day of celebration. Almost all the Who's Who of the writing circle were present at the party, watching various programs and tasting the refreshments. Needless to say, it was not meant purely for pleasure and entertainment.

Groups were formed to discuss various topics. I was in the group of scholars on Chinese classics. To promote its prestige, Li Chun-min, the president of the publishing house, chaired this group, which consisted mainly of older professors and famous authors. As the only young man in this group, I did not feel very comfortable. Those old scholars were highly delighted by Li's presence, and many of them spoke with excitement. I was a little shy and kept silent.

Li Chun-min called the meeting to order and made a speech in which he stressed the importance of our cultural legacy. Besides citing quotations from Marx, Lenin, and Mao Tse-tung, he unintentionally let out the secret of a Communist's real thoughts by saying, "Chinese classics are now being published in large numbers in Taiwan. If we forsake the property that our ancestors bequeathed to us, Taiwan will get it all. Why should we concede the legacy to Taiwan?" I laughed in my sleeve. It was just like two unfilial sons scrambling for an ancestral inheritance.

However, I was still very impressed by the announcement Li Chun-min made at the conclusion of his speech: For the sake of enhancing the publication of classics, the classics section of this publishing house was going to be separated from the present publishing house and be a base for the establishment of a new publishing house in charge of the publication of Chinese classics only.

This party, especially Li Chun-min's speech, touched off my mental struggle for quite a few days. Although the Peking experience had made me sick of the organizational life-style characteristic of the revolutionaries and reluctant to accept any regular job in the state-operated apparatus, the lack of a permanent job did create a sense of insecurity. Now, here came a job editing Chinese classics, which had long been my first preference. If ever I wanted to land a job, it was now. There was no other job that would be more suitable for me than this. Furthermore, I was well disposed toward Li Chun-min, who had made an impression on people more as a learned and kind-hearted intellectual than as a Communist bureaucrat. I also had a favorable opinion of Chien P'o-chen, the chief editor of the classics section. Finally, I made up my mind to write Li, expressing my desire to join the newly founded classics publishing house. Before long, I received a handwritten reply from him, welcoming me to work there. Thus, I was reemployed and once again became a public employee. This was in late autumn, 1956.

The controversy over my past remained. My secession from the revolutionary ranks by resigning from the Hsin Hua News Agency and my dismissal by the Bureau of Education of Shanghai were regarded as mistakes and blemishes, though I considered the original conclusions and accusations false. The leadership of the publishing house suggested I break away from my past and look forward. I was, therefore, offered the new job neither as a reallotment after an offense, in which case one should have some demotion in rank and salary, nor as a rehabilitation, in which case he should enjoy the original rank and salary. I obtained the same rank and salary as a new graduate from the university. That is to say, the period after my graduation did not count whatsoever. Besides working as an editor during office hours, I was allowed to do translation and annotation in my spare time and to earn royalties just as other authors did.

Li Chun-min, besides still holding the office of the president of the original publishing house, was the head of the newly established Chinese Classics Publishing House. The body of the editing department was enlarged from a few staff members of the classics section of the

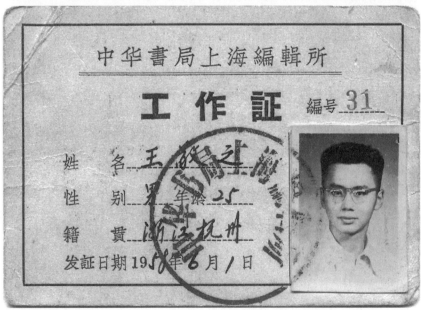

*My identification card from the Chinese Classics Publishing House
(above), which was later turned into the Shanghai Editing Bureau of
Chung-Hwa Printing Company, hence another card (below).*

original publishing house to ten or more, I being one of them. In addition to the editing department, there were other departments like the supply, communication, personnel, and finance offices. The entire Classics Publishing House occupied a townhouse with a beautiful garden in which there was a swimming pool. The editing department was on the third floor. Looking out the window, I could catch sight of verdant grass, and around my desk were piles and piles of ancient books. I liked this job because I liked reading, especially the Chinese classics. To work was just to enjoy. Moreover, Li Chun-min treated me with utmost consideration, not because I had anything special from which he could benefit personally, but because he had a disposition to take good care of youth. As I was young, he put me on the list of persons to be fostered and nurtured. Every time some important persons visited the publishing house, Li never forgot to introduce me to them, saying, "He is the new rising force in our ranks." He really entertained high hopes for me.

Alas, it was not too long before something went wrong. This time it was totally my fault. The period of my unemployment had been a period of Communists clamouring to "hold in high esteem the contributions of intellectuals" and reinforcing the unified front. Branches of the so-called democratic parties and the Chinese People's Political Consultative Conference at various levels actively developed their own spheres. The Political Consultative Conference of Ching-an District, in which I lived, approached me by sending me tickets for assemblies, movies, dramas, and other activities. I was reluctant to accept these invitations, as I was very busy with translations and annotations.

But I did not refuse to attend their weekly politics study session, because in this "heavenly society" everyone had to belong to some "organization." Normally, the unit one worked for was one's "organization." Since I was unemployed, the policeman in charge of household registration in the area where I stayed often dropped in at my house to chat with me, and those grandmas and aunties in the so-called neighborhood committee often called on me to engage in "heart-to-heart" talks with them. The gate of my house was disregarded by these people, because they, representing my organization, were entitled to come and go anytime they thought fit to help me "progress" politically. I was, accordingly, eager to link up with an organization like the Political Consultative Conference, so that I would be able to shake off the pestering of these semi-literate people. In the end, I did extricate myself from this predicament, only to be caught in another.

In the study group of the Political Consultative Conference, there was a member who was an actress with the Peking Opera, quite famous in the old days, but at that time already retired from the stage since her marriage to a rich merchant. Sexy, social, and several years older than I, she was like my elder sister and soon became intimate with me. Her husband had been out of town for months, so she invited me to her house to drink and sing. Then we played Adam and Eve. This happened on the eve of my entering the Chinese Classics Publishing House. It was, of course, a mistake, as both she and I were married.

In addition to this blunder, I made other mistakes. After I entered the Chinese Classics Publishing House, I accidentally found that this publishing house was trying to hire some hands for copying manuscripts. I talked to the head of the communication office, who was in charge of this kind of work, and said that I knew someone who was able to do the job. In my mind the job of copying seemed to be very simple, and anyone who could read and write would be equal to the task. I intended to have my mistress fill the vacancy. Nearly all the staff members in the editing department were unimpressed with the head of the communication office, as they thought this fellow had no other talent than fawning upon the leaders. He might have felt flattered when I, as a staff member of the editing department, took the initiative to make some suggestions to him, or he might have thought that I was President Li's favorite. Whatever the reason, he complied with my request instantly. Thus, the actress joined this publishing house, and we met each other daily. But her working there lasted for only a short while. No sooner had she entered this job than it was revealed that she was not competent for it at all. Besides, she was so audacious and aggressive that she never bothered to avoid doing anything that might arouse our colleagues' suspicions about our relationship. I did caution her, but was only sneered at by her as being timid and chicken. She thought that as long as there was no evidence, we were safe. What she did not anticipate, however, was that even if people failed to discover any evidence to sustain their suspicions, they could employ other pretexts to destroy what they disliked. Before the end of her one-month probationary period, she was released from the job on the grounds of incompetence.

Deprived of the convenience of working in the same unit, we were compelled to find time to date each other. One day, in our eagerness to get together when there was no reason to ask for a leave of absence, I suddenly hit upon a way. I called my office, stating that my wife had had a miscarriage and that I could not go to work that day. Because it was known to the publishing house that Jane was pregnant, I thought there would be no danger that anything would go wrong with this. The lie seemed to be working, because I was granted one day's leave without question. But I did not expect that the "organization," in order to show its concern for me and my family, should do something right for them and wrong for me. Just as I was having a very good time with my favorite actress, a representative from the personnel office of the Chinese Classics Publishing House made a phone call to the school where Jane was teaching and asked for the location of the hospital Jane was in, because they intended to pay her a visit. This goodwill phone call laid bare my lie.

Jane was just stepping into her office during a break when this phone call reached her school. She was, of course, astonished and very upset by this false alarm, for this denoted that something must have gone wrong. Then, the representative of our personnel office made a special trip to Jane's school to console her, promising to find out what had really happened. Jane was asked to be calm and do nothing to me, leaving the whole thing entirely to the "organization."

When I went to work the next day, I was called to the personnel office. Without mincing words, they told me everything they had heard and done the previous day, and asked for an explanation. They were straightforward; therefore, so was I. I made a clean breast of everything, but I stressed that I assumed full responsibility for the affair between the actress and me. I would accept any punishment my "organization" would give me, but I implored them to leave the actress alone in order to avoid causing any trouble in her family. However, they had already dispatched another official to the actress to verify their suspicion about our relationship. I found out only later that the actress did exactly what I had done—instantly acknowledged everything during the official's visit. Separately, we told the same story. The only difference was that each of us claimed responsibility. This time was different from the last time, when I was teaching. The organization of the

Chinese Classics Publishing House did not care much about responsibility. What they cared most about was my ideology. The actress did not belong to this organization, so they just ignored her. Thus, they told me to forget about responsibility but to criticize my own ideology.

It was no joke. They put ideology above everything. I still remember the serious talk that the head of the personnel office had with me that day, when he stated, "Your conduct has done a disservice to the Party and to the revolution. It has especially let President Li down. He always thought highly of you and took good care of you, just like a father does with his child. He was furious when we reported this matter to him. He gave us detailed directions, which I am now going to relay to you."

Then the head of personnel relayed Li's words: "It is not accidental that Wong has committed mistakes in his personal life over and over again. The decadent ideology and philistine ways of life of feudalism and capitalism are the root causes of his repeated mistakes. He should take full responsibility for his mistakes, but the repetition of his mistakes also had something to do with the fact that he had been simply expelled from the revolutionary ranks without receiving any revolutionary education. This time we should deal with him differently. Our goal is not to push him away from the revolutionary ranks but to pull him to our side, and we should adopt the approach of 'curing the disease to save the patient.' Therefore, we should not be indulgent of Wong's mistakes. What we should do is purge away all rotten ideologies from his mind, so that he may learn from past mistakes and avoid future ones. Tell Wong to take a correct attitude toward this matter and thoroughly and clearly understand the nature and the root causes of his errors. Then, as I earnestly hope, he will be able to turn over a new leaf and begin his life anew. For our part, we must be stern to the errors of a young man, but we must also be lenient if there is some change in his attitude and some sign of his repentance. Right now, our first step is pressing Wong to make a serious self-criticism."

Then the head of the personnel office closed his notebook and continued, "Per the order of President Li, you have to write a self-criticism. Be serious, because we will draw our final conclusion according to your attitude toward your mistake."

In retrospect, despite the severity of President Li's direction, he had really intended to protect me, and I should have been grateful to him.

But at that time I was totally annoyed by this revolutionary jargon and paid no attention to it. "Love affairs are something personal," I thought. "If it is wrong, then it is wrong. The ones I should apologize to are my wife and my family. What does it have to do with your Party or your revolution?" However, under the pressure of seeking leniency, I still wrote a self-criticism, although it was strongly repugnant to me. In the self-criticism, I truthfully admitted my faults and sincerely apologized for them. I actually had qualms of conscience, and felt remorse for unfaithfulness to my wife. I decided not to commit such errors again. Up to this point, I had truthfully recorded what I thought. If I had stopped there, the self-criticism might have been considered insufficient and unsatisfactory by the leaders. So I went a step further. Out of an aversion to the garrulous talk about linking one's personal love affairs to a certain kind of ideology, such as "proletarian ideology" and "bourgeois ideology," I gave rein to my self-criticism by making superfluous remarks and said that this kind of behavior had long been the bad habit and corrupt custom of intellectuals. Then I used as examples some famous writers and poets in the Tang and Sung Dynasties who are known for their romances. I also cited a contemporary example: Kuo Mou-jo, who, as is well known, had had many love affairs from his early years up to the very days when I was writing the self-criticism.

I was quite sincere in my self-criticism. Even the superfluous paragraphs represented my true thoughts. But they contained an underlying message. Since some high-ranking people had done the same thing, why should you be so harsh to me? But such controversial self-criticism was intolerable to those revolutionaries. President Li flew into a rage. Previously, he had instructed the personnel office to handle this matter in a behind-closed-doors style—keeping other colleagues in the dark. Now he lifted the ban by issuing an order that the manager and deputy manager of the editing department, along with the head of the communication office, attend the meeting of "helping and criticizing Wong." The head of the personnel office dropped a hint to me that the attendance at the meeting could be further increased if my self-criticism continued to be unsatisfactory. Needless to say, more attendance denoted more seriousness.

Both the manager and deputy manager of the editing department were about ten years older than I and, therefore, they were much more experienced. Neither of them was in the Party. In private, they were just as liberal-minded as I was. The romances of Kuo Mou-jo which I cited in my self-criticism had actually been learned from them just recently. But at the meeting to "help" me, each of them became quite different from in private. They talked about revolutionary ideals and the lofty goals of life. They gave reasons for my errors from the Marxist and Leninist points of view. The chairman of the meeting apparently was very happy with their harangues, so he concluded the meeting by saying to me: "Your self-criticism is totally unacceptable. You should take these comrades' words seriously and rewrite your self-criticism."

I hated saying and doing the same thing repeatedly. Into the first self-criticism I did pour some of my thoughts and expressed some of my innermost feelings, such as my sense of guilt toward my wife and my determination not to commit the same error any more. There was no way that I could force myself to make another self-criticism with the same degree of sincerity. But this was something I had to go through. What should I do?

The harangues of the two heads of the editing department gave me great inspiration. I came to understand that what the Communists liked was just the stereotyped stuff and that they did not care about what I really thought. Fortunately, it was common practice for the person being criticized at a meeting to take down the words of those who were criticizing him in order to show his repentance. I had had these two persons' speeches recorded in writing. Now all I had to do was piece together what they had said. I rearranged their words in a more logical sequence and rigged up an essay in which the second person was changed to the first person. Almost without effort, I concocted a piece of self-criticism full of revolutionary jargon from the high plane of Marxism-Leninism.

This was an essay entirely different from my real thoughts and feelings, following my grandfather's teaching: "In dealing with the Communists, you have to suspend your conscience temporarily." The authenticity of Grandfather's teaching was borne out by the different results of my two self-criticisms. The one that somewhat reflected my true ideas was rejected, while the one that contained nothing but nonsense was accepted.

A few days after I submitted my second self-criticism, I was summoned to the personnel office and formally informed of the conclusion of the "organization:" "With the assistance of the organization, you have made some progress and begun to understand the nature of your mistakes; therefore, we have decided to take disciplinary action and put your error in your personnel file. But if your performance improves in the future, this record will be subject to cancellation. We can simply take it out of your file. But that will depend upon your performance."

That was at the beginning of 1957. I believe those words were said with good intentions. But I failed to live up to their expectations, which could, in fact, never be realized. Finally, the organization could not make good on the kind offer because things were out of its control. There was no time when the organization could cancel this penalty, because it was only a few months later that the storm of the Anti-Rightist Movement began and swept me into the camp of "cow ghosts and snake demons"—the special term concocted by Mao Tse-tung to describe the politically lost wanderers. Compared to the label of rightist, the disciplinary action they had taken to put my romantic error on my personnel file was not even worth bothering about.

CHAPTER 6

A Lost Wanderer

THE MANAGER AND DEPUTY MANAGER of the original classics division of the New Literature Publishing House, Chien P'o-chen and Wang Mien, became the leaders of the editing department of the Chinese Classics Publishing House. They acted as chief and deputy chief editors, but maybe because neither of them was in the Communist Party and both of them were intellectuals with liberal thoughts, or for some other reason, they did not have any formal titles. By that time, there had been complaints about the "lack of power to exercise the function of one's title." In the case of these two gentlemen, however, the situation was just the reverse. They lacked titles matching the functions they exercised. Later, in the Anti-Rightist Movement, both of them were labeled as "rightists" and found guilty because they had the audacity to complain about lack of titles.

Prior to the Anti-Rightist Movement, they were big shots shouldering the responsibility of assisting President Li in recruiting editors for the newly established Chinese Classics Publishing House. These editors can be said to have been a group of weirdos, of whom none was in the Party.

The oldest member of this group was Wang Yuan-fang, then already around seventy, but tall and robust. He was a so-called capitalist, while in fact just the owner of a small bookstore, Yia-tung Publication Company, Limited, which had been merged into the New Literature Publishing House several years before. As a capitalist, he was entitled to a job, according to the Party's policy. And as an elderly person at least familiar with some old stories, he was offered a job in the Chinese Classics Publishing House. Always smiling, never complaining, he made a favorable impression on both the leadership and rank and file. But as a townsman of Hu Hsih who formerly had had some of his works published by Wang's company, this old gentleman could not now resist prating about his willingness to assign his copyright to Hu Hsih's works unconditionally to our publishing house for republication. No matter how hard people explained to him the impossibility of Hu Hsih's works being republished here owing to Hu's "reactionary" background, he never gave up talking about it. Apart from this mistake, he never pointed his finger at anybody or uttered one word against anyone. Therefore, his talk about publication of Hu Hsih's works was considered just an unrealistic well-meaning prank, not a political blunder, even in the Anti-Rightist Movement.

Another elderly gentleman, Lee Wei-chin, came from a bordering province and could not speak the standard Chinese dialect of Mandarin. This hindered his way of communicating with others considerably, and for others to communicate with him. So during the Anti-Rightist Movement he was quite carefree, free from struggling against others and being struggled against. But after the movement, he was suddenly sent to the forced labor camp and an announcement stated that he had, decades ago, committed the grave crime of having beaten the buttocks of the Communists he had arrested when he was a county magistrate in the old regime.

Mei Ling was a special figure. First of all, he had abandoned his surname, Chang, which he had never used and by which he had never been called by others. He originally had been deputy editor in chief of the New Literature Publishing House, and had been arrested during the Anti-Hu Fengists Movement on the charge of being a friend of Hu Feng.* He had been released in the autumn of 1956, but had not been allowed to do his original job, and had been appointed editor of this

---

*Hu Feng, a Communist writer and critic, was accused by Mao of being a leader of a counterrevolutionary camp, because he openly disagreed with some of Mao's literary viewpoints. With his arrest, Mao even triggered a nationwide manhunt campaign in 1955.

newly established Chinese Classics Publishing House. Though a well-known critic of modern literature, he knew almost nothing about Chinese classics. But I liked one aspect of his character, that he never did pretend to know something about the classics. He frankly admitted his ignorance as well as contempt for the classics, leaving others to wonder why he should have been assigned to work as an editor in this department and why he should have accepted the job. Though not a member of the Communist Party, he posed as a sincere revolutionary, an authority on the theory of Marxism-Leninism. He used to start talking like this: "I, as a Marxist-Leninist...." He particularly stressed "ist" by uttering it loudly, as though to declare that this was not something ambiguous.

Whenever we had a group discussion, he was sure to speak. He did not just speak, but always gave a lengthy oration. However, this was not too bad for me, since I hated speaking. He helped to while away the meeting time; therefore, pressure on others to speak was reduced. But he had a very unpleasant habit of sitting and smoking during the meeting without uttering anything until the last minute. When the meeting was drawing to an end and most of the colleagues were at the end of their patience, he began to clear his throat and said, "Now, just a word."

After pulling a cigarette from his pocket and lighting a match to it, he would steadily inhale the cigarette once and let out the smoke slowly. With this preamble finished, he began his speech, and all through his lengthy talk he would never bother about the cigarette again, but let it burn away in his fingers. He never forgot to point out that something had been missing in today's discussion and that we should have focused the discussion on such-and-such. Some of the participants were so irritated as to refute him. "Our meeting has already been going on several hours. If you had this kind of opinion, why didn't you make it known earlier? Now, it's only a piece of belated advice." But whenever refutation arose, Mei Ling would be even more enthusiastic about speaking, with the result that the meeting became even longer. He never yielded to different opinions, nor did he ever tolerate being interrupted.

Sometimes I was glad that he had stopped, and thought that it would be the end of his speech. However, he would start again, "This was point one." Oh, my God! It was only point one! I never really listened to him, nor did I ever dispute with him like others did. All I cared about was that the meeting would not last too long. Later, I found that the length of Mei Ling's speech was calculated neither by his mind nor by his mouth, but by the cigarette between his fingers. When the cigarette burned his fingers, he would be startled and then instantly press the butt against the ashtray. His words, "That's all I wanted to say today," came simultaneously with the extinguishing of the cigarette. After making this discovery, I was able to stop him in a very natural way. Whenever he was going to continue his speech, regardless of the lunch hour, I would all of a sudden scream as though in alarm, "Lao Mei, the cigarette is going burn your fingers!" This innocuous prank of mine would make him throw away his butt with his habitual statement, "That's all I wanted to say today."

Ho Man-chih was another Hu Fengist working with us. Like Mei Ling, Ho had also been released from jail. But unlike Mei Ling, who knew nothing about classics, Ho Man-chih was very learned and knowledgeable about Chinese classics. He was more haughty than Mei Ling. His sarcastic and swordlike words often hurt people, while Mei Ling only made people sick of him with his endless speeches. Personally, he was very kind, at least to me, although I could never agree with his pro-May Fourth Movement spirit and his adoration of Lu Hsun, whom I disliked.

Another gentleman, Chen Han-sheng, had originally been a clerk with some other department of the New Literature Publishing House for a few years, and was transferred to the Chinese Classics Publishing House at its establishment and promoted to editor. He had an impoverished family, and petitioned the "organization" for some free-lance job like making annotations. It was the custom in that society that an employee might request the organization to take his straitened circumstances into account, and it normally did comply with such a request if possible. Our department was no exception. The problem was that Chen was not able to suggest any topic that he was interested in, nor did he demonstrate his ability in making annotations. The manager, Chien, was pressed by the personnel department to give consideration to this old employee's request.

Just at that time, my free-lance compilation and annotation of the *Chinese Classical Travels*, which had been contracted with this publishing house before I entered its payroll as a permanent employee, was approaching its completion. At the same time I was being criticized for my affair with the former Peking Opera actress, which finally led to a disciplinary action against me. That error certainly had nothing to do with my job performance, let alone my work of compiling and annotating the *Chinese Classical Travels* which, as a matter of fact, was supposed to be guaranteed by the contract between the publishing house and me. But in that society whoever committed any error was of an inferior status. So Manager Chien forced me to collaborate with the old Chen. But the work had already been finished, and no cooperation was needed. It was obvious that they wanted me to share royalties with Chen out of concern for him. I had nothing against this old gentleman personally, but I thought the imposition was unfair and did not wish to allow myself to be ordered about. So I disagreed. This turned out to be another blunder; for not long after, I was labeled a rightist. Since my name could not be printed on the book, the *Chinese Classical Travels* I had worked on could never be published. Had I agreed to Chien's suggestion about the nominal cooperation with Chen, the book might have been published under his name and I would have been able to collect at least half the royalties.

Among my fellow editors, the one I revered most was Hu Tao-ching, a really erudite scholar still living in Shanghai today. Reticent but kindhearted, he always greeted people with a smile and a polite nod. Keeping himself in low profile, he just worked hard and studied diligently. I never saw him write even one cursive character. His docility and a kind of overcautiousness might have been due to his personal experiences. He had been, before the so-called liberation, editor-in-chief of the Shanghai branch of *Central Daily*, the official organ of the Kuomintang. The Communist liberators, in accordance with their policy that the personnel of old institutions should remain in office and be given jobs, and also in consideration of his specialty, assigned him to work in this classics publishing house when it was established.

He was not as well paid as he should have been for his qualifications and contributions, but he never complained. His clothes and shoes were all worn out, but he had no lament for that either. It was only in the early sixties, when Dr. Joseph Needham visited China as an honorable state guest and, it was said, expressed his earnest wish to meet Hu

Tao-ching, that the Communists understood what a treasure Hu was. In a frantic rush, the organizations, from top to bottom, ascertained Hu's whereabouts and, when they found out about his straitened circumstances, hurriedly bought some new clothes and shoes for him so that he could meet Needham without embarrassing the regime. From then on, Hu's situation began to improve.

Another very interesting figure in our group was Yang Yu-jen, about twenty years older than I. Graduated from one of the local universities in Shanghai, he liked to associate himself with those old scholars and pose as an old fogy. He was humorous, amiable, always trying to say something to make people feel good. On the other hand, he was very timid, always afraid that some misfortune might befall him, and a sincere believer in Lao Tze. He looked upon Taoism as the highest philososhy for handling human relationships and used it as a criterion to judge people's social behavior. He would say: "Such-and-such can be thought of as some sort of *Huang Lao*."* He even had the audacity to put Mao Tse-tung in the category of *Huang Lao*, by saying with his thumb up, "The Chairman is the best *Huang Lao* in the present era." It went without saying that Yang himself was at the pinnacle of *Huang Lao*'s achievements.

I did not really know what Yang meant by *Huang Lao*, but I did notice his originality in dealing with people. It was my chief enjoyment to watch him secretly and closely at group meetings. Whoever spoke at a meeting, he kept nodding his head and swinging slowly and slightly to show his attentiveness to the speaker. And whenever his eyes met the speaker's, he would look as though to say, "Ah, you are perfectly right. That's just what I am thinking." He even did that to me. At first, I was really pleased and flattered. The higher the position of the speaker, the more expression there was on his face. If the speaker happened to be the president of the publishing house, he would keep eyes looking straight, as though spellbound. When the speaker raised his tone to

---

*During the first millenium B.C., the semilegendary Lao Tan preached conformity with the Way of Nature, a system of belief later called "Taoism" which exalted the legendary Huang-ti (The Yellow Emperor, 2697–2598 B.C.) as its originator. Hence, *Huang Lao* became a special term denoting both the philosophy and the practitioner of Taoism.

stress a certain point, Yang would straighten his back and move his head in a big circle, as though delighted by suddenly seeing the light.

After long observation, I came to understand that despite his vivid facial expressions, he was actually indifferent. This is how I found it out. Sometimes when, after a meeting, I mentioned some points by which he had been so moved, he seemed totally ignorant of them. Very often, he revealed an expression endorsing someone's view, but a while later, when another proclaimed an opposite view, he would also express his approval by taking the same attitude. Apparently, neither of the speeches really interested him. All his expressions were but mechanical acts geared to fit in with the tone of the speaker. They were controlled by a computer, as it were, and did not in any way reflect his real feelings, which were concealed from others.

Even though he made no more mention of *Huang Lao* after the Anti-Rightist Movement, he still showed his habitual expression at meetings. This meant that his *Huang Lao* had been upgraded.

I am still of the opinion that Yang's attitude might be a proper way for surviving under Communist rule. Long before the Anti-Rightist Movement, when most people were intoxicated by the comparatively easy atmosphere, Yang had never relaxed his vigilance, and often alerted me, "Those who always behave arrogantly and do not know how to conceal their thoughts, like you and Ho Man-chih, are going to pay for it." Unfortunately, he was right.

The person Yang Yu-jen admired most was a deaf-mute, Chow Hwa-yen, a rather well-known, old-fashioned fiction writer and an owner of a publishing house before liberation. He was the author of *How to Write a Self-Criticism*, published soon after liberation, and the book, a best-seller, brought him a fortune. He was incorporated into the state-operated publishing house as a private entrepreneur. As a capitalist, good at making money, and as a writer full of reactionary thoughts, he should have been a typical target for criticism. However, thanks to his deafness and muteness, no one had any interest in setting him up as a target, because it was too difficult to wage an ideological struggle against a person who could only be communicated with through writing. His deafness and muteness were envied by Yang Yu-jen, who said, "How nice to be deaf!"

Among the staff members of our department, the one who had

already been most famous in the literary arena before liberation was Chin Hsin-yao. He had been very active as a writer during the Japanese occupation of China; consequently, he had been labeled a "collaborator writer." Actually, he had not held any post in the puppet regime, so he could not be said to be a traitor in its real sense, but could only be considered somewhat blemished in his personality and reputation. That was why he had never been put in jail by the Communist regime, and, owing to his accomplishments in Chinese classics, was assigned to a job as editor of the Chinese Classics Publishing House. His outstanding performance was his frequent statement of gratefulness to the Communist Party, "I was born by my parents, but I have been understood by the Communist Party." This sentence, said in his Ning-p'o dialect, sounded quite musical and not too nauseating.

A fellow who had formerly had no knowledge about Chinese classics and was now an editor in this publishing house was Chu Chin-chen. He had been an employee of the former Shanghai customshouse for many years until the liberation of Shanghai, and later associated himself with Ch'u Tui-chih, a remarkable scholar in Chinese classics who had served as minister of education during the Japanese occupation. Thanks to Ch'u Tui-chih's academic fame and erudition, he was imprisoned for only a few years, and since his release had been treated as an "object of the unified front." The Chinese Classics Publishing House gave Ch'u Tui-chih some piece-rate job to do, and the president, Li Chun-min, showed quite great respect for him. So when Ch'u introduced Chu as his outstanding pupil to President Li, Chu succeeded in landing a job in the editing department. It was totally incredible that a decade later, during the so-called Cultural Revolution, it was Chu who informed on Ch'u Tui-chih, and Ch'u ended dying in jail.

Another young man, Chen Wen-chian, worked in our editing department, even though he was not an editor. We were the same age. He was responsible for the office supplies, but he read and wrote diligently, and studied with Ho Man-chih. In their eyes, I was a fogy, but we got along quite well.

Roughly, this was the organization of the editing department. To launch any movement, the Communist party had to rely upon the power of the "organization," without which any success would be impossible. In the Communist lexicon, the "mass of the people" is supposed to be the base of the revolution. So in Mao Tse-tung's strategy in whatever movement, the primary task was to differentiate the class enemy from the mass of the people. And the mass in my organization was composed chiefly of the above-mentioned people when the Anti-Rightist Movement began.

It was 1956 when the outside world first witnessed the turmoil in several Communist countries, such as Poland and Czechoslovakia, and started to notice that the Communist world was not monolithic. In China, the ordinary people got excited by these incidents in the Communist camp, while the ruling hierarchy was frightened and confused. For a short period, the people enjoyed a little softening of the iron fist and did not have the least idea that this would be only very brief and presaged a much tighter grip on them. All the ranking Chinese Communist officials were deeply concerned about the pestilential democracy which the people in so many Communist countries were fighting for. It was a matter of life and death to all of them that the masses in China should not be infected by the bacteria of democracy. But all the traditional ways of controlling the people, which were in use at that time, were disliked by the paramount leader, Mao Tse-tung, who tried to take a different approach, an approach which temporarily puzzled most of his comrades.

After a brief period of relaxation ushered in under Mao's slogan, "Let a hundred flowers blossom and let a hundred schools of thought contend," this wily tactician adopted another strategy of "inducing the snakes out of their holes." Mao not only played sinister games with intellectuals, but concealed his real intention even from the majority of the Communist Party members. He solemnly called on the whole nation to participate in a movement of "free airing of views." His mobilization speech was given at a special "Supreme State Affairs Conference," over which he presided in person.

Chao Tan, the famous movie star living in Shanghai, attended this conference in Peking and relayed Mao's message to writers in a meeting held in Shanghai soon after he returned from Peking. Due to Li Chunmin's position in the Communist Party as well as his official title of "Director of Writers' Association," the staff of the editing department of our publishing house was invited to listen to Chao Tan. Chao Tan, in his forties or fifties at that time, spoke in a large meeting room remodeled from a parlor, as the Writers' Association occupied a big single house which before liberation was the residence of the Koumintang's Shanghai mayor. Thus I had the opportunity to hear the firsthand report of Mao's message. Chao Tan seemed to be deeply intoxicated by Mao's encouragement to air one's views freely. In turn, he intoxicated the audience with his optimistic sentiments. Almost everybody, including me, believed that all of a sudden democracy had come to China.

However, as most people in our department were experienced and sophisticated, they were reluctant to say anything themselves, although they had high hopes of enjoying some true democracy. In other words, they adopted the precautionary tactic of "wait and see." I had no such patience, and took exception to their cynicism. I did not expect a topmost leader to turn back on his own words delivered on such a formal occasion. I did not think that the Communists would retreat from the path of democracy; therefore, I expressed my mind without the slightest hesitation both at the meeting and in the "blackboard newspaper."

Nevertheless, due to the caution of the majority I described above, and thanks to the steady leadership of this publishing house which I was convinced did not share Mao's intention of laying a political trap, the policy of our publishing house did not deviate too far from the ordinary Communist line. The opinion I voiced in public was no more than that office hours were not necessary for the editors, who should be assigned a certain workload to be executed in places of personal choice, such as office, home, or library. I also aired my opinion of the necessity of raising pay and royalties. In the field of national policy, I advocated the principle of "befriending distant states while attacking those nearby," making a specific suggestion that China should align with the USA, resist the USSR, and boycott Japan. In addition, I could not refrain from being sarcastic about those Soviet movies and novels in vogue at that time.

All these statements, deemed "heresies" or "fallacies" by the Party, at that time were actually nothing extraordinary. However, upon hearing what I had said, most of the gentlemen in the editing department sighed and shook their heads when they met me in private. This was their way of expressing their anxiety for my safety, although a few of them might have gloated over my possible misfortune.

Yang Yu-jen was kind enough to give me advice. "You'd better be sensible. If you are swelled-headed like that, you'll surely get into trouble."

I was so arrogant that I retorted bluntly, "Why should you be so timid? Didn't you read the newspaper and notice Chairman Mao's words? How can the leadership go back on their own words?"

"You want to bet? For the Communist Party, changing its tone is as easy as turning one's hand. Either Chairman Mao makes another speech or *Renmin Ripao** carries an editorial. It would serve as a signal of change."

At this point, Chu Chin-chen, who sat opposite and shared a desk with me and was usually somber and glum, could no longer keep silent and sided with Yang, saying with his palm stretched out, "That's true. The Communists can change just like this." With that, he turned his palm over.

In a sense, Mao's trick of "inducing the snakes out of their holes" did not succeed in this publishing house, because almost no one believed in his sincerity. The only one who dared to follow my example was Chen Wen-chian, a young man as naïve as I was. But, as a whole, the staff had in no single moment deviated from the ordinary political path any other unit had taken. The extreme fallacy that "some of the Communist Party members deserve to be killed" which appeared in the newspapers of those days had never been heard in our office. But, still, something unexpected happened, and what was even more unexpected was that it had been touched off unintentionally by me. The story goes as follows:

Peng, a famous actress in Hunan Province, was visiting Shanghai at that time. She was an acquaintance of my mother. Aware that I was serving in the field of classic literature, she asked whether I could buy her a copy of *Chin Ping Mei*, for she needed it as a reference for a new play. *Chin Ping Mei*, a classical Chinese novel, was not sold publicly because of its sexual description, but was available to literary specialists in some bookstores. Peng, as an actress and the leading figure of her opera troupe, was entitled to purchase a copy, but only on condition

---

*Renmin Ripao (People's Daily), is the official organ of the Chinese Communist Party.

that she produce a formal letter from her "organization," while I, as an editor of classic literature, could order one without having to have a letter from the "organization." I did not think I would have any problem doing her a favor. I myself had never purchased any books, but aware that my colleagues often bought this kind of "books for internal circulation," I asked about the procedure for buying a copy of *Chin Ping Mei* when I arrived at my office the next day.

"Very simple," I was told, "just ask Yuan Ping, the head of the communication office, to get it for you. He goes to the special retail department of the bookstore almost every other day."

Thus, I went downstairs and asked Yuan to do a favor for me. He readily promised, "No problem. I will get it for you today or tomorrow. You can pay me back after you get it."

I always tried to avoid complications. "Why don't we do it this way," I said. "I'll give you a certain amount of money. You don't have to bring the book back to me. Would you please ask the bookstore to mail the book directly to Peng in Hunan Province?"

"What?" said Yuan, astonished. "Why should I tell them to mail the book to the actress?"

I did not blame him. It had been through him that I had introduced my actress-girlfriend to this publishing house. He must have felt embarrassed when that matter had such an ending. Now another actress came up, and he was naturally shocked. So I explained to him who Peng was. As the leader of a provincial theater troupe and a member of the Political Consultative Conference, she would not have had too much difficulty obtaining this book herself. I did it for her just because it was convenient for me.

Now, Yuan took up the official jargon. "The privilege of buying books for internal circulation is extended only to those who have the qualification for them. It is not allowed to buy them on another's behalf."

"Okay, okay," I conceded, "let's do just as you said a moment ago. Get me the book, and I'll pay you then."

"But now I know it's not for your own use. I cannot do that for you," he retorted.

I turned around and left in a rage. When I came back to my office, my fellow editors were astonished by my angry looks and asked me what had happened. Habitually reluctant to utter a word in an unpleasant mood, I just answered briefly, "Yuan refused." Unexpectedly, my answer caused havoc.

Most of the editors disliked Yuan, who, they thought, did nothing while receiving higher remuneration than most of them simply because he had been in publication circles for decades and was able to flaunt his seniority, which was the criterion by which one's salary was decided at that time. Very often he could be seen dozing at his desk. The editors were so eager to find fault with Yuan that they wasted no time in finding out the details of his conflict with me. They burst into an uproar on hearing the news that Yuan refused to buy the book for me. It is my habit whenever I am in a sullen mood to keep silent, so I neither joined in the uproar nor gave any further explanation.

Young Chen Wen-chian was the most vehement, because Yuan looked down upon him and this hurt his dignity. He was diligent in study and in the good graces of such major figures in the editing department as Chien P'o-chen and Ho Man-chih. He shouted and pounded the desk, "Damn! An editor is not worth a penny in Yuan's eyes. How come an editor is not eligible to buy a copy of *Chin Ping Mei*?"

"What's the good of being an editor!" someone chimed in.

"I don't want to do the editing anymore," said another and threw his pen onto the floor.

Then many more members of the department echoed, "Right, no more work. Get the leadership to come upstairs and make things clear."

The two vice presidents who were later to co-control this publishing house had not yet been appointed, and President Li was concurrently president of the New Literature Publishing House. The highest official in the building was in fact the head of the personnel office. He might have been greatly disturbed by those strikes which had just happened in Poland and Hungary and which all Communists around the world looked upon as scourges. As soon as he heard what was going on upstairs, he took it for a tumult and called President Li. "A disaster is imminent. A walkout. The editors are on strike. They want you to come over. Please come right away."

President Li arrived in a big hurry. "Am I supposed to attend the meeting? Do they want me to?" Li asked when he walked upstairs to the editing department on the third floor.

There were three rooms on this floor, and each room accommodated several editors. The biggest one was the site of our meetings. When a meeting was called, editors in the other two offices just pulled their chairs to sit at whatever spare space they could find in that room. This time we did the same way.

The president took a chair from downstairs by himself and sat down with us, and inquired about what had happened. The editors vehemently attacked Yuan for his refusal to purchase *Chin Ping Mei* for me. Li immediately summoned Yuan to the meeting for an explanation. No sooner had Yuan arrived than he came under fire.

Yuan did not give in, retorting succinctly, "Why don't you guys ask Wong to describe the details first?"

"Okay, let Wong speak first." All agreed. They apparently anticipated that my description would certainly turn out to be fatal to Yuan.

Under such a circumstance, I could no longer keep silent. And in no circumstance did I want to lie or conceal the facts. Since I had to speak, I could only tell the whole story about how I had requested Yuan to have the book mailed directly to someone else and how he had refused not only to mail the book but also to purchase it. Those who had cried out against an injustice were now stunned by my account.

My colleagues did know that I was going to purchase the book not for myself but for the actress from Hunan Province, because on that very morning when I asked about the procedures for purchasing the book, I had not concealed who was the real buyer. I had mentioned the name casually, but they had not conceived that I would be so stupid as to mention this to Yuan and make an impossible request that the bookstore send the book directly to someone else. As a matter of fact, in our department, purchasing "internally circulated materials for reference" for someone else was not uncommon at all. People did this all the time, but in their own names. None of them had ever acted as I had acted. Had they known, they would not have vehemently attacked Yuan's refusal to buy the book as an evidence of his failure to fulfill his job of serving the needs of editors.

They were even more embarrassed and frustrated when Yuan, after my description of the case, stated smartly, "Had Wong himself needed the book, or had anyone else in the editing department needed any job-related materials, I assure you, I myself and my colleagues would have been more than happy to be at his and your service." This made the strike seem ridiculous.

I left early that day, so I was not present at the latter part of the meeting, the sketchy picture of which I learned the next day. Since the battle array had been deployed, the warriors were reluctant to withdraw. But they were compelled to change their strategy and even their weaponry at the last moment, dropping abruptly the topic of buying *Chin Ping Mei* and picking up some other complaints. Chien P'o-chen complained about the lack of a legitimate head of the editing department, with the undertone that he had acted as a department head but did not have the title. At the meeting, Ho Man-chih blamed President Li on the spot for seldom showing up and asked the president not to lead this publishing house nominally but to give specific guidance, for instance by offering concrete opinions on the manuscripts to be published, not just make decisions by saying yes or no. This meeting was spontaneous, not well planned and, therefore, carried no weight at all and exerted no pressure on the leadership.

But in Shanghai, the grapevine report of the "walkout" in the editing department of the Chinese Classics Publishing House spread among all other institutions related to publishing. This happened to be on the eve of the Anti-Rightist Movement. And no wonder that in the Anti-Rightist Movement six rightists were from this publishing house, whose total employees were no more than fifty. Among the six rightists, five were from the editing department, which had a staff of less than twenty people.

As to the "walkout," the role I had played was subtle. I could be regarded as a major culprit because it was I who had sparked the event. On the other hand, I could be considered to be "clean," because I was not the mastermind nor did I chime in with my colleagues in criticizing President Li. In fact, I should have been credited with the truth I had told when questioned about the whole story. Furthermore, I had been reluctant to attend that meeting at first and chickened out in the middle of it, thanks to my *tai-chi* boxing class.

As described earlier, I was learning *tai-chi* with Master Yue. The time of his class was quite strange, only Sunday noons and Tuesday evenings. I took *tai-chi* as a first priority and never missed the class. While doing the teaching job, I had requested that I not be scheduled to teach on Tuesday afternoons, so that I could attend the *tai-chi* class regularly. After I entered this publishing house, which was a state-operated institution with strict office hours, I had to observe the regulations. I had written a report about my personal health, in which I mentioned my tuberculosis and pointed out that this disease had been cured only after I had learned *tai-chi* with Master Yue. I therefore formally requested that I continue my *tai-chi* class for the benefit of my health which, I stated, was the basis for making my contributions to the revolution. I also made it clear in this report that Master Yue gave classes on Tuesday evenings. In other words, I had to leave earlier every Tuesday afternoon. Strictly following the organizational procedures, I had submitted this report to the personnel department, which forwarded it to President Li, who then gave approval. Therefore, justifiably I left my office before three o'clock every Tuesday. The so-called walkout happened on Tuesday. It was already past two o'clock when President Li arrived in a big hurry. At first I did not want to attend the meeting, because I had my *tai-chi* class to attend, but was prevented by them. "You should not be absent. Everybody has to attend." So I attended unwillingly, and after I had told the story about the bickering due to the purchase of a book, I thought my job had been done. When they changed the topic and started making other complaints, I left.

Another subtle complication lay in the fact that later Chien P'o-chen was regarded as the mastermind of the "walkout" and the leader of an anti-Party clique. As mentioned earlier, after I got my disciplinary penalty because of my romance, Chien proposed to me that my work on the *Chinese Classical Travels* be considered a joint product between Chen Han-sheng and me, and I had flatly refused the proposal. Then he put a hold on the publication of my work; therefore, I got more angry with him than he with me. One day, as head of the department, he assigned me to a certain editing job on which I held some different opinions from him. This was not unusual, and in normal cases we could just discuss our opinions and find a way out. No big deal. But this time, I intentionally embarrassed him by saying, "I don't want to have anything to do with such unreadable rubbish!" I then threw the documents that he had passed to me back onto his desk. He trembled with anger, and immediately lodged a complaint against me with President Li, who ordered the personnel department to solve the problem by persuading both of us to calm down. After that, everyone, from the leadership to the rank and file, knew that Chien and I were antagonistic toward each other, and for this reason I could no longer belong to his clique. For a period of time they seemed not to know which category I should fall into. Neither did I know myself, and I did not bother to find out.

At the beginning of June 1957, there appeared in the official newspaper two editorials, later widely known to be written by Mao Tse-tung himself, which launched a vehement attack on intellectuals. The whole nation was shocked. Intellectuals were especially sensitive. The older gentlemen in our publishing house were on tenterhooks. Even young men like Chen Wen-chian were scared. As a member of the Youth League, he attended the League meetings regularly. One day, with a serious, nervous, and frightened countenance, he told me in private that at one such meeting political classifications for all the employees were discussed and determined, and that according to the discussion he and I fell into the same category. I still did not feel uncomfortable at that time, maybe because I was too slow and insensitive to sense any imminent danger. I even retorted to Chen with a joke, "Ah, if I could be ranked in the same category as you, I should feel honored, shouldn't I?"

"Come on, don't be so silly," said Chen. "What I am worried about is that you and I might be classified as rightists."

"Rightists?" I shouted, "I don't care at all! I don't mind being termed a leftist or a rightist. I myself know very well that I am neither."

"How come you are so naïve? In terms of revolutionary theory, the rightist belongs to the enemy camp."

"In that case, people in our editing department, including you and me, all share the same political attitude. How can just two of us be singled out as enemies?"

What I failed to comprehend then, however, was the traditional Communist tactic of singling out certain people to be struggled against as foes by the rest of the people. As a matter of fact, by that time, some rightists had already been selected from the central organizations. The official newspaper *Renmin Ripao* (*People's Daily*) carried every day a list of newly ferretted-out rightists, which almost corresponded to a Who's Who in China. With so many outstanding scholars and scientists labeled as rightists, this term which I had initially been indifferent toward now carried prestige. This might be part of the reason why, while most of people turned pale at the mere mention of this word, I could take it easy.

Mao always boasted of the Anti-Rightist Movement as the product of his *yang-mou* (meaning explicit scheme). This may be true. The scheme was masterminded only by himself, or by some of his cronies at most. As far as I could see, our publishing house had no such scheme. It is true, there existed various conflicts in our department. For example, Chien P'o-chen and Wang Mien both assumed the responsibility of editor-in-chief, but neither had acquired a title other than that of editor. Of course, they were unhappy and felt frustrated. On the other hand, since they had the responsibility, they had to order people about; and since neither was in the Communist Party, Party members in other departments naturally felt jealous of them. Moreover, the editing department, though the pivotal section of the publishing house, possessed not a single Party member. This was sufficient for people in other departments to look askance at the editors. Within the editing department itself, ten people entertained ten motives and tended to scorn one another. Human relations were very complicated in Chinese society, and this editing department was no exception.

The leadership of this publishing house at that time had no intention to carry out any anti-scheme. Up to the eve of the Anti-Rightist Movement, the leadership had been devoted to the development of this institution. As President Li was concurrently the president of the New Literature Publishing House and could not devote his time exclusively to the business of our publishing house, he started to recruit some senior assistants. Two vice presidents arrived, one after another. First came Chen Hsiang-ping, a bureaucrat just in his prime, learned and knowledgeable. He had been in the Communist Party for many years. For the major part of his revolutionary career he was an underground worker in the Kuomintang's newspaper. As he described himself, he was able to deceive some Kuomintang leaders while engaged in underground work. Apparently, he was very capable. The other vice president, Ch'i Min-ch'u, a Communist military man and very loyal to the Party, came later. He too, was interested in Chinese classics.

Besides the above two high-ranking Communist officials, two non-Communist senior editors came in. One was Liu P'ai-shan, a professorial-looking scholar. As he suffered serious tuberculosis, he only showed up in the office two or three hours each day, making decisions only on editing techniques. He seldom attended political meetings and never uttered a single word on politics. At first, I really wondered how one could manage to be above politics in any state-operated organization, and was surprised that the leaders of our publishing house tolerated this apolitical attitude and were very polite to him. It was some time later that I learned by chance that he was a brother of one of the deputy mayors of Shanghai at that time.

Another senior editor, Lu Chen-pai, was unique in other ways. It seemed that he had never gone to a modern school, since he knew nothing but classics. He was not sixty years of age yet, but he looked much older by wearing old-fashioned cloth shoes and walking in a doddering way. Before liberation he had long been secretary to Wu Mei-sun, a well-known authority on Chinese classic literature, as well as an entrepreneur. With this background, he was believed to be some authority on classics. At least President Li looked at it that way. Lu Chen-pai knew nothing about modern political theories, let alone Marxism. Neither was he familiar with political jargon. For this reason, he was totally unable to speak at any political meeting, but the leadership seemed very tolerant of him.

Lu knew the subtleties of traditional bureaucracy very well and was familiar with red tape. Furthermore, he deftly employed the unnecessary elaborate formalities of the old society to impress the bosses of our publishing house. His performance in this respect reached the acme of perfection, and Marxist revolutionaries like President Li and the two deputies were all very comfortable with him and commended him as a model worker.

He was really successful in creating an image of diligence for himself, keeping himself constantly busy in everybody's presence at anytime. On numerous occasions I went to his office for some business—in China you do not have to call to make an appointment before you go to see someone, as in the U.S.—and noticed that he was enjoying having tea while reading newspapers. As soon as he was aware of my presence he would suddenly drop the newspaper and resume an appearance of being busy. On catching sight of me and before I went up to his desk, he would wave to me forcefully and hurriedly and say, "Come on, come on, come on, I just wanted to talk to you. Here is a job, very, very urgent. I think you can do it this way or that way. And then, you have to.... You know, President Li takes it seriously and he wants it done as quickly as possible. So now I need your help. You'd better hurry up. Oh, my God!"

He never chatted with anyone else. Whenever he was away from his desk and dropped in at offices of other editors, he always seemed to be in a great hurry, as though he were being pressed by something urgent. In the presence of the president or deputy presidents, he would pretend to be even busier. But no matter how "busy" he was, on no single occasion would he overlook etiquette. He never straightened his back when the bosses were present, keeping it hunched. However, he never acted to the extent of making people nauseous. He won respect by using his seniority. He had smooth sailing for almost ten years, until the Cultural Revolution, during which he had a rough time with those Red Guards who were ignorant of etiquette and lacked the ability to appreciate his excessive courtesy. But I should now return my narration to the Anti-Rightist Movement.

Other evidence showed that the leadership of our publishing house did not conceive of any plot for the movement. At the beginning of 1957, when the political atmosphere was most free, this publishing house had set up a regulation allowing each editor one sabbatical month each year for doing research. The publishing house not only paid salary but covered all travel expenses, excluding room and board. To obtain approval, each editor had to submit his plan specifying time and place at the beginning of the year. So far as time was concerned, everyone wanted to enjoy the sabbatical leave as soon as possible, for it was quite uncertain that the regulation would last forever. But the leadership allowed only one editor to have it each month. As I was not senior enough to take my vacation at the very beginning of the year, the earliest month available to me was July. As for the place, everyone could make his own choice. As I had a cousin in Chingtao, a coastal city known for its beach, it was convenient for me to go there. I therefore submitted my plan for visiting Shangtung University, which was located in that city at that time and which was strong in classical Chinese literature. Of course, my chief motive was to bathe on the beach and swim in the sea, but I did not include this intention in the written plan.

Those who had approval for vacations in January, February, March, April, and May took turns going to their preferred places. Yang Yu-jen, who was scheduled for June, was so scared by the seemingly imminent political storm that he did not dare to go and, eventually, gave up his right. I insisted on my plan. Chien P'o-chen, the head of the editing department, also scared by the unpredictable situation, refused to make any decision and referred this matter to the leadership. It was at this moment that the new vice president, Chen Hsiang-ping, arrived, and he reviewed the report and approved my plan. So on the first day of my vacation, July 1, I left Shanghai aboard a train heading to Chingtao.

In those days transportation was not as difficult to obtain as nowadays. I was very comfortable on the hard seat of the sleeping car on which, according to regulations, I was then eligible to ride. The next morning when I woke up, I was fascinated by an impressive mountain outside the window. By reading the signboard on the station, I knew it was Taishan. I made up my mind within five minutes to get off at that station. Again, it was quite easy in those days to get on and off trains, even if the decision was made at the last minute.

I fully enjoyed the wonderful sights in this magnificent mountain area that, more than two thousand years before, had attracted Confucius, who then ascended it, marveled at the view from the top, and then remarked, "What a small world!" I spent two days on the mountain before I was driven away by fleas, which were very rampant during the night. There was no hotel at that time and I could only take refuge in a native hut.

After leaving the mountain, I resumed the train trip, my interest in continuing my journey undiminished. I stopped in the city of Jinan to visit Damin Lake and some cultural places. Several days later I arrived in Chingtao.

As the trip was nominally a studying vacation, the first thing to do in Chingtao should not be to visit Laoshan Mountain and swim in the sea. I had to visit Shantung University, so that I could prepare a report on its library's collections of Chinese classics. But my initial impression of this campus was terrible: *da-zhi-pao* (big-character wall posters), were hanging almost everywhere, condemning Professor So-and-so or student So-and-so. It seemed unlikely that students were taking classes or that the library was open. I thought I had better pay a visit to someone I knew. I dropped in at the office of Professor Huang Chia-te who had formerly been dean of St. John's University and head of the journalism department while I was a student there and had been teaching English in Shantung University since the closing of St. John's.

I was almost stunned at the sight of him. Still immaculately dressed as always, but no longer calm, natural, and unrestrained, he had an expression and attitude which I had never seen before. He looked not only ghastly pale, but sad, helpless, and depressed, like one of the cows waiting to be butchered in a slaughterhouse. I appreciated his willingness to receive me under this circumstance, although he had little to say during our meeting. Besides giving conventional greetings and telling me his situation after the closing down of St. John's, he asked the following question over and over again: "Did your leadership approve of your leave?" Even after I gave him an affirmative reply, he still repeated this question, as though he were incredulous of my answer. When I said goodbye to him, he sincerely advised me, "This is not a place for you to linger in. Better not to come back again. I would advise you to return to your own unit as soon as possible."

But how could I give up my vacation without cause? I did not want to part with the lovely beach of Chingtao until the end of the month.

I felt as if I had arrived in an alien place when stepping into my publishing house after the vacation. A Chinese proverb goes: "Having spent seven days in a remote mountain, one would find the mundane world has been changed as though a thousand years had elapsed." According to this rate of change, after one month in the mountain and on the beach, I felt as if I had been absent from my work unit for at least four thousand years. People no longer smiled and chatted with one another. "Hello" and "hi" had disappeared. When I gave a nod or smile to my colleagues, they either avoided meeting my eyes or showed indifference as though we did not know each other at all.

"I am back," I said in bewilderment, approaching the desk of Chien P'o-chen, manager of the editing department, and reporting to him. He looked at me in even more bewilderment, and uttered not a single word. Then I reported to the deputy manager Wang Mien, who shared the same office with me, and announced, "I'm back." He simply said, "You had better go report to the personnel office."

I did. The head of the personnel office—a bald old man, illiterate, but with a long revolutionary history—was totally different from the two editing executives. He was now confident and complacent, totally different from the former days, when he felt inferior to the executives of the editing department since his educational level was quite low. He first reprimanded me, "How come you returned so late?"

"I do not think I am late. My vacation ended yesterday, and I came to report to you today," I retorted.

"We called your home many days ago, asking you to come back to the office. Why did you not come until today?"

"When you called, I wasn't home. There was no way that my family could contact me; therefore, I did not know you called me."

"Well," remarked the personnel manager, "it was for your benefit that we called you. It was your loss that you missed the meetings. A great movement is now underway. Everyone has to participate. The revolutionary situation has been developing very rapidly. Now, you have to catch up. One way for you to make up for the missed lessons is to read all the *da-zhi-pao* carefully."

Chen Hsiang-ping, the vice president, who had given me final permission to take the holidays, summoned me to his office for the ostensible purpose of listening to my report on Shantung University. He stopped me abruptly after I had briefed him on the wall posters I had seen there and the seeming suspension of the classes and library and also my failure to locate professors of classical Chinese literature. Apparently, he was not interested in academic research activities, which my vacation was supposedly intended for. He brushed aside the topic of vacation and sternly informed me of the policy regarding the Anti-Rightist Movement in this publishing house.

"You did and said something wrong in the past. Some of your acts and deeds should be deemed crimes. However, having studied your case meticulously, we, the leadership, are of the opinion that we should take into consideration the fact that you are still young, you have no complicated relations with the old society, and so far you have a clean political record. Therefore, we do intend to help you out by not labeling you a rightist. But this is not what we are in a position to decide, and you control your own fate. Whether you will be labeled a rightist totally depends upon your performance in this movement. If you make a serious self-criticism, make a clean breast of all your anti-Party words and acts, and with all the weight on your mind gone actively expose and struggle against the crimes of any rightist you know, then, I am sure, you might be given leniency. Otherwise, you will be a de facto rightist, and all we'll have to do is just put the right hat on the right head. You have the option, but the time available for you in choosing your way is running out. You have to make up your mind right now, and we are waiting to see your performance to make our final decision."

In retrospect, although his remarks implied intimidation, his attitude was sincere. He meant what he said about their reluctance to label me a rightist. The leadership expected me to extricate myself from a possible predicament by fighting with them against others. It was a shame that at that time I did not have the least idea that I was embroiled in a political entanglement. I would not have appreciated being called a leftist. In fact, I had no aversion to the so-called rightists. As so many outstanding scientists, writers, and artists in the society had already been labeled rightists, that title seemed to me to have a halo around it. I would not have had the slightest objection to being placed in the same rank as these honorable and famous people. So I took the words of these leading Communists half-seriously, if not lightly.

After having read carefully all the posters on the walls, I got a rough idea of the great revolutionary situation: We were struggling against the rightists. Chen Wen-chian, the young man in the editing department, had already been struggled against. It seemed that the struggle against him was temporarily over. Now, it was Ho Man-chih and Chien P'o-chen's turn. The Communists were not efficient in anything except in the struggle against someone.

Reading, writing, editing, and publishing were no longer the routine operations of our unit. We were just to participate in the movement, writing posters and attending meetings. The meetings were attended by all the employees of the publishing house, so they were held in the conference room on the second floor. At first, I acted like a fool at the meetings, not knowing how to make a speech and just sitting there and listening. But being reticent in the movement was a blunder, or even a crime, so I lost no time in learning how to play the role properly. At each meeting there was a person to be struggled against. He was supposed to make a self-denunciation first, and then all the participants vied with one another in criticizing him.

Compared with the Cultural Revolution, meetings in those days were much more civilized. The target of the struggle was even allowed to sit on the kind of chair used by the rest of the attendees. There was a table in front of him, because he had to write down other people's criticisms made of him after his self-denunciation. By so doing, he showed his gratitude to people struggling against him and his repentance for his crimes of opposing the Party, the people, and the socialism.

As an evaluation of the harangues of all the masses, those from other departments were not too critical. The heaviest punches usually came from fellow editors. I suddenly realized that intellectuals were the most apt to struggle against one another. One week one had been blue in the face denouncing his colleague as a rightist; however, all of a sudden he himself became a rightist next week and was attacked by other colleagues with just as stern a voice and countenance as his had been. Of course, not every hero in the Anti-Rightist Movement became a rightist himself later on. Some of them, like Chin Hsin-yao and Chu Chin-chen, got promotions after the Anti-Rightist Movement owing to their meritorious contributions to the struggle against rightists.

After having learned several lessons, I became familiar with the pattern of struggling. Take the form of address for example. A target of struggle, no matter how critical the accusation was, could still be addressed as comrade, if the accuser chose. But when the leadership formally declared someone a rightist—usually the announcement would not come until the last meeting designed for struggling against this man—then nobody was supposed to address him as comrade anymore. If someone inadvertently called him comrade, there would arise a protest, such as, "Why do you call him comrade?" or "Is he your comrade?" Thus, the ineligibility of being addressed as comrade served as pressure brought on those "politically lost wanderers."

This kind of meeting was under strict control of the Party, headed by Chairman Mao, who was particularly fond of stirring up excitement. They were not dull. The usual method of creating liveliness went like this: While someone was exposing a certain "criminal's" anti-Party words and deeds, another would break in: "Is that true? Such-and-such [the criminal], you should answer his question honestly." If the "criminal" gave an explanation or said no, then the group would shout, "You are dishonest!" "Liar!" "You are seeking your own destruction."

If he said yes, then he would be showered with questions: "Why did you do that?" or "Why did you say this?" Then, of course, he had to explain why. The masses would shout, "Don't deceive us!" "Cunning!" "Tricky!" "Worldly-wise!" "Quibbling!" And if the accused did not want to answer sincerely and just said, "I oppose the Party and social- ism. I am guilty," still he would be shouted down: "You are acknowl- edging your guilt in a general way. Don't conceal your initial motive!" "Confess your crime honestly!" All in all, there was nothing right in whatever the "criminal" answered. These meetings, ironically enough, were then termed "debates."

As a matter of fact, whatever the inquisitors shouted, one did not have to take their words at face value. They were just shouting; they did not expect their words to affect the criminal. Deep in their hearts, the only audience for their performance was the leadership. Only when the "criminal" got a clear understanding of this point did he manage not to be overwhelmed by this situation. He did not need to be upset by whatever these people criticized or shouted, nor did he need to be influ- enced or misled by them. In the end, criticisms or shoutings from his tormentors carried no weight.

What was important was the conclusion the leadership drew. If the conclusions read, "The self-criticism that So-and-so has made today is totally unacceptable," or, "So-and-so has not yet taken a correct atti- tude toward his self-criticism." That meant he still needed to act on the stage at least once again, until the leadership stated at the conclusion, "Thanks to the struggle and criticisms, So-and-so has started realizing his crime of opposing the Party, the people, and socialism. But as his understanding is far from profound, he has to continue to enhance his sense of guilt and try to perform meritorious service to atone for his crimes; that is to say, he has to take an active part in struggling against other rightists uncovered during this movement." That meant that al- though he had not really finished his ordeal, he was at least temporari- ly relieved.

The leadership of our publishing house was very skillful in setting the time for the meetings, which were never arranged in such a way as to have one "criminal" come onto the stage after the disposition of a former criminal. When the current major "criminal" had already undergone several sessions of meetings and the struggle against him was seemingly drawing to an end, the next one would start to the stage, and another next to him would be told to make preparation for his self-criticism.

Take myself, for example. I was the last, or the sixth, to be denounced and labeled as a rightist. They attacked me by name in public as early as the final session against the second rightist, Ho Man-chih. In this way, they intended to stimulate me to get ready for self-denunciation. That session took place in a big hall of the Shanghai People's Publishing House and it was attended by the employees of the whole publication system in Shanghai. For such a huge audience, the entire performance, including denunciations by some members from the group and the acknowledgment of crimes by Ho Man-chih, was rehearsed like a drama. One of the speakers was an official of the personnel office of our publishing house. She intentionally made mention of me in her denunciation of Ho Man-chih, saying, "Ho Man-chih was swollen with arrogance when he took advantage of the quarrel between Wong and Yuan over the purchase of the book *Chin Ping Mei*. He forced our President Li to attend a meeting in an attempt to have President Li agree to his terms. Now, to give you some information, I have to tell you who this Wong is. He is a very, very bad element, leading a loose life."

It is the practice of Communists to mention a name at a mass rally in order "to set a tone," that is, to try to influence public opinion. So the next morning, when I arrived at our publishing house, I was summoned by the director of the personnel office. I was not surprised when he asked, "Did you hear what the group was saying about you at the meeting? Now you can see how you incurred popular indignation. You should instantly straighten out your confused thinking and take a correct attitude. We gave you plenty of time, and we are going to take time and give you more time to prepare your written self-criticism. We will not subject you to mass criticism until you get ready a presentable self-criticism; otherwise, it will waste the masses' time."

I did not challenge him; instead I agreed to write my self-criticism. The time allowed me was really plenty, more than I needed. After Ho Man-chih bowed off the stage, the major negative role was played by

Chien P'o-chen, with Wang Mien as the supporting villain. Then after Chien, Wang Mien, the supporting actor, was given a major role, while the finance manager, Liu, played another villain. I was the last villain of our publishing house during this movement.

Each of those who had been labeled rightists before me had undergone numerous "struggle meetings"—some three or four, and others six or seven. Almost none of them was willing to acknowledge he was a rightist, and each tried to explain that he had no intention to hurt the Party, socialism, or the people. It was only after repeated struggles that he had to accept the title of "rightist." I was proud that I helped accelerate the process of the movement by turning the spearhead of the struggle against myself after only two such meetings. I saved everybody's time as well as mine.

At the first meeting held to struggle against me, Vice President Chen began with this prologue: "Our Party has always brought up youths with loving care and adopted the approach of curing the sickness to save the patient in dealing with those who committed mistakes or even crimes. As to Wong, we did help him at first. We gave him plenty of time and opportunity. While we were struggling against the other rightists, we expected Wong to take the initiative in acknowledging his own crimes and actively expose others. It is a shame that he has lost his chance by pretending to be calm and doing nothing, neither sincerely acknowledging his guilt nor exposing others. This shows how reactionary he is. We simply cannot let him escape."

Actually, in my first self-criticism, I listed all that I had said and done. None of the attacks denouncing my "crimes" had anything more to expose. All they could add was a series of adjectives or adverbs, such as "towering crimes," "cunning" and "incorrigibly obstinate." Some of the editors would add some literary grace to these clichés. Mei Ling's speech is an example. "Wong, as a young man living in this great socialist society, has been embraced by happiness and well-being. Nevertheless, he not only took his good fortune for granted but, like a venomous snake, incessantly concentrated his poison on our beloved Party."

A few members of the group, like Hu Tao-ching, still addressed me as "comrade," because at the first meeting I had not yet been proclaimed a rightist. This label came only after an entire day's meeting.

Ch'i Min-ch'u, the newly arrived secretary of the Party branch, announced at the conclusion of that day's meeting, "Wong's self-criticism today is totally unacceptable. His attitude is especially intolerable. Here is an example to illustrate how ugly his attitude is. Criticism of him from the masses should be seen as great help to him, and each word is very precious. But he certainly did not look at it that way. Instead of listening carefully and taking notes from beginning to end, he left in the middle of the meeting. Three times he was seen going to the restroom, and once he spent almost half an hour there. In view of his attitude and crimes, I, in the name of the 'organization,' announce that Wong is a rightist. From the next time onward, Wong, you should make preparation before attending the meeting, and you won't be allowed to leave while anyone is speaking."

This was the first speech Ch'i made to the subordinates with whom he was to work for the next few decades. There is an old Chinese proverb, "A new official adopts strict measures on his arrival," and I was lucky enough to be the first to be blessed with his first strict measures. Two decades later, in 1979, when he was promoted to the position of vice director of the Bureau of Publication in Shanghai, I got approval from the Bureau of Publication to travel to the U.S. I shall be grateful for the rest of my life for his allowing me to leave the country.

His observation about my going to the restroom was correct. I went there not because there was an emergency, but because I was fed up with taking notes of others' criticisms all day long. Not in the least did these assailants bother me, because I clearly understood that their words were not meant for me. I just served as a topic about which they could say something to distinguish themselves in the eyes of the Party. What tortured me most was not the boredom of listening to those speeches, but the hard labor of incessantly taking notes. With my neck and back aching, I felt my whole body stiffen like a rock. Therefore, from time to time I slipped into the restroom, which was a big family-style bathroom—a pretty nice place in which to take a break. Since the newly arrived leader had pointed out it was a crime to stay in the restroom, I decided to atone for it.

So at the next meeting, which I had not expected to be the last to criticize me, I took notes of the criticisms of all those anti-rightist fighters from beginning to end, enduring it all with dogged will, clenching my teeth. The physical pains were compensated for by the leader's remarks that I had shown improvement in my attitude toward this movement, and he also spoke favorably of my self-criticism.

In fact, I spent less time on this second self-criticism than on the first. I just briefly mentioned concrete deeds and words that I had already confessed in the first self-criticism, and then acknowledged that I was a rightist. Not only did I not hesitate to label myself a rightist, but I also quoted Mao's words: "Some people do not like this socialist country of ours," and told them frankly that I did dislike socialism. None of the people labeled rightists before me were willing to acknowledge this point until they had been exhausted by several struggle sessions. But I was not reluctant at all to do so. First of all, it is true that I dislike socialism, and I like to tell the truth. Secondly, I was so naïve at that time as to fail to comprehend why it was sinful not to like socialism since, as I understood it then, likes or dislikes were simply a personal matter. So I felt neither fear nor regret. But my frank and straightforward acknowledgment that I was a rightist might not have been appreciated by heroes of the movement because it put an abrupt end to the play. The main goal of struggle meetings and the chief pleasure derived from them lay in making every effort to compel each target to confess his or her crimes of opposing the Party, socialism, and the people, and acknowledge he or she was a rightist. The more evasive and resistant he or she was, the more high-spirited the heroes in the campaign became. I had the honor of being the rear guard of this movement, the last one labeled a rightist.

At first, I did not have the idea that the rightists were to be subjected to further punishment, because I thought that what rightists had done was just thinking in a different way and that, after all, they had already been criticized and pleaded guilty at the meetings. However, several months later the punishment was announced. During these several months I had had a very good time, as life and work had returned to normal. I enjoyed my job, and had a good appetite and sound sleep. I did not care much about the invisible rightist hat at all. Deep in my heart I was quite proud to be able to be ranked among first-rate scientists and scholars.

As a matter of fact, even in the course of cruel and vehement struggle meetings—or "meetings of debate," as they called then—I felt very calm, as if nothing had happened. One of the "debates" I was forced to attend happened to fall on a Tuesday, the day for my *tai-chi* lesson, and I went to learn *tai-chi* as usual, but in the evening. And after being labeled a rightist, I did not look crestfallen and behaved in a normal way. One day at Master Yue's house, while I was changing my clothes for exercising, I overheard two fellow students chatting outside of the dressing closet.

"I was told that Wong had been labeled a rightist."

"Yes, that's what I heard, too. But he doesn't look like a rightist."

"That's what I am wondering about. I guess he may just have been criticized instead of being labeled a rightist."

"I think so. It is impossible that a proven rightist like him should be so happy and relaxed."

This unintentional eavesdropping delighted me, but also alerted me to question myself, "Why should I keep it a secret?" From then on, in my contact with any person, whenever possible, I would intentionally inform him or her that I had been labeled a rightist recently, without any comment or apology, but the undertone was clear: "I do not hide anything from you. Whether you want to make a clean break with me or not, it's up to you." Although the Communists highly stressed the importance of drawing distinctions between different classes and between the people and the enemy, I felt very lucky and happy that not a relative or friend of mine, except my colleagues in the publishing house, severed relations with me.

My only regret was that the rightist label damaged my personal relationship with my engraving tutor, Chen Chu-lai. It was not because he or I wanted to draw a line between us, but because a misunderstanding arose when he was ferreted out as a target by his "organization," the Chinese Painting Academy of Shanghai, while I was struggled against in my "unit."

Mr. Chen actually had not aired any political opinions that offended the Communist party. He liked gossiping, especially about others' personal lives. Not that he harbored any ill intentions, but he was very interested in finding out what was happening in real or false love affairs, including those of his closest friends and even his brothers or relatives. He had entered the painting academy as an prominent artist a couple of years before the Anti-Rightist Movement began. He did not discard his old habit of gossip after he joined that academy. He could not comprehend that it was an official institution and all staff members belonged to the revolutionary ranks. Gossip could always arouse indignation from the victim or anyone who thought himself a victim. In the revolutionary ranks, a private affair could turn out to be a political problem. Worst of all, Chen's gossip was not only about ordinary colleagues, but about leaders as well. Thus, he provided his victims with excuses to accuse him of anti-Party crimes.

Even Lu Hsiao-man, who was supposed to be Mr. Chen's good friend, could not escape his gossip. He always told others how great, kind-hearted, and sincere Lu was, while spreading stories about her relationships with this man or that man. Lu was aware of his behavior, but refrained from haggling with him, still treating him as an old friend. As Lu Hsiao-man and Chen Chu-lai were in the same Chinese Painting Academy, she witnessed how Chen was struggled against and told me about his trouble with deep concern.

According to Lu's observation, the situation of Mr. Chen as a target of the movement was somewhat different from that of other targets. To struggle against him, the leadership did not have to mobilize the masses and make special preparations beforehand. Fierce assaults from the masses came almost automatically. Once at a meeting someone attacked Chen like this, "Chen Chu-lai, why did you tell me at such-and-such a time about Jack's what-and-what? Is it an act of sowing discord?" Then Jack, flying into a fury, jumped up and scolded Chen, "What! How dare you say so? You liar! As a matter of fact, on another occasion, at such-and-such a time, you told me about Mary's what-and-what. That's the same kind of act of sowing dissension." This filled Mary with hatred, and then she exposed another slander of Chen's about someone else who, burning with anger, in turn came to expose his mistake of gossiping. It turned out that almost all the individuals in his organization had been the objects of his gossip.

To top off the public wrath, Chen caused himself further trouble by adopting the most improper attitude toward this kind of situation. At the struggle meetings the target being struggled against invariably assumed the stance of "lowering his head and admitting his guilt." Not a word of retort. Any modest explanation could be interpreted as a counteroffensive. Even if the accusation was totally untrue, the target should not reply, although he might deny it when he talked with the leadership in private. Direct contradictions in public were a crime. This is what the "debate" was like. Mr. Chen Chu-lai was so naïve that he always refuted his colleagues' accusations, and sometimes even said "Wrong!" at the top of voice. His performance just added fuel to the flames. Therefore, at first he was labeled a rightist, but later was relabeled a "bad element." This was a "promotion," because a "bad element" fell into another category of "enemy," and usually received harsher treatment than a rightist and could be sent to stay in a labor camp for several years.

As our tutor-student relationship had been known in the engraving art circles during the period that both of us were being struggled against, each of us was forced by his "organization" to write materials to expose the other's "criminal words" spoken in private. This was a prerequisite before one was "qualified" to pass the ordeal of the movement. According to what Chen told Lu Hsiao-man, he had exposed my crimes, such as longing to study abroad and dreaming about a change in the social system. Given that his words were true, such exposure did not hurt me at all, because I had already confessed these crimes in my self-criticism.

The materials I wrote to expose Mr. Chen's mistakes could harm him even less. He was by nature a person who readily made his thoughts known to anyone he met. Besides teaching me the techniques of seal engraving, he also told me what he had already told others. So the materials I wrote about him were no more than what his colleagues had already exposed at the struggle meetings.

I did "expose" some of his so-called crimes, which, if they had been seriously and intensively considered by the leadership, could have helped to redress his grievances. I learned from Lu Hsiao-man that at the struggle meetings Chen was also accused by some people of gossip about romances of the First Lady Chiang Ch'ing during the early 1930s in Shanghai. These were not rumors but facts. Mr. Chen was a friend of T'ang Na, Chiang Ch'ing's first husband, so the stories about Chiang Ch'ing had been favorites which he had told to almost all his acquaintances. Stories about romances of Chiang Ch'ing were taboo.

In the Cultural Revolution, spreading these stories could incur a death sentence. It was fortunate for Mr. Chen that in the Anti-Rightist

Movement gossiping about Madame Mao was not a capital crime, but it still could cause serious trouble. I included this issue in my written exposure of him, but added one paragraph to the effect that before the so-called liberation he had told me some romances of Madame Chiang Soong Mei-ling. I wrote this material with the intention that if what I wrote was to be submitted to any logical leader, Mr. Chen might be cleared. My implication was that since he had made the same kind of remarks about Madame Chiang Kai-shek under the rule of the Kuomintang, then his gossip about Madame Mao should be regarded as his habit, not a political plot. Of course, I did not know whether any of his leaders were governed by such logic. What I intended to do was to protect him in my own way.

It was the common practice of Communists to obtain confessions by compulsion. They pursued a policy of "leniency to those who confess their crimes and severity to those who refuse to." This policy was never really implemented, but was designed to draw people out. They would intimidate Jack, "Mary has already exposed your such-and-such mistakes or crimes. You should take the initiative so as to obtain leniency." In the meantime, they would say to Mary, "Jack has fully confessed his crimes and we know you were his accomplice. If you refuse to make a confession, you are sure to get a severe punishment." It was no surprise that they dealt with Mr. Chen in this way. When the struggle sessions were almost over, and before he was sent to the labor camp, he told Lu Hsiao-man one day that he hated me because I had exposed what he had said.

"I saw with my own eyes the materials Wong had written," he said angrily.

That I believe. I can imagine that his leadership must have pressed him to confess as much as possible. They must have used me as bait. It was highly possible that, in order to convince him that they had already obtained evidence, they showed my materials to him. Needless to say, they were not so stupid as to show him the whole text of my exposure of him. They must have concealed anything in my written materials that would be favorable to him. It was a pity that he was so credulous and fell into the trap.

What astonished me most was his analysis of my motives. He told Lu Hsiao-man, "Wong has good reason to betray me. First, he was eager to perform merits to atone for his own crimes, or so the official from his publishing house told me. Second, he took advantage of this opportunity to retaliate against me because it was I who first discovered his affair with the actress and reported it to the leaders."

He communicated the above ideas not only to Lu but to our common acquaintances as well. Whenever his accusation was related to me, I dismissed it with a laugh. It became a part of my personality not to care about whatever comment I might meet, good or bad, especially when someone drew a totally wrong conclusion about me. I would be indifferent and have no interest in refuting it or giving any explanation. Thus, it often seemed that I had acquiesced to it. Even Lu Hsiao-man, who regarded me as her own child, thought that way and believed in Chen's talk. One day, she seriously discussed this matter with me and candidly accused me of having been so blasé as to frame my teacher. Under this circumstance, I could no longer laugh her accusation off.

Then I told Lu Hsiao-man what had happened in detail. If I had really wanted to do so-called merits to atone for my "crimes," I said, I should have done so in my own "organization," which was the unit having direct bearing on my fate. There was plenty of opportunity for me to perform this kind of merit in our publishing house, and I had never done so; therefore, why should I have taken advantage of my teacher?

Furthermore, I told Lu Hsiao-man, I had never had any idea that Mr. Chen had informed of my affair with the actress until he acknowledged it. Even then I still could not believe it, because I was pretty sure he had not been the first to report this romance to the leaders. I knew he was not an informant, but was fond of making inquiries into this kind of thing. When he heard of my romance, he must have spread it far and wide, as if it had been a piece of top news, but I believe he did not do it with any ill intention. How could I be serious with him? Moreover, even if he had been an informant, and this was pure supposition because I did not believe it to be so, I could have had no choice but to resign myself to the fact. How could I have revenged myself on my tutor, who, according to my moral concept, was someone second only to Heaven and Earth, Sovereign and Parents.

It was fortunate that I kept on file all the manuscripts I had submitted to the leadership. Then I showed them to Lu Hsiao-man. Lu, who had seldom been in a mood to read anything other than fiction and review the personal report I had written for her, unexpectedly had the patience to read through my handwritten manuscripts attentively. She was very concerned about the morality of friendship.

"Now I am pretty sure that you did not mean ill toward Chu-lai. On the contrary, you tried to protect him. If I have any chance to meet him again, I will surely vindicate you of his accusation," she said after reading my manuscripts.

I still feel sorry that at that time Mr. Chen was in the labor camp. Several years later Chen was released, but Lu had already died and I was reluctant to make any social contacts for I was concentrating my efforts on leaving the country. Only after I had arrived in the United States did I write a letter to him. Just a brief explanation was sufficient to make him understand what had really happened. He sent me a copy of his newly published *A Collection of Seal Prints of Chen Chu-lai* with his autograph and inscription on the flyleaf. The inscription reads, "This book is given to my student Ching-chih as a keepsake." This meant the restoration of our friendship. A few months later, he passed away.

CHAPTER 7

The Triumphant Sufferer

TOWARD THE END OF 1957, THINGS SEEMED to return to normal. The struggle meetings against the rightists were over. Editors, with or without the hats of rightists, resumed their original jobs again. I was happy to be able to read classical Chinese literature again, and anticipated that the sun would shine again after the rain. However, my anticipation was wrong, for the rain would never end and the sun would never shine. First of all, labeled rightists were not just dealt with by putting "hats" on their heads, as I had thought. No! A "hat" was a nominal thing. They were substantially "treated."

Punishment was meted out by the Party to each rightist in a very scientific manner. Six categories of punishment were announced; however, not a single rightist was executed. Although we listened to and discussed the directive on punishment at that time, I cannot recollect the details. The only thing I can remember is the punishment I received, which was demotion and a drastic reduction of salary. My title of assistant editor was revoked; however, my workload and job requirements remained unchanged. Before the official announcement of my punishment, I was summoned to Vice President Chen, who said, after informing me of the decision, "You can look all across the country, and will surely find that those who have been labeled rightists no longer remain on their original jobs. Rightist actors cannot play on the stage, rightist teachers cannot stand on the platform, and rightist editors cannot sit at their desks. This publishing house has been allowed to adopt a slightly different policy and keep you on the original job because, on the one hand, we are short of people specialized in classical literature, and on the other hand, you are still young. We are keeping you here on condition and with the hope that you will accelerate your remolding." The undertone was clear: I should be grateful and, henceforth, more obedient. I understood and accepted the undertone. The reason was that I liked this job. It was as simple as that.

Firmly believing in the Chinese tradition of always stressing the past, not the present, I had never been stingy with time spent on Chinese classics. Now, as I was paid to read and study those precious treasures, what could I lose by so doing? Even though my salary was cut and my name could not be printed on the publications I edited, I was still satisfied with this job, which I thought could not be matched by any other in the world. In compliance with the special unwritten law for rightists, I was not entitled to meet the authors in the name of the publishing house and put my signature on any correspondence with the authors regarding their manuscripts. However, I did have the obligation to express my opinions to the authors about the improvement of the publications, because that was one of the requirements of an editor, though the memo which conveyed my opinions should be sent in the name of "the editing department." This kind of practice fitted in exactly with my wishes, for I like reading and studying more than contacting people.

In the years to come I was to annotate as well as edit quite a number of selected works which were later to become best-sellers, such as *Loose-Leaf Selections of Chinese Classics*, the popular edition of *One Hundred Tang Poems*, and the popular edition of *One Hundred Sung Poems*. Among the authors of the publications that I edited, there were a few big shots. One thing that gave me great comfort was that some authors known for their hot tempers and haughtiness not only accepted my opinions but wrote to the leaders of our publishing house expressing their appreciation for the anonymous editor's suggestions.

The salary cut was tough for me, not because I got a harsher cut than others, but because my original salary had been low and even a smaller reduction of it would have driven me into straitened circumstances. When I first entered this publishing house, I was given the same rank and salary as a graduate from the university, with the job title of assistant editor and a salary of sixty-five RMB per month. They promised to give me a pay raise after a three-month probationary period. Owing to my affair with the actress, which resulted in a disciplinary action against me in the probationary period, it was only too natural that the supposed pay raise was never to be mentioned after the probation. Then came the Anti-Rightist Movement. Now, my salary had been reduced from sixty-five RMB. Though the leadership was kind-hearted enough to slash just a small percentage and set my new salary at forty RMB, it was still rather tough for me, for by now my wife had already given birth to three children—thanks to the crackdown upon Malthusianism several years before, and a population-increasing policy obstinately pursued by Mao Tse-tung, which made contraceptives unavailable on the market.

I tried my best to keep the daily life of my family from being affected by my punishment. I resumed my occasional contributions of literary features to the supplementary pages of newspapers, as I had done before the Anti-Rightist Movement. In theory, writing for the newspaper was a kind of free-lancing and, therefore, had nothing to do with my "organization." Thus, I had never mentioned this matter to my leaders. Unlike most of the Communist supporters, who regarded the Constitution as invalid, my leaders were clever enough not to interfere openly with my personal constitutional right and refrained from talking about it with me directly. What they did was to block my way in a subtle way.

Each newspaper gladly accepted my first article, but after its publication refused to publish my further contributions. If I tried another newspaper, the same thing happened—all my subsequent articles were rejected after the first had been published. Then I tried still another. Fortunately, there were many provinces and municipalities in China and each of them had a newspaper, so I could try any of my articles several times. However, I did not try all the newspapers, because after several of them had accepted my first articles, they rejected my subsequent articles; the remaining newspapers rejected all my articles, including the first. Later, I realized what had really happened: As soon as my "organization" noticed my name in a certain newspaper, an official letter was sent to that newspaper informing it of my status. No newspaper would venture to knowingly accept any rightist's contribution, as all these newspapers were run by the Communist administration. As newspapers could refuse to publish articles without giving any reasons, they just rejected my manuscripts by returning them. Several times later, my organization must have tired of seeing newspapers publish my articles one after another, and then just informed all the newspapers of my situation to prevent the publication of any subsequent articles.

However, my "organization" had no intention to drive me into a cul-de-sac. They did take into consideration my financial situation after the Movement, and offered some substantial subsidies to make up for the reduction in my salary. In other words, they did not like me to help myself, but only allowed me to accept their favors. Some overtime work, such as punctuating or annotating Chinese classics, compiling indexes, and writing book reviews, was reserved for me. As these kinds of work were done in my spare time, I was paid according to the normal standard of royalties but, of course, my name could never appear in any publications.

I believe that the main purpose of arranging for me to do some additional work was to compensate for my salary cut while trying to turn this arrangement in the leaders' favor, for they thought that the overtime job would greatly reduce my trick of asking for sick leave. In the "heaven-like" socialist society, all employees in the state-operated institutions enjoy free medical care.

Free medical care is not the same as health insurance in Western countries. Most of China's institutions have their own clinics with one or two physicians and are linked to nearby hospitals. Any employee who has fallen sick should go to the clinic first, where the physician often refers the patient to the related hospital after giving a checkup and deciding that it is necessary to do so. Diagnosis and medications are free. Patients have paid sick leave, if the physician of the clinic or the related hospital prescribes it. The sick leave prescribed by a physician working in any other clinic or hospital will not be approved by the "organization." Some regulations have been made regarding sick leave. For example, a person who has a temperature below a certain degree would not be given sick leave. If he has a temperature above it, he will have a certain number of hours' or days' sick leave. Similar regulations have also been laid down concerning hypertensive patients. No one can get sick leave by making verbal complaints. The physician needs physical data before signing a sick-leave certificate.

I had no difficulty obtaining a sick-leave certificate when I needed it. As I practiced *chi-kung*, I could temporarily raise my blood pressure by means of *chi*, which was imperceptible to anyone else. The indicator on the pressure gauge was sufficient for the physician to issue a sick-leave certificate to me. However, I never wanted sick leave, since reading classics was an enjoyment to me and I took my job as a joy rather than a burden. One thing most abhorrent to me was political study.

Thanks to the three very loyal Communist leaders of this publishing house, political study was seen as a first priority. Even during the ordinary days when no movement was under way, regular political study times were not to be altered under any circumstances. In every week, a half workday was used for political discussions, and another two hours on one of the evenings were alloted for reading political materials. On that evening, no one went home after office hours and everybody had supper in the cafeteria, and then went back to sit at his or her desk to read the Red canonistic materials. During these hours of political study, I felt as if I were sitting on a bed of nails, because it was just a waste of time. I wished I could be excused, but politics had already been deemed a first priority in this society and no one was supposed to be absent during the political study sessions. In order to avoid political study, I had to go to the clinic and spend the whole day trying to obtain a sick-leave certificate for all that day. People did have some suspicion about the fact that I was always sick on the days of political study, but what could they do to me? Unlike some others, who were often caught red-handed when they either asked someone else to visit the physician and get the sick-leave certificate or took some medicine to create symptoms, I relied on myself and was never discovered. Offering me some after-office-hours jobs could be thought to be the only effective way to prevent my asking for sick leave, because of the simple logic: If I was sick during the day, how could I do any job in the evening?

In order to get some side work to maintain the basic economic situation of my family, I could not avoid all those political activities. The Anti-Rightist Movement was followed by a campaign of "Laying Bare One's Heart to the Party," which was a campaign involving all intellectuals, leftists, rightists, leaders, and the rank and file. Everybody was required to write wall posters or reports, confiding his or her nonproletariat thoughts to the Party. Evaluation of one's performance in this campaign was based on the quantity and quality of those reports in which one had laid his or her "black heart" bare to the Party. The slogan of this campaign ran like this: The more one writes to lay bare his or her "black heart," the more loyal to the Party one proves himself or herself to be.

In some places, the campaign of "Laying Bare One's Heart to the Party" was designed as a sequel to the Anti-Rightist Movement, and more people were labeled rightists. In others, this campaign was just a gesture. For instance, the leadership of the Chinese Painting Academy in Shanghai just asked Lu Hsiao-man to submit to them a written report of "Laying Bare One's Heart to the Party," since she was free from the obligation of going to the office. Thus, she had no opportunity to read and write wall posters unless she made a special trip there. Again, she entrusted me with the job. She just gave me some general ideas about the report. After I had finished writing the report, she did not even bother to read it through, but just signed her name on it and then requested me to mail it for her. Beyond our expectations, when she met her leaders later, she was told, "Your 'Laying Bare One's Heart' report is well-written, very sincere and truthful. It means that you are faithful to the Party." What they did not know was that this faithful report had actually been produced by a most unfaithful hand.

However, in my publishing house, thanks to the three very devoted Communist leaders, Li, Chen, and Ch'i, every single call issued by the Party was always implemented to the letter. They did not allow the campaign of "Laying Bare One's Heart" to go through the motions. They played the leading roles by taking the initiative of laying bare their hearts first. To set an example of fighting selfishness and repudiating all nonproletariat thoughts, they in turn made a "Laying Bare One's Heart" report at the general meeting of all employees. In so doing, they brought pressure on all employees to lay bare their hearts. They claimed that this would be a test of each one's attitude to the Party and the revolution and that rightists should lay bare their hearts to the Party more thoroughly so as to prove their sincerity about remolding their ideology. Therefore, nobody could be exempted from the campaign, especially not rightists like me.

This campaign did not last as long as the Anti-Rightist Movement. Although I have no particularly bitter memories of this campaign, I experienced some of the ugliest scenes of human relations.

The Communists are adept in the use of figures of speech. For example, giving someone a political label is called "putting a hat on his head." Now, during this campaign, following Mao's teachings to the effect that all members of the revolutionary ranks should be concerned with and help one another, they invented metaphors such as "taking a bath" and "scrubbing each other's back" to lure people into not only confessing their own wrong thoughts but exposing those thoughts of others. Hence, some farces and comedies.

Chow Hwa-yen, deaf and mute, had formerly aroused nobody's interest in struggling against him. He had the advantage of being naturally immune to all absurd political activities. Maybe owing to his being unreconciled to loneliness, he volunteered to act as a hatchet man in the Anti-Rightist Movement by contributing a written speech at almost every meeting. Since he had never attended any meeting before the movement and, owing to his muteness, was also free from any "queue,"—a figure of speech referring to a recorded mistake or crime. Thus he was able to play the role of hero in the movement. He regarded himself as versed in Marxism-Leninism, so his criticisms of each rightist-to-be were decorated with much lengthy theoretical and literary jargon. Lengthiness was not the fatal weakness of his speeches. The worst thing was that he tried to please the public as well as himself with claptrap and many inappropriate jokes. Sometimes he set the whole room rocking with laughter, and the person who was reading his written speech could not help bursting with laughter. This spoiled the atmosphere of struggling.

I still remember one of his criticisms of me in which he compared me to a naughty young monk deserving punishment by the elder monk. No sooner had his criticism been read through than someone refuted his comparison with a question, "Then who is the elder monk?" Apparently, it was a serious mistake or crime to give the great and honorable Communist party the image of a fierce and tough old monk. However, it was very inconvenient to struggle against him, since he could be communicated with only through writing; therefore, people would disregard him, and no misfortune would ever befall him. Now came the campaign of "Laying Bare One's Heart," one of whose characteristics was putting up wall posters. The masses' attention was naturally focused on Chow because he had already distinguished himself for his ability to prepare written speeches quickly. People urged him to "lay his heart bare" as actively as he had done in the Anti-Rightist Movement. Some of them pointed out in the wall posters that Chow Hwa-yen harbored quite a number of evil ideas which, in Chinese, they called "black hearts." However, he refused to give in.

Just as he was actively engaged in writing polemics on the wall, a "bomb" was thrown at him. Ho Man-chih, a rightist who was endeavoring to demonstrate his penitence, wrote a wall poster exposing the following story: Soon after he had been "crowned with the laurel" of a rightist, Chow Hwa-yen had approached him in private. "There is no way for a rightist to have his article published, so you will be deprived of earning royalties in the future. But no problem. You can use my name and address to send your articles." His sympathy with the newly "crowned" rightist proved that all his criticisms of the rightists in public were phony.

Chow did not refute Ho's exposé, which was apparently true and had put Chow in a fix. I knew Ho was not a malicious person, but very forthright. Why then should he have exposed this kindhearted gesture of Chow's, which was meant to help him out of dire straits? It was not until later that I understood the real reason. Neither of them was bad. It would have been too much of a risk for Ho to keep silent on this matter. In the campaign of "Laying Bare One's Heart to the Party," people were compelled to search their own minds and make as thorough a self-exposure as possible. If Chow picked up this matter as one of his "black hearts" and lay it bare, Ho would be punished for concealing this fact. As a person with two "hats" on his head already, that of a Hu Fengist and a rightist, he could not stand the mere rustle of leaves in the wind. He had to protect himself. As to Chow, although this exposé had brought him under fire from wall posters, he was not disturbed by the possibility of wearing any "hat." After all it would take too much labor and energy to struggle against a deaf-mute, and it would be no fun for a person who hated writing or reading.

Notwithstanding, Ho Man-chih still failed to escape the fate of being sent to a remote province when, not long after the "Laying Bare One's Heart to the Party" campaign, came another campaign called "Supporting the Construction of the Border Areas."

There are extreme differences in the standards of living between metropolises like Shanghai, which is a very modern city, and the remote border provinces. There is a lack of free choice of professions, which tends to cause one to work all his life where he was first assigned. It is, therefore, a calamity for one who worked originally at Shanghai to be sent to a remote area. However, no one dares to reveal what he really thinks.

The Communists conducted this campaign in this way: To begin with, a mobilization meeting was called, at which a bureaucrat from a higher level made a mobilization speech, announcing a mission of honor to develop a certain remote area and expounding its importance. His speech straightened out the confused thinking of the audience like a magic key. Then the audience members vied with each other to try to take the floor. An exciting scene of snatching the microphone occurred. Everyone wanted to be the first to sign up. Some people cried and shouted, and others even bit their fingers to write a statement of determination in blood on the spot. Anyway, all the rank and file were expected to express their attitude of unconditional obedience toward this revolutionary call. At the same time they were very nervous until the list of those who were to go was finally announced. Then, those who were not to go were relieved of anxiety. Those who were on the list had no choice but to leave Shanghai.

By that time I had begun to waver in the belief that the Communist regime would not last long and that any job assigned would be short-lived. I determined not to leave Shanghai, because someone who had been assigned to work somewhere else would not be able to relocate as he desired. At the same time, I was disgusted with those who pretended to be enthusiastic about the Party's call while very reluctant at the bottom of their hearts to respond to it. Watching people feign enthusiasm nauseated me. On the other hand, I, as a rightist, should feign more enthusiasm to show my willingness to remold myself, but I had neither the desire nor the ability to feign.

Pressure was irresistible, but I did not want to resign myself to my fate. I had to do something to protect my job in Shanghai before the announcement of the final list. The only way out was for me to be on sick leave. It was not difficult for me to obtain a sick-leave certificate of one day or two days for my high blood pressure, which I could contract through exercising *chi-kung*, but temporary sick leave was useless.

Only a chronic disease could save an employee from being forced to leave Shanghai. Thus, I used the spots on my lung X-ray as a magic weapon. I had had dark spots on my lungs since my childhood. I learned from my uncle, who was a well-known lung specialist, that it was impossible to determine precisely whether or not one was cured of tuberculosis until the physician compared two X-rays, between which there should be an interval of at least a couple of months. Accordingly, I went to the hospital with the permission of the clinic of my publishing house. I strictly followed the fixed procedures. As it was the first time I had visited the lung department of that hospital, they had no record of my lungs. The dark spots on the X-ray of my lungs seemed new to the physicians there; therefore, they prescribed a sick leave of three months for me. The "organization" deprived a tuberculosis patient like me of such an honorable duty of developing border areas. By the time I was able to report back after my prescribed sick leave, three months had passed and the campaign of "Supporting the Construction of the Border Areas" was virtually over. I was safe, but this situation did not last very long.

"Living and working in peace and contentment" had long been the traditional dream of the Chinese people, but after the Communist takeover, this dream was shattered. The Communist Party of China is a revolutionary party whose self-imposed task is to lead the revolutionary ranks in constructing a revolutionary society. It always offers the people a grand opportunity to "make revolution." Not long after the tide of supporting the border areas had ebbed came the call for transferring public employees to do manual labor in the countryside.

According to the solemn call of the Party, in order to keep socialist China from changing her political color, it was critical to reeducate all public employees, and the best way to guarantee against their becoming revisionists was to have them do physical labor with poor peasants. So, it was said, it would be the Party's long-term policy for all public employees to be transferred to "strike root" in the countryside and work for the revolution shoulder to shoulder with poor peasants. Again, a solemn report was delivered at a mobilization assembly, followed by a wave of wall posters written by individuals expressing their determination to go to the countryside and their strong desire for the approval of their application by the leadership.

Again, I had to conjure up some disease that could come to my rescue. My determination not to go was unswerving, especially because by that time I had already had some short experience of country life. In the previous year most of the employees of our publishing house had gone together to the outskirts of Shanghai to assist in the three autumn jobs of harvesting, plowing, and sowing for two weeks. I had not had the least aversion to the peasants nor any disdain for manual labor. On the contrary, I liked them. The only thing I was terribly disgusted with was the collective life. Living under the same roof and eating from the same pot with these revolutionary comrades was a nightmare. It is all right to live together for a period of, at most, two or three weeks, but to do it longer than that would be unbearable for me. It would be worse than living in jail.

Alas, no disease could be my savior now. The dark spots on my lungs, like a one-way ticket, became worthless once used. With two or more X-ray negatives of my lungs placed on file, the physicians could easily ascertain that no tuberculosis was developing. Thus, no more sick-leave certificates. However, there did exist one last resort, the sputum test. Each time I went to see the doctor, he asked that my sputum be tested. I was told that only after several consecutive tests proved negative could it be concluded that the disease was fully cured. If only one test proved positive, then it meant tuberculosis was still in its developing stage.

With this knowledge in mind, I made every effort to contract tuberculosis. My mother-in-law, a tuberculosis patient in the late stage, was in the hospital at that time. On the reports, her sputum tests were marked positive. So I asked her for a small bottle of sputum. At first she refused. Then I told her why I desperately needed it. I also told her that without the help of her sputum, I would have to follow in the steps of other public employees and live in the countryside for a long period. I would rather be handicapped by the disease. Realizing that I was not trying to intimidate anybody and that I was very determined, my mother-in-law finally complied with my request. Her sputum saved me from being sent to the countryside. However, the Chinese Communists were "uninterrupted revolutionists," as they claimed, and they never stopped disturbing the people's normal lives. A few years later they issued this kind of call again. Unfortunately, by that time, my mother-in-law, who had once given me her precious sputum, had passed away.

Hopelessness sometimes leads to desperation. I became a thief. The sputum sample delivery spaces in the laboratories of the hospitals were unguarded. People went to the laboratories and left the sputum samples at an allotted location. Then the samples would be collected regularly at a certain time during the day. No one ever thought of taking precautions against burglars. It took little effort for me to pick up a dozen small sample bottles if I pleased. The difficulty was that I had no idea which bottle contained a sample which was to prove positive. Besides, I hated to take away the samples of those who were really sick and, therefore, delay diagnosis of those patients. I did it this way: I took ten or more bottles to a quiet spot, and poured a tiny bit of sputum from each bottle to an empty one. Then after the empty bottle was filled with sputum, I sent it to the laboratory as my sample and returned the other bottles. I did not think that loss of a bit of sample in each bottle could affect its test result. I endeavored to be a thief who did others no harm.

By being a thief of this kind, I managed to evade responding to successive revolutionary calls. But intermittently I did some physical labor in the countryside, each time for about two weeks. I was praised by the leadership for being "good at manual labor" since I really liked various kinds of farm work. I was particularly fond of "making steel by the indigenous method," because in doing so I did not have to be away from home and went to the office as usual. The only difference was that we did not enter our offices but instead made steel in the garden of the publishing house. It was just like a tea break. I was interested in carrying two baskets of cement or brick on a shoulder pole. It was true that it turned out to be a nationwide waste of raw materials and manpower to make steel by the indigenous method, but during this campaign, instead of losing anything, I gained some strength and two big calluses on my shoulders. At the same time, I earned some praise for my good performance in physical labor.

However, my reputation of being good at manual labor did not help me to get rid of my rightist hat. The difficulty involved in getting rid of my hat should be attributed to my leaders' strong Party spirit. I was glad that this publishing house had strong leadership. All the leaders were very considerate of the employees. For example, they made up for my financial deficit by offering me some overtime work or granted

Steelmaking by the indigenous method. I am second from left.

permission for all my sick leaves prescribed by the doctors, but politically they were very firm. Both the vice presidents talked to me about my hat and said: "You were labeled a rightist because of your political views. The only way to have your hat taken off is to change your outlook on life. We admit you are diligent in your work and have done very well in manual labor, but the most important thing is to transform your ideology." They were too shrewd not to know my real political views.

At first, I had been glad to be labeled a rightist, for I took pride in ranking with famous scholars and scientists. Then, when I saw almost all the rightists surrender at the struggle meetings, or "hang their heads and admit their guilt," an idiom meaning not only pleading guilty and imploring leniency but also exposing and reprimanding one another, I was disappointed and astonished at the ugly aspects of human character. These outstanding intellectuals, who were equivalent to ancient China's gentry, did not dare to demonstrate rudimentary dignity as a human being under pressure from the Communists. As I lost my respect for them, I no longer felt proud of sharing the same label with these famous figures.

Before long, the Communists came up with a brilliant stroke of politics. On the eve of October 1, 1959, the so-called National Day, in celebration of the tenth anniversary of the founding of his republic, Mao gave amnesty to some high-ranking Kuomintang officials captured in the civil war and at the same time began "delabeling" those rightists whose ideology was said to have been transformed. The offer of "taking hats off" was itself a move designed to raise the hopes of the immediate relatives of rightists, and encourage them to persuade their rightist loved ones to transform their thinking. For the rightists, the clause "whose ideology has been transformed" served as a sort of pressure. Those who failed to have their "hats" taken off were regarded as not having made sufficient effort to remold their world view. As more and more rightists had their hats taken off, pressure on the remaining rightists became heavier and heavier. I was an example.

My parents, my wife, my brother, and even Lu Hsiao-man, who was always carefree, asked with one voice: When would I have my "hat" taken off? In their opinion, I was young and had not really committed any serious offenses against the Communists; therefore, I should be among the first to be delabelized. They were disappointed when they learned on the eve of the tenth anniversary of the founding of the People's Republic of China that I was not on the list. Then came the spring festival, the Chinese New Year. I was not on that list of delabelization either. I was sad that their disappointment spoiled their happiness during this important traditional festival.

Then came May 1, Labor Day. Disappointed. Then National Day again. Disappointed again. In the end, I was in such despair that the approach of every festival in which a list of delabelization was to be announced would make me feel as if I were facing a bowl of bitter medicine which I would have to force myself to gulp down. To me, festivals were no longer holidays, but ordeals. I was never in a mood to celebrate them. Out of concern for me, my family and friends seldom touched this topic in my presence, except Lu Hsiao-man, who occasionally discussed with me how to get delabelized. However, I understood their feelings. Once Granny Liu, my mother's nanny who had stayed with our family all her life and who was illiterate and knew nothing about politics, told me inadvertently that my eldest son, who had just entered elementary school, had asked her about "Papa's hat." I felt so bad that tears rolled down my cheeks. Apparently, even a little kid had been hurt by my rightist hat.

I went to the personnel office and requested that my hat be taken off. My request elicited a quiz: "Do you think your ideology has already been transformed?"

I approached Ch'i Min-ch'u, vice president as well as secretary of the Party branch of this publishing house, and asked frankly, "Would you please have my hat removed? I would greatly appreciate it if you could do so."

"It is good that you have this desire," he replied, "but it was you yourself who put the hat on your head, and now it is also up to you to decide when to take it off. Remold your ideology, and your hat will certainly be taken off. Remember, it is better to go back and make a net than to stand by the pond and long for fish."

When the majority of the rightists across the nation had been delabeled and I was the only person in this publishing house still with the rightist "hat" on, it seemed that I had been singled out as "a teacher by negative example." I talked with the other vice president, Chen Hsiang-ping.

"I am the youngest of the rightists in this publishing house. I had no reactionary record under the old regime. I have committed no more crimes since the Anti-Rightist Movement and have been hanging my head and admitting my guilt. Many rightists have been delabeled, but I still remain a rightist. I would like to ask you to help me out," I told Chen.

"You are very stubborn," he said frankly. "It is true that you have not done anything wrong since the Anti-Rightist Movement. Outwardly, you are faithful and diligent and have done your work quite well. The key point is that inwardly you have different ideas and feelings from us. I can surely tell that you have not accepted even a little bit of Marxism in your soul. Verbally, you have changed a great deal. Deep in your heart, you haven't changed at all. How can we have your hat taken off?"

I was fully convinced by all his words, except the last sentence. What the devil does "hat" have to do with the soul?

I resorted to human nature, which I assumed was something that human beings, including Communists, had in common. In 1962, I submitted to the leadership a formal but unusual report, in which I omitted all political terms and refrained from talking about politics. I just talked about my mother's fiftieth birthday and the filial piety I should pay to my parents. As my parents had been hurt so much by my rightist label, I would endeavor to have my "hat removed" as a most precious birthday gift to my mother. My parents could not be made happier by any other gift than by this one. I racked my brains to make this essay soul-searching and heart-rending. However, these "Bolsheviks," as they styled themselves, were really made of some special material, just as Stalin said, and were not touched at all by my article. My goal of having my hat taken off was not achieved, and I was severely criticized because of this report. They asked me to read it at the meeting as my monthly ideological report and subjected it to criticism by the masses, who accused me of continuing to spread feudalistic poison.

The foremost necessity for a rightist was "accepting supervision by the masses." Who were the masses? All those unlabeled persons around you were the masses, and they were eligible to supervise you. As I was a staff member in the editing department, all the supervisors were intellectuals, since all of them were editors.

Not long after the Anti-Rightist Movement, the publishing house moved from a single house to a big building, formerly the site of the China Academic and Artistic Institute. The Chinese Classics Publishing House was merged into Chung-Hwa Printing Company and now called the Shanghai Editing Bureau of Chung-Hwa Printing Company. Our original scope of business and individual job descriptions remained unchanged. Most of the original Chung-Hwa personnel merged into other departments, and the composition of the editing department basically remained the same, with only a little adjustment. Wang Yuan-fang and Chen Han-sheng had retired, and Li Wei-chin had been arrested. Ho Man-chih and Chen Wen-chian had been sent to border areas. Wang Mien had also been arrested. Added to the list of editors were Wu Tie-sheng from the former Chung-Hwa Printing Company, and four others from the original proofreading section. Two editors from other publishing houses were transferred to our department, one of them also a rightist. The entire editing department was divided into two groups, one headed by Chin Hsin-yao and the other by Chu Chin-chen. Their appointments as group heads were probably rewards given to them for what they had done in the Anti-Rightist Movement. However, as neither of them was in the Party, both were "helped" by a

Communist deputy newly transferred from some other system. Another young Party member, Nee Mo-yen, who had just graduated from a university after majoring in Chinese literature, was also assigned to work in Chu's group. So there were now three Communist Party members in our editing department, which had not had a single one previously.

For the first time our editing department had a female. Ms. Chen was assigned to work in the same group as I. She seemed to know very little about Chinese classics, yet she was given the title of editor. She posed as a 100-percent "Bolshevik," although she was neither a Party member nor a League member. Undoubtedly, the easiest and most efficient way of demonstrating one's leftist stance was to supervise the rightists and give them a hard time. I was subjected to her supervision. Thank God, she was very kindhearted by nature and lacked a real understanding of the theories of Marxism-Leninism. She never found fault with me as some people did, nor did she ever preach any lengthy sermon. All that she did was to summon me to report my thoughts to her from time to time, and echo slogans printed in the day's newspapers, since she could never make any clear and logical analysis by herself. Very good. She saved me a lot of time. Except for supervising me, she did nothing. However, all the leaders were very nice to her. One or two years later she quit, but she refused to say where she was going to work. She only gave some hint that she was going to Hong Kong. It happened in the period of "lockstitching border," when nobody was able to leave this country, but she managed to do so. I did not reason why, but terribly envied her. It was only when I happened to read a biography of Chen Yee, a high-ranking official of the Kuomintang who had been executed by Chiang Kai-shek for his attempted defection to the Communists, and I saw the picture of his daughter, sometime after I arrived in this free world, that I came to realize that Ms. Chen was none other than Chen Yee's daughter.

As a rightist, I was required to write an ideological report every month and read it to the masses at the meeting for their review. On my written reports, sentences like "I should apologize to the Party," "I should apologize to the masses," "I am grateful to the Party," "I am grateful to the masses," and "I hate myself for having launched frenzied attacks against socialism," appeared over and over again. No matter how tired I was of writing the same things, I still had to repeat them. The reports should be neither too short nor too long. They each averaged 5,000 to 10,000 characters. In other words, on the average, I wrote 100,000 characters annually. If published, the ideological reports I had written during that decade would pile up from the floor to my waist.

In comparison with being criticized by the masses, writing reports was easy. Eager to demonstrate their progressiveness, the masses vied with one another to disparage my ideological reports. They not only never put in a good word for me, but also found fault with me by hook or by crook. If the report was a little longer than usual, they would assert that I was attempting to drown the masses in a sea of words. If it happened to be shorter than usual, they would rip into me, saying I was unwilling to make any self-criticism. If it gave a detailed account of my activities of the past month, they would discredit it as a day-to-day account without any new substance. If it was theoretical self-criticism, they would claim it was empty talk.

I could tell from their criticisms that most of the time they had no patience to read or listen to my self-criticisms, for their comments were not directed at what I had written but at some trivial things of daily life, about which they would raise a fuss. The following are some examples:

"Recently, Wong walked with a springy step. This demonstrates that he does not feel guilty. He looks so happy and relaxed."

"Lately, Wong walked with heavy and sluggish steps. His attitude constitutes a sharp contrast with that of the masses, who are full of vigor and vitality. It shows Wong has an antipathy to the Party's policy, and that he lacks determination to remold himself."

"These days, whenever we attend a general meeting and listen to political speeches, I notice that Wong chooses to sit conspicuously in the middle of the front row. This demonstrates he is getting cocky."

"The other day, while we were listening to the political report in the meeting, Wong was seen sitting in a corner. I can smell a rat in his mind, something that could not be exposed to the sunlight; otherwise, he wouldn't have been so furtive and stealthy."

My fellow editors were good at phrasing, and skilled in confounding black and white. They disregarded facts whenever they needed to. When they could not find fault with my way of walking or my seat in

a meeting, they could make a fuss about the wording of my self-criticisms. For example, whenever I had a slip of tongue and said, "I regret
that I committed serious mistakes in the past," they would point out in
no time, "No, what you rightists committed were crimes, not mistakes.
It is only the people that commit mistakes."

I still remember many platitudes uttered by these commentators, such
as "It should be thought that our great Party was trying to deliver a
youth like you from hell when it labeled you a rightist. You should be
grateful to the Party for its profound kindness, for it gave you the opportunity of remolding yourself thoroughly and beginning your life anew."

"The very fact that we, who have so many other things on hand,
have spent so much time sitting here and attending a meeting held for
you denotes that our Party still pins its hopes on you. Otherwise, why
should we bother to make so much effort to pull you to our side?"

Lying with sincerity and raving with seriousness did not make me
angry. Listening to these nonsensical words might be taken as some
kind of amusement. What made me really angry was their desire to
prove how stubborn my anti-Party standpoint was. They tried with all
their ingenuity to find the evidence. This kind of sinister scheme could
only be employed by intellectuals. Here are some instances.

As I intensely hated Mao's "reform" of the Chinese writing system,
which I regarded as a true destruction of Chinese civilization, I never
wrote the simplified characters which constituted an important part of
his reform plan. As a matter of fact, some of the simplified characters
had been adopted as early as the pre-liberation days and had been in use
for a long time. Now, since these characters had been introduced into
Mao's reform plan, I refused to use them. But I made an exception; that
is, I used simplified characters only in my manuscripts for the purpose
of making things easier for the typesetters, because, in most of the publications, they were supposed to typeset simplified characters only. On
other occasions, I wrote old characters. This never caused people inconvenience, for almost no one, including those who fully endorsed Mao's
plan, could remember all the simplified characters. Inevitably, people
would sometimes write some words of old characters. Once at a meeting held to discuss my ideological report, someone, either because he had
nothing else to say or because he had some ill intention, spoke thusly:

"If you want to know how stubborn Wong is, it is very simple. Just look at his written self-criticism. From beginning to end, there's not a single simplified character, all old ones. This is full proof that Wong is a young man with the mentality of an old fogy and a surviving adherent of the Kuomintang regime."

This comment was echoed by someone else, who began to make a further analysis. "This is not just a question of mentality. In Wong's case, this is a reflection of his firm reactionary political stand. As we all know, the reform of the Chinese writing system was initiated and led by Chairman Mao. Thus, Wong's rejection of simplified characters is in fact an opposition to Chairman Mao and the Communist Party."

In the summary, made by the leader at this meeting, these comments were praised for their keen insight. After the meeting, my group leader came up to me and said, "The leadership acknowledged that you have been working hard recently and that you have always admitted your crimes. So we are considering taking off your hat. But in view of the opinions of the masses, we don't think that they will agree to the removal of your hat."

Of course, these words could not be taken seriously. They were spoken to give me some consolation. Whenever the Communists want to do something, they never care about the opinions of the masses. Anyway, at that time I had no doubt that the opinions expressed by these intellectuals greatly helped to keep my hat on.

Even trifling things like bickerings between husband and wife could become things of political significance. Jane bought a radio without consulting me and I was unhappy about that. I found fault with her and said that it was a luxury which we could not afford given our current financial situation. I wanted her to return it and get a refund, but she refused. Thus, we quarreled. I refused to have the radio in my room, and Jane refused to part with it. So she moved to the attic. She was good-natured but very naïve. In the past, whenever a quarrel arose between us, she, unable to settle it herself, always turned to others. She would call my best friend, Yue Tan, Master Yue's son. She would call Lu Hsiao-man. She would call anyone who she thought had the ability to convince me. This time she thought I was obedient to my "organization," so she called my group leader, Hwa Shou-yi, a Communist. Hwa was in charge of my ideological reports and presided over the monthly meetings of mass criticism held for me. So at the next meeting, after I

had finished reading my written self-criticism, he informed the participants of my wife's complaint about our quarrel over the radio. He dealt
with it as if it were a political matter: "From this incident we can see
that Wong is still very arrogant and stubborn," he said.

Perhaps it was beyond Hwa's expectation, but the incident became
very serious in the mouths of the intellectuals. One intellectual said,
"This matter does not simply involve a radio. The radio programs
nowadays are designed to propagate our Party's policy and Mao Tse-
tung Thought. What Wong resists is not the radio, but Marxism and
Mao Tse-tung Thought."

Another made some additional remarks by using poetic language.
"Exactly! Wong is tenaciously entrenched in his rotten, mildewy king-
dom while desperately trying to ward off the brilliant sunshine of Mao
Tse-tung Thought." I appreciated his beautified wording, and acknowledged in my mind that he was quite right. Fortunately, this meeting did
not cause me too much trouble other than that I was ordered by my organization to give in to Jane, and she moved into my room with the
newly bought radio.

I was much more fortunate in the next incident. In the summer of
1960, Master Yue, my *tai-chi* tutor, was seriously ill. Observing the
age-old Chinese tradition of the tutor-pupil relation, I attended to him
by doing the chores of serving tea, boiling water, washing his spittoon
and chamber pot, et cetera. As Master Yue's house was close to my office, it was for my own convenience, as well as his, that I stayed at his
house taking turns to attend to my tutor during the day or night. Jane
was unhappy about it, and again turned to my "organization." This
time she complained to the female official in the personnel office, who
had visited her when she was pregnant with our second son. Then this
official came to attend my ideological report meeting for the first time.
She probably did not know how to link the tutor-pupil relation to feudalistic morality and criticize me from the high plane of Marxism, because, after all, she was not an intellectual. She just sat there and waited until the close of the meeting, then she began to mention to the surprised participants Jane's complaint about my staying at my tutor's
house. She treated the trifling matter lightly, saying, "I am ordering you
to move back to your home immediately. You don't have to go to any
tutor's home. He won't improve your ideology. At present, all you need

is ideological transformation." Then, without waiting for any answer from me, she announced abruptly, "The meeting is over."

After the meeting, one of my colleagues, who knew me very well but was not very nice to me, came to ask me, "Now what are you going to do?" Pretending to raise a casual question, he was in fact gloating over my bad luck. Almost all of the people around me knew that I had been dedicated to *tai-chi* for a long time and that I would not succumb to any pressure brought on me to give it up. At the same time they knew that the personnel department in any organization in Communist society was very powerful. No matter how rash and indiscreet the order was, as long as it had been issued from the mouth of the official of the personnel office, it had to be carried out. Whoever dared to challenge it would be down on his back.

I replied to this seemingly casual question calmly but firmly, "Everything goes as usual." This man and other people around were astonished to hear my answer. No one uttered a word. I was pretty sure that they were saying to themselves, "We're going to have something interesting to look at!" I thought the same way that they did, but in a different mood. I was prepared to be jailed.

I was really lucky that only several days after the meeting, this official from the personnel department had a childbirth. She must have been engrossed in her newborn baby, because when she returned to work after her maternity leave of about two months, she seemed to have totally forgotten about the reckless order on which she had hastily staked her prestige. The false alarm was over.

In comparison to the boorish Communist officials, the intellectuals were much more dangerous. They could kill you, as it were, without spilling blood. They killed others as well as themselves. They were so erudite that they could make endless enlightening judgments. At one time, I was working hard and no one made any complaints about me, so it seemed about time to take my hat off. At the meeting for my ideological report, the participants again could not find fault with my report or my performance. Instead of talking about my ideology and my work performance, they directed attention to my clothing.

"I have the feeling that there is something political behind Wong's clothing. Why does he always wear such rags?" someone raised the question.

"Terrific! You have a keen political sense. Wong's financial situation is not so bad that he should be dressed like that. Look, he is out at elbows. His big toe can be seen through the hole in his shoe. He has been protesting his salary cut since the Anti-Rightist Movement," someone chimed in.

Then another stepped in to try to sound more frightening, "No, it is not merely the salary cut that he has been protesting since the Anti-Rightist Movement. As a matter of fact, he has been using this method to vilify the socialist system as a whole."

"I agree. By wearing rags, Wong tries to embarrass the Party and uglify socialism. Comrades, this is a challenge he is deliberately posing to all of us. We must not relax our vigilance."

I am pretty sure that those who had uttered those words did not believe in them themselves, but the leaders were readily taken in. According to what the group leader told me, the question of "taking my hat off" would again be shelved. In fact, it is my nature to be carelessly dressed. Now I am in the United States and can afford good clothes, but I rarely buy them. Each time my present wife, Carin, wants to buy new clothes for me, she has to waste some energy persuading me to agree. However, it is futile to explain to the Communists what one's nature is. So I kept silent.

My habit of saying something humorous could not be changed. When a colleague, a rightist transferred here from some other publishing house after the movement, expressed his concern and sympathy for my much delayed "hat removing" during our private conversation, I returned his kindness with a confidential self-sarcasm, "I did not expect that the worn-out shoes on my feet could have something to do with the hat on my head." Who would have thought that at the next meeting of my ideological report, this fellow, in order to show his loyalty to the Party, cited the above sarcastic expression of mine as evidence of my stubborn refusal of ideological transformation and my abhorrence of mass criticisms. Needless to say, this exposure, which he used to ingratiate himself with the Party, caused further delay in taking my hat off.

I was slow in drawing a lesson from this experience. After this incident, I still could not refrain from confiding my real thoughts to him. We still talked to each other. This was because our desks stood side by side. One day, as if nothing unpleasant had ever happened, he expressed his admiration for me, saying, "I admire your editing. You see, in our publishing house, we have some kind of campaign almost every other year, the purpose of which is to censor recent publications and see if there are any political blunders in the content. You have edited a lot, but no serious mistakes have been discovered in the publications you edited. How is it possible?"

I could not help showing off. "Very simple. There are two knacks. First, you have to pay attention to the interval between editing and publishing a work. When the political atmosphere of the society is relaxed, our leaders often asked us to lower the political standard. I don't have the least doubt about our leadership's sincerity. The problem is that before a work comes out, several months or one or two years have elapsed. By this time the political ambience of the society has already changed, usually from relaxed to restrained, and censorship has to be conducted by using the strict point of view prevailing at the moment, not the view prevailing in the period of editing. My way of dealing with this is that, no matter how relaxed the atmosphere is while I am doing the editing, I use a tone three times as leftist as the tone prevailing at the moment, so that the publication will be able to withstand censorship if the atmosphere changes. Second, my sole criterion in evaluating literary works is to faithfully use my own conscience, or I should say, diametrically running against my own conscience. Whatever strikes a sympathetic chord in my heart must be something poisonous, something related to the theory of human nature.* So I just do away with it. Any work which gives me a sense of beauty, loyalty, purity, and peace must be reactionary and, therefore, should be avoided. On the contrary, anything that is dull, dry, and insipid, I recommend with confidence that it won't cause me trouble in future censorship."

He appreciated my words with a knowing look, but at the next meeting of my ideological report, he betrayed me again and exposed this private conversation. Using me as his stepping stone, he succeeded in

---

*Mao Tse-tung considered the theory of human nature a fallacy put forward by the landlord class and the bourgeoisie, which denies the class character of human nature. Hence, any literary work with ideas praising human nature was poisonous and dangerous.

having his hat removed not long after. He was not the one with whom I felt most angry. After all he was a rightist, and to have his hat taken off he tried to achieve his goal by fair means or foul. Although I did not like his unscrupulousness, I was fully sympathetic with his goal.

What I could not forgive was the selfish behavior of some people. Most of my colleagues had escaped being labeled rightists simply because the number of rightists, including me, had met the quota set by Mao for each organization. If I or the other rightists tried hard enough to show our repentance and expose the so-called crimes of others and succeeded in escaping being labeled, then other people would have to fill the vacancies. Therefore, they became my supervisors instead of being themselves objects of supervision, at least partly because I was labeled a rightist and met the quota. In other words, they slipped through the net only at my expense. Now, instead of showing me any gratitude, they ceaselessly dropped stones on me, a person who had fallen into a pit, for almost a decade. They hit me even harder after I had fallen down. As the Chinese idiom goes, they requited kindness with enmity.

Owing to my apathy to the entire social system as well as my indifference to my colleagues, I was not in the least uncomfortable, whatever they said. I knew very well that they were just using me as their topic, but not as their audience. The real audience was the "organization," which not only controlled my fate but theirs as well. I had to react to their opinions carefully, but I never accepted them in my heart. The following instance reflects how I treated the ideological report and mass criticisms.

As a lover of nature, I am fond of traveling. In a socialist society, we worked six days and were free Sundays. As we had only one day off, we did not have sufficient time for any long excursions; therefore, the three festivals, namely, the spring festival known as Chinese New Year, May 1 (Labor Day), and October 1, which is the Communists' National Day, are the only opportunities available for traveling. Each of these festivals, plus a Sunday, usually lasts three to five days. I never gave up the chance to travel, and usually went to a scenic place that was within a distance of several hours' train ride from Shanghai, such as Hangchow, Soochow, Wuhsi, and Yishing. I could not travel to places farther than these, which took more than three or five days, nor could I afford the expense. I budgeted my trips carefully. Take a trip to

Hanchow, for example. The express, which took three or four hours to reach the destination and cost an equivalent of less than two U.S. dollars, was not affordable to me. I would take the boxcar, which cost half as much and which was normally used for shipping freight and transporting travelers during festivals only. It was a car without seats. A large wooden bucket, placed in a corner and separated from public view by some curtains, was used as a makeshift lavatory. Travelers could choose to sit any place available on the floor. If I was so "lucky" that the only available "seat" I could find was a place right beside that bucket, then I had to "enjoy" the smell all the way. Sometimes I was so fortunate as to ride on a car with very few travelers. Then I could lie down on the floor and sleep all night, as it used to take seven or eight hours for this kind of car to reach Hangchow. It usually left Shanghai late in the evening and reached Hangchow early the next morning. I made visits to various scenic spots on foot and put up for the night in a cheap inn or in the lounge of a hotel or in a school classroom, which charged one tenth as much as a regular hotel room.

In spite of my hard life and low income, I still enjoyed my travels, but for each trip I had to pay a certain amount of spiritual cost, that is, "self-criticism." The Great Leader Mao issued a special instruction to the effect that the downtrodden had to recite the following quotation loudly during the festivals: "The day of joy for the people is a day of woe for the counterrevolutionaries." Each "organization" summoned its ox monsters and snake demons, class enemies of all descriptions, on the eve of the festivals and admonished them: "All of you should behave yourselves during the coming festival." What did "behave yourselves" mean in this context? No clear definition was given. However, whether the definition was clear or not did not matter. What was important was to exercise dictatorship. Thus, each time the prefestival admonition was followed by an order: "When you come to work after the holidays, each of you should submit a written report on what you do and think during the festival."

I faithfully reported my trip during the festival. At first, I had thought there was nothing wrong with traveling, but the masses, who were supervising me and who were all intellectuals, thought otherwise. They were so intelligent that they could, in the comments they made on my report at the meeting held to criticize me, make a convincing

Pictures taken while traveling.
For each trip I had to be criticized and self-criticized.

analysis that my traveling was a revelation of my tacit protest against this social system. They cited many instances of ancient scholars who were famous for their spiritual sustenance through withdrawing totally from society and living in seclusion in some scenic places after their banishment from the court. These instances led them to conclude that my travels were of the same nature and were manifestations of my dissatisfaction with reality. Thus, I had to write another self-criticism because of my traveling.

Notwithstanding these criticisms and self-criticisms, my interest in traveling did not abate. I continued to travel whenever there was a vacation of two or three or more days. Since my writing of self-criticism after each trip was such a wet blanket, I later became more clever. I wrote my self-criticism before setting off on the journey and kept it in the drawer so that I could submit it as soon as the holidays were over. Thus, I did not have to worry while having fun with the mountains and waters.

I had a strong aversion to any meeting. Whether it was a general meeting or a small discussion group, or whether I was listening to a harangue or political documents, I was always fidgety, because I could not help thinking, "Oh, part of my life is being wasted again!" With the passage of time, I gained some experience in dealing with any kind of meeting.

I did not waste any time listening to political harangues at the meetings. I took advantage of the common practice in that society of taking notes while listening to harangues, especially those which were made by high-ranking officials. I always had a notebook on my knee and I put some materials I wanted to read under it. The notebook was small, and the materials were larger but folded neatly. It looked as if I were using these materials as a kind of pad for the notebook, and I kept making random marks on the notebook with my pen as though I were taking notes. In the meantime, I concentrated my eyesight on the materials under the notebook, and read them line by line. Of course, I had to move the notebook slowly so that it could cover the part which I was not reading at that moment. When I had finished reading a page, I pretended to pay attention to the haranguer by staring at the platform while turning over a sheet casually. Then I started reading again.

It was more difficult for me to make up the waste of time duing our collective reading sessions. During such sessions, everybody sat at his or her own desk reading the "sacred" documents. It would have caused suspicion if you had put some irrelevant materials on the desk. For such occasions, I had to make some preparation beforehand. Then, during the collective reading, I kept my eye on the sacred documents while trying to memorize the materials I had prepared, such as some classical poems or English vocabulary.

It would have been one of my crimes if I did not say something during the discussion on either the political harangues that we had recently heard or political documents we had read. Even at such meetings, I tried to save as much time as possible. My trick was to take the first chance to speak. There were three reasons for doing so. First, in the eyes of the leaders, speaking actively meant a positive attitude toward political study. Second, if I was speaking at the time everybody else was considering his own speech, few people would bother to listen to me and thus be able to find fault with my speech. Third, and most important, once I got rid of the burden of making a speech, I could use the rest of the time to exercise my brain in whatever way I wanted to.

While my brain was concentrating on something meaningful during political study, I was very cautious not to reveal any indifference to the nonsensical talk around me. I developed a habit of staring at the speaker without paying the least attention to what he was saying, but whenever his eyes met mine, I would, as a natural reaction, nod slightly as though I were listening to him. This was a trick which I had learned from another editor, Yang Yu-jen, and in which I was now more proficient than he through the frequent use of it.

Another unbearable suffering was being forced to go to the movies or the theater. The tickets were always free, but I always felt annoyed. During the period between the end of the Anti-Rightist Movement and the eve of the so-called Cultural Revolution, which was actually an Anti-Culture Movement, watching movies or dramas was as important as attending political meetings. At first I had no idea about the importance of theatergoing and, therefore, declined the tickets. As a result, I was severely criticized for resisting political study. According to their analysis, this was a reflection of my continuing antagonism to new things: the new era and the new society.

Again, I gave in. However, while watching this kind of movie or drama, I could not help regretting having my precious time wasted. Again, I thought of a trick.

These movies or dramas were not entertaining at all, and very few would care to watch them. The audience chiefly came through block booking. In our case, it was always the official Union of Publishing Workers that chartered the whole theater and distributed tickets among all the publishing houses. To show no discrimination, the Union gave different classes of seats to each publishing house, which got the same percentage of good seats, bad seats, front seats, rear seats, and balcony seats. The same principle applied to each department. Therefore, the staffers of the same department did not usually sit in the same row. Thus, when I was in a theater, the audience members around me came from different publishing houses and did not usually know one another. When it came to my mind that this was a loophole, I wasted no time exploiting it.

Each time I was asked to choose a ticket, I, unlike others who tried to get tickets for good seats, adopted the attitude appropriate to a rightist and picked the worst seat, or, instead of choosing a ticket, just said "Please give me the worst." This attitude complied with Mao's instruction of "tucking one's tail between legs," and got some good comments from the masses. I used to go to the theater several minutes before the show was over, and wait in the restroom. When the audience walked out of the theater after the show, I mingled with the crowd and intentionally jostled my way into it to be seen by as many of my colleagues as possible. If it happened that no colleague was in this crowd, I would go to the bus stop and slowly promenade from the head of the line to the rear.

Sometimes I did the opposite. I went to the theater several minutes before the show started, and pretended to look at the playbills or posters, in order to be seen by as many of my colleagues as possible. I tried carefully to be seen by my colleagues, who then would get the impression that I was in the theater. Thus, no one would blame me for my absence from those revolutionary lessons, while actually I had saved a lot of time for myself.

Needless to say, group discussions were frequently held in the publishing house, in which everybody had to talk about what they had learned from the movie or drama. What did I do in such discussions? No problem at all. I took several minutes to read a review in the newspaper or summarized my impressions of the pictures hanging on the walls of the theater before I talked about a movie or a play in the exaggerated way they required. There was a conventional way of talking: How brave, how great, or how extraordinary the hero in the show was, or how ugly the negative character was. I never forgot to link myself with the negative character. I would say, "While I was watching the show, I was so upset or so angry with what So-and-so did. But then I said to myself, 'Isn't he the mirror of my former self?' When I committed the rightist crimes of attacking our greatest leader and Party, was I even more ugly than he? I really feel ashamed and remorseful. This show educated me a great deal, and made me more resolved to remold myself and redeem myself from crimes."

In dealing with my colleagues in the publishing house, I had to put my conscience away for a while because in my thoughts none of us was a human being in the real sense of this word. I only wanted to keep my job, and it was only when I was reading classics that I could temporarily divorce myself from the ugly reality and sense the value of human beings as well as my own existence.

As to my editing work, there was a blemish on my otherwise perfect record. As the entire editing department had been divided into two groups after the Anti-Rightist Movement, I was in the group headed by Chin Hsin-yao. I felt happier to be under his leadership than that of Chu Chin-chen, who had headed the other group. However, I was much more interested in working in the latter's group, which marked punctuation and did textual collation of various editions of classics, while my group made selections and wrote annotations. To do this kind of work, one had to use the current viewpoint, that is, the Communist one, which I hated. Moreover, the new editions of original classics used old characters, while selections employed simplified characters, which I detested. Unfortunately, as a rightist, I had no choice but to be satisfied with whatever job I was assigned as long as it was related to the classics. Therefore, I made every effort to do well in the work for which I was responsible.

Embarrassed by the unprecedented famines which took place across the country in the wake of the Great Leap Forward, the Communists comparatively slackened their control for several years. These saw a bumper harvest in publication of classics. However, this was not divorced from political reality. It even caused some ripples in the waters of diplomacy. This may sound like a legend, but was a fact. At one time, our publishing house launched an internal campaign of "publication investigation," in which we censored all the books we had published and manuscripts about to go to press. We were told to underline those sentences and paragraphs which, so to speak, "involved foreign affairs or foreign nationals." Did they suggest any pacifism? Poems, lyrics, or essays containing antiwar, peace-loving, or humanitarian sentiments were harmful to world revolution and, therefore, should be weeded out. Most important of all, did they contain any wording that might hurt the feelings of those nationals who were our brothers—the Vietnamese and Koreans?

At first, I could not understand the real purpose for frittering away our time on such nonsense. Then, to make us aware of the importance of this campaign, it was revealed that a story in a newly published classical Chinese novel depicting the execution of a pair of minority sisters over a thousand years ago had greatly offended the Vietnamese, who regarded these sisters as national heroes. The Vietnamese ambassador in Peking lodged a protest with the Chinese government. As everybody knows, publication of a classical novel is a purely domestic affair; therefore, the protest was groundless. However, even more senseless was the fact that the Chinese Communist regime accepted such a protest. The reason was that, at that time, the Chinese Communists were enthusiastically propagating the notion that Vietnam and China were fraternal countries. While on a state visit to Vietnam, Chou En-lai made a special trip to pay tribute to the two sisters' tombs, by way of apology.

My tasks fell into two categories. One was to edit the selections and annotations made by modern scholars, whom we deemed authors because the real authors lived hundreds or even thousands of years ago. Among those scholars, some were quite famous. For example, I was responsible for the publication of *The Selected Readings of Yang Wanli*, and the author, i.e., selector and annotator, was famous for his quick temper as well as his learning. He used to be fussy about comments on his work. On my part, there was an unwritten law in this publishing house that the editor had the duty to make comments on the manuscripts and return them to authors for revision. The manuscripts would go back and forth once, twice, or even several times. No manuscript could be published as it was. The quantity of comments was one of the criteria for judging the performance of the editor. If I made no comments, how was I going to account for this to my leadership? However, I was fully aware that if there was only one slip in my comment, I would be ridiculed by the author. Fortunately, Yang Wanli, the original writer, was not only a poet and essayist but also a statesman and philosopher. His work contained quite a few discussions of *li-hsueh* (neo-Confucianism), which I knew was the annotator's weak point. So I directed my comments to this part. My comments were sent to him in the name of the editing department, and this author returned a letter of appreciation, which, of course, was addressed to the editing department. Nevertheless, the fact that the editing department received a letter of appreciation was very helpful to me, because my leadership noticed it and knew who was to be credited with the work.

Another aspect of my work was the selection and annotation of classics along with other members of our group, because there were times when something had happened to the authors, especially when they were perplexed by some restrictive political situation, and were reluctant to submit their manuscripts. I was assigned to work in the group selecting and annotating *One Hundred T'ang Poems*. The T'ang Dynasty was distinguished for its poetry. The T'ang poems now available amount to almost 100,000, so it was difficult to select 100 best poems from among them. However, in the past decades there had been several authoritative collections. If you want to publish a new collection, you have to beat the existing ones by showing how yours would surpass theirs. As the first step, we had to read through the other selections as well as the *Full Collection of T'ang Poetry*. This was not too difficult. We just divided the whole workload and each individual was assigned part of it. Each was required to select the poems he thought were the best. Before long, we assembled a considerable number of best T'ang poems after pooling our selections. Then, in the discussion of these selections, difficulty arose. Each argued for his favorites. Arguments, of course, would only end by arbitration by the leadership. The most difficult problem was that the leadership did not consist of just one person; therefore, they had their own arguments which, of course, were subjected to arbitration by higher leadership. Furthermore, the higher leadership did not consist of one person either. Some liked butter and others preferred cheese. There was no end to the arguments. Worst of all, the leaders never issued their orders in the form of documents, but just oral commands. At this time, one of the vice presidents of our publishing house went to Peking and got word that So-and-so, an authoritative figure, was of the opinion that "Ode to Everlasting Regret" and "Song of P'i-p'a," the two long poems of P'ai Ch'u-yi, which had been passed from generation to generation in China, were incompatible with the current atmosphere of the Great Leap Forward. When the vice president had relayed this instruction to us from the center of authority, we had to abandon our selection and work out another table of contents. Several versions were developed and submitted to the leaders in Peking for approval. Then we got word from another even higher-ranking leader, "How can you call it a selection of T'ang poems if it does not even contain the 'Ode to Everlasting Regret' and 'Song of P'i-p'a'? In order to surpass the existing editions, you have to include the best poems that they collected." The higher the position from which the instruction came, the more importance and "truth" it contained. We gave up the second plan and returned to the first.

This time there came another instruction, of course from a high-ranking official, "Why have you included 'The Memorial Poems for a Deceased Wife' in your version? Though they have been famous through the centuries, their weeping tone is out of step with the Great Leap Forward." This mandate we could not but obey, so we started all over again.

Then came some new instructions. This time Shanghai's First Party Secretary growled, "What on earth is this collection of T'ang poems? It does not even contain the most famous T'ang poems. 'The Memorial Poems for a Deceased Wife' reflect people's common feelings and can be appreciated by anyone. Although I myself have never had the experience of losing a wife, I can fully appreciate the beauty of these poems and have never been made to feel depressed by the weeping tone." The opinions of Shanghai's First Party Secretary were the last we wanted to overlook. It would be wiser to insert these poems in the new version again.

The book was finally published after several setbacks. This was a typical example. Almost all our publications had to go through the same kind of trials. I envied the job of the other group—punctuating and making textual collation on different editions of original classics, because this job did not involve political points of view. During that period a certain number of ancient works with modern punctuation were published and their various existing texts were collated. As each of these texts inevitably carried this or that mistake, the collation was valuable. Since I had no hope of being transferred to the other group, I decided to do this work in my spare time as a sideline job. I had to look for an ancient work which had never been punctuated and whose various editions had never been collated and which would be acceptable for publication. This was difficult. Those important ancient works which were obviously worth the effort had already been contracted by the publishing house to famous scholars. The publishing house had no faith in "small potatoes."

Again, I was fortunate to work in this publishing house, which had a library with a rich collection of Chinese classics. One day, *Chi-ku lu*, a work by the great historian Ssu-ma Kuang, happened to attract my attention. *Chi-ku lu* is an annotated annal of China from the twenty-fifth century B.C. to the eleventh century A.D. I thought, "Gee, isn't Ssu-ma Kuang on the list of the Communists' unified front?" Another monumental work of his, *Tzu-chih-t'ung-chien*, was the first large volume of classics ever published with punctuation under the aegis of the Communist regime. "Why don't I try to work on *Chi-ku lu*, which is but one tenth the volume of *Tzu-chih-t'ung-chien*?" I thought I could do the job singlehanded.

It was no accident that I chose *Chi-ku lu* to work on. Before that, I had spent a lot of time reading *Tzu-chih-t'ung-chien*. As my job was to edit Chinese classics, reading *Tzu-chih-t'ung-chien* had been part of my work and, therefore, had not caused any criticism. However, I had not read it for fun but as a kind of "Bible," on the recommendation of Master Yue, my *tai-chi* tutor.

After the Anti-Rightist Movement, Master Yue treated me just as before, as though nothing had ever happened. One day, while waiting on him in private, I told him for the first time that I had been labeled a rightist, because I did not want to conceal from him the fact that I was now a lost wanderer fleeing from all men.

At first he did not say anything, but just sniffed through his nostrils with a grimace. A little later, he said, "Go and read *Tzu-chih-t'ung-chien*, from beginning to end. Don't miss a word. Pay special attention to Ssu-ma Kuang's comments."

I accepted his suggestion and said, "Yes, it's worth reading. In modern as well as ancient times, many history students devote themselves to reading *Tzu-chih-t'ung-chien*, but very few have enough patience to read it from beginning to end."

"You seem not to have fully understood what I said. I don't mean you should read it from the academic point of view. This is not what I want you to do," Master Yue said. Before I could make an answer, he noticed my bewilderment and added, "Neither do I wish to use it as a sort of spiritual sustenance for you. The reason I want you to read *Tzu-chih-t'ung-chien* is that through reading it you will get a better understanding of your present situation, which has no fundamental difference from the ancient society, and find a way out."

I did what he told me. After reading *Tzu-chih-t'ung-chien*, I found I had benefited very much from Ssu-ma Kuang's ideas. His purpose in writing these annals was to provide some moral and practical lessons. Whoever was enlightened by these lessons would be able to help the ruler provide peace and happiness for his country if he happened to live under a reasonable ruler, or avoid both being persecuted and being dishonored by involvement in dirty politics. I am sure that had I read *Tzu-chih-t'ung-chien* before the Anti-Rightist Movement started I would not have fallen into the trap set by Mao Tse-tung. However, it was never too late to learn, so I tried to make the best of it, for I believed it might help me survive this regime. The more I read *Tzu-chih-t'ung-chien*, the more I respected it and the more I adored Ssu-ma Kuang. That was why I was so interested in punctuating and collating the various editions of *Chi-ku lu*, another historical work of Ssu-ma Kuang.

Frankly, when I started to work on *Chi-ku lu*, I had no idea how big the job would be, because it was not clear how many editions of this book existed. My original intention had been to punctuate it and get it published so that I could obtain some royalties. Then, as I delved into it, I gradually realized the value of studying Ssu-ma Kuang and his achievements in writing historical works. I found that different editions were needed for cross-reference in textual collation. I put in all my energy and no longer thought about the remuneration. I concentrated my attention on solving the questions that I continued to raise. I was just like a person who has stopped halfway on a mountain and suddenly found some scenery of exceptional charm, with beautiful flowers and trees and distant waterfalls thundering down. How would he feel seeing such a sight? He would walk on in spite of himself.

In retrospect, I am glad that I started this project soon after the Anti-Rightist Movement, because it was followed by a comparatively tranquil period of several years, in which I was able to concentrate my effort on this task and complete it just before the start of the so-called Cultural Revolution. Otherwise, if I had been only halfway through with this work when the Cultural Revolution took place, all my previous effort would have been wasted.

I also feel fortunate that I had Hu Tao-ching as my colleague in the publishing house. He was a real scholar, but as he had been a high official in the Kuomintang's news media before liberation, he had been subject to "internal control" by this "organization." It was not until Dr. Joseph Needham visited China and asked the Chinese high officials to arrange for him to meet Hu Tao-ching that the Communists began to realize the value of Hu. This took place after the Anti-Rightist Movement.

During the movement, in order to protect himself, Hu had had to criticize me at the meeting. All that he said was meant to show his submission to the Party rather than do me any harm. To me, this kind of "criticism" was nothing, but apparently it was something on Hu's mind. After the movement, he became especially polite to me. When there was someone around, he just greeted me with his eyes. Otherwise, he would greet me with a broad smile. But still we did not talk to each other very often, so that nobody noticed that he was very friendly to me. However, he was very much concerned for me. I had never told him about my *Chi-ku lu* project, but he might have found it out by the books I checked out from the library. He offered to introduce me to the Department of Rare Book Collections of the Shanghai Municipal Library, where I obtained valuable assistance in finding some precious editions. He also offered to introduce me to some rare-edition specialists in libraries in

Peking and Hangchow, with whom I later kept correspondence and from whom I acquired a lot of valuable knowledge. I cannot imagine that without Hu's help I could have completed this project smoothly.

While I was fortunate enough to be favored with Hu's assistance, I had the bad luck to have on the rightist hat all these years. In order to carry on my project, I often mentioned it in my monthly ideological report with a tone of self-criticism. I said I gave too much attention to something old when I should direct more attention to new things. Then I reported how much of my leisure time I had spent on this project and how many reference books I had consulted for the sake of textual collation and how valuable *Chi-ku lu* was to the study of history. Actually, my mention of it was designed to serve as an advertisement, so that my leadership would be attracted by it.

It was just before the end of the period which intervened between the Anti-Rightist Movement and the so-called Cultural Revolution that I finished punctuation and textual collation of the various editions of *Chi-ku lu*. As I still had the rightist label, it was too early for me to request the publication of my works. I played a game that appealed to the Communists. On the eve of the so-called National Day, which falls on October 1, I handed my manuscript of *Chi-ku lu* to Hwa Shou-yi, the group leader, and said that I presented it to the Party as a gift to our beloved great National Day. Because of this pretext, he gladly accepted it, although he, a very smart fellow, must have tacitly understood my real intention. I was pretty sure that he would register my manuscript in accordance with the established procedures, transfer it to the other group which was responsible for this kind of work, and arrange for some editors in that group to review my manuscript just as they did the unsolicited ones coming from the society at large. The whole process would probably take one or two years. I thought that by the time they finished reviewing my manuscript and decided to publish it, my rightist hat might have already been removed and the political factor that hampered its publication might no longer exist. According to my knowledge of Communists, once the book was published, they would pay me the royalties in full, regardless of my declaration of presenting it as a gift. The Communists like to hear and encourage people to say high-sounding words, and never mind if they are not practiced.

My estimation turned out to be totally wrong, for I did not expect that I would have to wear that "hat" for another half decade. Neither did I expect that during the long period after I presented my gift, not a single publishing house other than the press which was solely responsible for the publication of Mao's works would publish anything. The publication of *Chi-ku lu* was, of course, out of the question.

Still, I have to say I was a lucky man, for I handed in my manuscript on the eve of the National Day of 1965, the year before the Cultural Revolution took place, and there was no better place for my manuscript to stay than in the publishing house during the tumult. After the publishing house went out of business, they were ordered to keep all the files and manuscript intact for the sake of any possible investigation. As they were inaccessible to the Red Guards, it was as though my manuscript was locked in a safe. Had I kept my manuscript in my house, it definitely could not have survived the "revolution," for either the Red Guards would have destroyed it or I myself would have burned it. Anybody else in my situation would have done so. Compared with the safety of my whole family, the manuscripts were nothing.

Nonetheless, I have some pleasant reminiscences of the period when I was a rightist. One of them happened at the beginning of 1960, one of the three years of famine, which the Communists insist on calling "the three years of natural disaster," but which were actually caused mainly by human error.

Place: the Cultural Club of the Political Consultative Conference. I frequented its restaurant, of course, not as a rightist, but as a guest of Lu Hsiao-man. The Political Consultative Conference was a tool used by the Communists to promote the Party's "unified front" work, and its club was only open to the objects of the unified front. Under this heavenly social system, people are rigidly stratified. The objects of the unified front are classified into several grades: the state, the municipality, and the district. Lu Hsiao-man fell into the category of municipality. People of this grade could each get fifteen tickets for admission to this club-restaurant each month, one ticket being good for only one order. Compared to the ordinary local residents, whose monthly ration was only a couple of dozens of grams of meat and oil per person, the objects of the "unified front" could be said to live in luxury, for they could enjoy fifteen extra good meals each month.

Treating me like her offspring, Lu Hsiao-man used to take me to the club for lunch or dinner. Sometimes she gave me the ticket and let me go there by myself. Though I was reluctant to share her meager ration, I could not resist the temptation. We used to eat in the section where Western-style food was served, because there only one ticket was required to order a bowl of soup, a piece of meat, and two pieces of bread with butter. Buttered bread was my favorite. Each bite made me feel so delicious that it totally satisfied my gluttony. I could not imagine what else in the whole world could taste better than buttered bread.

This was why in the first year after I arrived in the United States I had buttered bread for three meals a day. I tried to make up for what I had missed in the past thirty years. Regretfully, I have to acknowledge that the butter made here does not taste as good as that of China. It seems to me that China makes the best butter, because I never feel so satisfied with the buttered bread here as in China in those days.

Another reminiscence of that period is about manual labor, which I did willingly and which was totally different from what I was wont to do. It was in the cold winter of 1960. I was one of several young men who were pulling a two-wheeled handcart, on which lay a coffin, from a funeral parlor in the downtown area to a cemetery on the outskirts of Shanghai. We started pulling the flatbed in the evening when the moon had just risen, and were greeted by the rising sun when we got to the cemetery. In the coffin was the body of Master Yue.

At Master Yue's death at the end of 1960, his family was faced with choice of the form of burial. Traditionally, the Chinese people have preferred burial in the ground. The Communists advocated cremation. It was not easy to change the time-honored habit. During the first period of Communist rule, people were free to make their own choice. Then, gradually, the Communists made things difficult for people who chose ground burial. Still later, cremation became the only form available.

Yue's family wished the master to be buried in the ground. However, by the time of his death, the situation had developed to such a stage that people could not easily make a choice in matters of burial as in previous days. At that time there still existed coffin stores, and the ground for burying the corpse was still available in some cemeteries, but all cars were controlled by the government and no transportation was allowed for coffins. Also, while the funeral parlor did not refuse to put the body in the coffin, it refused to sell any coffin. In that case, it was almost impossible for ordinary people to choose any burial other than cremation. But Yue's family had the help of Master Yue's pupils, including me. Although all the cars were under the control of the government, it was not too difficult to borrow a two-wheeled handcart. We purchased the coffin and transported it to the funeral parlor on this cart. From the funeral parlor to the cemetery on the outskirts was a long way to walk. Futhermore, the cemetery only sold the ground but refused to provide gravediggers. We also had to do that ourselves. In order to complete the burial within one day, we had to set out the previous night. We transported the coffin to the cemetery early in the morning and then started digging, lowered down the coffin, and finally covered the grave with cement. We did all these things on our own. Among us there was a construction worker who was also Master Yue's pupil. Several years later, when the Red Guards began smashing all the tombs, under cover of darkness we went to the cemetery where Master Yue was buried and, by way of precaution, opened the grave, dug it to a greater depth, buried the coffin under water, and then covered the grave with soil. We sacrificed another night's sleep but saved our master from the hands of the Red Guards forever.

CHAPTER 8

"The Cultural Revolution is Good!"

THE CULTURAL REVOLUTION, WHOSE FULL official title was "The Great Proletariat Cultural Revolution," did not start in 1966, as is popularly believed. Even before Chiang Ch'ing, Mao's wife, distinguished herself by producing eight plays with modern themes and started to censor all other plays for the purpose of establishing the "eight models of revolutionary drama," as they were then termed, sporadic omens portending cultural calamities had already emerged. While I was touring Solitary Hill in Hangchow in 1965, I discovered that Lin Pu's tomb and the Crane Gazebo, the two historic sites that had helped to increase Hangchow's beauty and fame, had been destroyed. Lin Pu was a literary figure in the Sung Dynasty, famous for his hermit aloofness from the secular world. He never married and refused to enter officialdom. He devoted himself to cultivating plums and raising cranes. To declare "war" on Lin Pu meant to be antagonistic to all intellectuals except those who were in the bureaucracy.

If traced back further, the source of the Cultural Revolution can date back to the Anti-Rightist Movement, for no sooner was the movement over than the slogan of "Stressing the present, not the past" was raised and began to haunt intellectuals for several years. It was only when the Communist regime was embarrassed in the early 1960s by the unprecedented famines caused by its incompetence and miscalculation that the Communists cut out this slogan and reinstated the theory that history could not be severed and that each social phenomenon must be considered in its historical context. For a while intellectuals relaxed, and some of the prominent scholars were even brave enough to make special trips to pay tribute at the tomb of Confucius. However, their audacity and the economic recovery made the Communists think it necessary to tighten the reins again. The then First Secretary of Shanghai, who was Mao's crony, put forward the slogan of "Concentrating on writing about the past thirteen years."* The pendulum swung to the left once again.

During the one decade of political fluctuations, the political climate cold in one period and hot in another, Chinese intellectuals as a whole seemed never to understand the lesson. In each comparatively relaxed period there would always be some who were bold enough to step out and frankly express their original views concerning such subjects as literature, philosophy, and history. Their sincere wishes for participating in pure academic research ended in their being targets of criticism when the tide turned. For instance, one old pedant delved into the philosophical idea of "two combining into one" and became obssessed with this academic topic, when all of a sudden he found himself under fire and accused of disseminating a revisionist concept diametrically opposed to the Marxist-Maoist view that everything in the universe works on the principle of "one dividing into two." Another pundit, whose research on one of the leaders of the Taiping Rebellion had led to a conclusion different from those of other scholars, came under attack and was charged with trying to protect the traitors of the present age by defending the big traitor of the past.

Each of these examples further convinced me that whoever reposed full confidence in the Communists and attempted to have a sincere exchange of views with them would get into trouble in the end. Only those who hypocritically fawned upon the Communists could be safe. After I discovered this truth and acted accordingly, I committed no more serious mistakes.

---

* "Thirteen years" meant the period from 1949, when the Communists took over mainland China, to 1962, when this slogan was coined.

One of the important peculiarities of the Cultural Revolution was the game of "declaring one's stand." From the highest bureaucrat down to the rank and file, everybody was incessantly under pressure to take sides with either of the two leaders who seemed of equal importance to him before the disclosure of their feud. For example, Mao condemned all those high officials who had faithfully followed Liu Shao-chi at the time Mao openly claimed Liu as one of his close comrades-in-arms. Likewise, each of the local Party leaders expected the masses to make known who they would take sides with, him or his political enemy. Each thought himself a representative of the correct line and his opponent of the erroneous line and wanted the masses to make the choice before the differences between him and his rival were brought to light. The Maoists even employed the dramatic terminology "striking a pose on the stage" or the military term "line up" to press all officials and the masses to declare their stands or state their views.

We were just like people gambling on politics all day long. This weird way of doing things was not a sudden result of the Cultural Revolution, but a traditional style of the Communists. For example, when Mao first raised a quarrel with Nikita Khrushchev, it was never made known to the public. Then, during the Cuban missile crisis, the official newspaper only released the news of the USSR withdrawing missiles from its base in Cuba under pressure from the United States. Even though the public had never been told about the USSR having a missile base in Cuba, the Communists expected the bewildered, misinformed masses to make correct comments on this kind of event.

Officialdom had never publicly said anything against Russia; therefore, the people had the impression from the Anti-Rightist Movement that whoever criticized the Russians would ask for trouble. Who dared to repudiate them? However, I was lucky this time, for long before the Cuban missile crisis occurred, Master Yue had been the guest of quite a number of high leaders, such as Lin P'iao, Chou En-lai, Ke Ching-shi, and Chang Chun-chiao, and one of them had disclosed to him the topmost secret of the Sino-Soviet split either intentionally or unintentionally, and he had in turn relayed it to me.

"I will tell you an important piece of information, but you should keep it to yourself and not impart it to anyone else," Master Yue said in a serious tone one day while I was attending to him during his illness, some months before he passed away, "Mao has made up his mind to break with the Soviet Union and label Khrushchev a revisionist. Although it hasn't been made public and we ordinary people should pretend to be unaware of it, I think it may be beneficial to you to let you know what's what, so that you can refrain from writing or saying something that may cause you trouble again in future."

With this predisclosed information in mind, I felt sure that something had gone wrong and that this was a signal that Mao was about to start his campaign against the Soviets. Thus, at a group meeting, while most of my colleagues were hemming and hawing, making comments on the USSR, I stated explicitly that Khrushchev, as a revisionist, had betrayed the international proletariat revolution. My learned coworkers were shocked by my speech, looking at each other, not knowing how to respond. No one dared to say either yes or no. They were probably thinking that misfortune would befall me again and that the Party would settle accounts with me after the autumn harvest. Fortunately this time, before the Party had time to settle accounts with me, the Chinese and Russian Communists had already begun to quarrel.

Later on, in so many years to come, whenever the leaders, in reviewing my ideological renovation, thought it necessary to put in a few good words for me to balance some harsh comments, they cited my early awareness of the Soviet degeneration and attributed my political consciousness to the Party's education, as being their education.

As a matter of fact, it was only because I totally lost confidence in the Party and socialist society as a whole that I could deal with any situation with ease. I followed a simple logic: All the principles of value should run counter to my conscience. Anything which I found right and which I felt comfortable with must be erroneous, and anything which my conscience did not allow me to accept must be right with the Communists. Following this logic, I was no longer at odds with the Communists.

I never understood the contradictory characteristics of the Chinese intellectuals of my generation. In assailing a fellow intellectual, they could be so ruthless and treacherous as not to show the least mercy. In dealing with the Party, they were faithful, sincere, and aboveboard. They seem never to have learned the lesson that being open and aboveboard with the Party meant being subjected to harrassment by the Party. Many people disregarded the infallible truth that as long as one deals with a socialist society, one should never try to be open and aboveboard with the Party.

By the eve of the so-called Cultural Revolution, which I would prefer to call the Anti-Culture Movement, there were some signs of the approach of an enormous political storm, for more and more intellectuals had slipped back into the ways of the older generation, talking about the merits of faith, loyalty, sincerity, and straightforwardness. Even the old officials of intellectual origin, such as our President Li and two vice presidents Chen and Ch'i, began to dwell with great relish upon the merit of telling the truth. Vice President Chen went so far as to wonder why people could not trust each other through heart-to-heart talks. During a discussion of contents for a certain set of selected works edited by our department, he expressed his disapproval of those editors who were under the influence of "being left rather than right" and tended to select materials with dull and inhuman themes. He would ask, "Please tell me the truth, do you really like these works? If you yourselves don't like these kinds of stuff, how can you expect the reader to appreciate them?" Well said. The question he raised was very reasonable, but his criteria for a good publication were inapplicable. I used to say to myself, "My job is not meant to do what I like. All I am concerned about is guarding against any excuse that the Marxist critics may use to oppose me."

Such was the general atmosphere in which the majority of the masses lived and worked when an essay titled "On Hai Rui's Dismissal from Office" first appeared in the newspaper. People who have not lived under the Communist system can never imagine what a big impact such an article could make. Hai Rui was an official in the Ming Dynasty about four hundred years ago, and because he was extremely honest and upright and free from corruption, he became a legendary figure whom the Chinese people had adored through the ages. The newly-published drama *Hai Rui's Dismissal from Office* was written by Wu Han, who had been a professor of history but became deputy mayor of Peking after liberation. On the surface, the essay "On Hai Rui's Dismissal from Office" was just a criticism of a historical drama. Who could have imagined a drama review was to whip up big surf that would engulf the entire country?

The writer of this essay was Yao Wen-yuan, who was nicknamed a "cudgel" because he had written practically nothing other than articles attacking other writers. As was known, Mao highly appreciated one of the anti-rightist articles Yao wrote when still obscure. Now, this long article covered the front pages of almost all the newspapers and, after its publication, the Party branch of every system and institution arranged for people to discuss it in groups as though it were the Central Committee's directive. People sensed that this article had some powerful backing, but just could not understand the purpose of launching such a strong offensive against Hai Rui. In our publishing house, we spent half a day every day discussing how to evaluate the "good officials" of ancient times. Since the leaders of our publishing house called upon us to "speak the truth," my lovable colleagues expressed their doubt about the validity of Yao's arguments that all good officials were but the tools of the cruel, feudal ruling class.

I felt very relaxed in this period. Unlike the other intellectuals, I did not believe a single word of the front-page articles in the Communist newspapers; consequently, I rarely bothered to think seriously about or argue against their views. Whatever they proposed, I readily agreed with. During the group discussions, to be in tune with Yao, I deliberately asserted that "all officials in ancient times were bad and there was no difference at all between 'good officials' and 'bad officials.'" Deep in my heart, I was certain that when an administration advocated such a ridiculous theory it meant that the regime had gone mad and was approaching its demise.

Regretfully, I could not feel totally at ease, for my manuscript on *Punctuation and Annotation of Chi-ku lu* kept worrying me. An insane movement seemed to be imminent, and I was deeply concerned about the probability, following the development of the coming movement, of being accused of editing this book. This manuscript might be used as a testimony to the collaboration between Ssu-ma Kuang and a rightist. What punishment would await a rightist for colluding with Ssu-ma Kuang in opposition to the Party? I struggled with myself, "Should I request the withdrawal of my manuscript before they have time to review and make a decision about it?" I also debated with myself, "Will it be taken as a manifestation of my guilty conscience if I withdraw my manuscript at this moment?" To withdraw or not to withdraw, that was a question that troubled me greatly.

Thanks to the rapid development of the revolutionary situation and the new chapter of history opened by Mao's "My Big-Character Poster" which, even though badly written, had the magic power of sending the whole nation into boiling water, those suave meetings and pedantic talks ended in the publishing house.

In our editing department there was a young editor by the name of Nee Mo-yen. He was a Communist and had graduated from the university not long before. President Li liked him very much and had set him up as a model of being "both Red and expert," a Communist phrase meaning being both socialist-minded and vocationally proficient. Nee, in turn, thought himself a typical "proletariat successor." He regarded Yao Wen-yuan as an idol. Years before the Anti-Culture Movement, I had heard him declare time and again, "I will study hard enough to be able to write with the same quality as Yao Wen-yuan." When people began to engage in the hot debate about Hai Rui, several months before the start of Anti-Culture Movement, Nee mysteriously disappeared. It was vaguely known that he was participating in some kind of "study team" organized by the Municipal Party Committee. He was still seen in the publishing house sometimes early in the morning or late in the evening; because his family was in Shaohsin, he had taken a room in the first floor of our publishing house since he came to work there. I seldom talked to him, let alone inquired about his work. I assumed that he was making preparations for the oncoming movement, probably arranged by President Li or Vice President Ch'i, who acted as a political commissar in the publishing house.

One day, unexpectedly, he beckoned me into his room and solemnly said to me, "You have been in this publishing house for so many years. You know a lot of things and persons here. Now, try to recall conscientiously whoever has opposed Mao Tse-tung Thought. Write the names down and give them to me. This is an opportunity to have your hat taken off. Remember, consider everything from the standpoint of Mao Tse-tung Thought. Whoever said or did anything against Mao Tse-tung Thought was wrong, and you must let me know. Don't be afraid. Now, Mao Tse-tung Thought is the sole criterion for evaluating everything."

At the moment, I could make neither head nor tail of his words, so I answered irrelevantly, "I am the only remaining rightist in this publishing house. If you ask who deserves to be criticized most, it is me. I am also prepared to willingly accept criticism, for it means that the

Party and the masses are trying to rescue me." These clichés I could recite fluently without using my brain.

He laughed. "Come on," he said and still smiled. "Your thoughts
are trammeled by conventional ideas. First of all, you have to break
away from notions about positions or other considerations, and concentrate on thinking what words have been said or what actions have
been done against Chairman Mao's teachings. Otherwise, you could
never discover the anti-Mao materials in our publishing house." Notic-
ing that I was still puzzled, he gave me some encouragement. "As a
matter of fact, you do have some degree of political sensitivity. For example, you were among the first to take a clear-cut stand against
Khrushchev's revisionism. Another instance is that during the discussion on *Hai Rui's Dismissal from Office* you took the side of opposing
'good officials.' This shows you are not handicapped by stereotyped
thinking and are able to accept newly emerging thoughts. Now all you
have to do is discard all the outmoded notions and evaluate everyone's
words and actions, using Mao Tse-tung Thought as the sole criterion.
I'm sure you can find some problems."

I was too slow. The problems came before I had found them. A few
days later, the news media published and broadcast Mao's approval of
the "first rebellious big-character poster in Peking University." Our
publishing house became restless.

When I stepped into the publishing house that morning, a crowd of
people were standing in front of a big-character poster hanging from
the banister of the stairway. It was written by Nee Mo-yen. It severely
criticized President Li by name, asserting that Li was the fierce enemy
of the socialist society, because, as the poster said, "Li has always opposed the Party, socialism, and Mao Tse-tung Thought." Accordingly,
it called on those who wanted to follow the Party and Chairman Mao
to struggle against Li. It was characterized by exactly the same tone as
the rebellious "big-character poster" Mao had eulogized.

Slow as I was, I realized at once that this poster had some kind of significance. I could tell from the facial expressions of others that they were
thinking the same way. No one was talking, and Li was standing in front
of the poster, speechless and expressionless, like a defeated rooster. The
airs of a leader, which he had put on all those years, suddenly disappeared.

A while later, wall posters began to appear one by one. They invariably declared their support for Nee's viewpoint and their determination to struggle against Li along with Nee. That whole day, I did not know what to do. Nobody dared to pull out the manuscripts from their desks to do editing. I either sat with boredom or went in and out to read the new big-character posters.

The next day, another of Nee's big-character posters mentioned me by name, describing me as standing by with folded arms. It pointed out that I should perform meritorious services to atone for my past crimes and that the meritorious service I could perform at that moment was to write big-character posters. The crimes of which Nee accused Li were recruiting renegades and traitors and harboring "monsters and demons" and promoting the publication of "poisonous weeds," a term employed by Mao for all the writings he thought harmful to socialism. Thus, Nee Mo-yen had set the tune that most of the editors were evildoers and most of the publications were bad. To this tune, a farce was to be staged.

Nee Mo-yen opened another chapter of the history of this publishing house. With the appearance of his big-character posters, everybody did nothing from then on except read and write big-character posters, and the walls of the whole building were left with no space. In this case, strings were pinned from wall to wall so that people could hang their posters from them. Lines and lines of wall posters were the only scene in this building, and people were actually surrounded by a sea of posters.

Believe me, in that sea I was swimming smoothly while others suffered hell. This should be credited to my belief that the Communists were not persons you could reason with and that they and I were not the same human beings. With this belief in mind, I did not trust one single word on their big-character posters, nor on mine. All nonsense. On my big-character posters, I criticized myself severely. Echoing Nee's view, I acknowledged that I, as a "monster and demon," had been shielded by Li. I also acknowledged that all the publications I had been in charge of were poisonous weeds, deserving to be burned.* I myself

---

*This is the actual servile statement made by Kuo Mou-jo, a man of letters with no morality, who before the start of the Anti-Culture Movement showed his servility to Mao and his wife by claiming publicly that all his previous works were worthless and should be burned.

did not believe a single word I wrote on my big-character posters.

Not everyone did the same. Intellectuals used to try to assuage their consciences with the desire to follow the Communists. They could not run counter to their own consciences, nor could they refuse to identify themselves with the Communist theory and Communist regime. As a result, they failed both to have a clear conscience and to keep pace with the leadership. They did not understand that communism and conscience are as incompatible as fire and water.

The so-called Cultural Revolution was the result of the extreme development of the Communist rule. Only when one had determined to discard all preconceived ideas of morality and logic could he move about with ease. In the chaotic struggles of the Anti-Culture Movement, there existed nothing worthy of being considered truth. Later, when the incident was over, it became crystal clear that the Shanghai Municipal Party Committee, for the sake of saving themselves, had made scapegoats of four people, and Li was one of them.

One of Li's alleged crimes was his fiction *Tu Fu Returning Home*, which had been published a couple of years before. It told the story of the famous poet of the T'ang Dynasty who lamented over the dead bodies of the starved while on his way home. Li Chun-min was accused of attacking the "Great Leap Forward" by innuendo. It was alleged that, while he was working on his book, enemies both at home and abroad were blaming our dearest, infallible, great Communist Party for the famines taking place in China. This was the typical logic used during the Anti-Culture Movement. It was most satirical that these four sacrificial lambs did not lend much help to the Municipal Party Committee, which was later to be disbanded by Mao. Since Li was labeled an anti-socialist, the masses were required to shout the slogan, "Down with Li Chun-min!" Although it was very evident to everybody who was not an idiot that Li was innocent and wronged, about two decades of brainwashing made people do whatever the Party told them.

The sense of justice and righteousness, however, is not easily erased from human beings. If someone unconsciously showed a flicker of conscience, then he would cause himself trouble.

In one department, there was a good-natured old man who was in the Party. I had no idea how he had become a Party member. All I knew was that he had been with the Chung-Hwa Printing Company for many years. It was possible that when the company became a joint state-private enterprise, he was young and it was, therefore, relatively easy to join the Party, as was often the case at that time, because the Party was badly in need of recruits from the rank and file to assist in organizing the enterprises and remolding the capitalists. Anyway, he was not a diehard Party member. Now he was apparently not very comfortable with the chorus criticizing Li. In his big-character poster, he attempted to make a sincere analysis of how Li, an old man with a military background, had degenerated into an anti-Party, anti-socialist revisionist. He reached the conclusion that it was due to the fact that Li had rested on his laurels complacently. "Move forward, or you'll fall behind," his poster warned. "This is the lesson each one of us should draw from Li's degeneration, which has resulted from the loss of his initiative and enterprising spirit and the relaxation of his efforts to re-mold his world outlook continuously." I believe he was telling what he really thought, and trying to give a reasonable explanation for reconciling the unreasonable current situation with his conscience.

One would be doomed if he tried to have a good conscience. Such was the case with this poor fellow. I posted a big-character poster in refutation of that man. In a typical tone prevailing at that time, I chided him for trying to defend Li with the technique of bogus criticism and genuine cover-up. I contended that Li, as a counterrevolutionary revisionist, had committed the crime of opposing the Party and socialism, and that his crime was a contradiction between ourselves and the enemy, not just a question of ideological remolding. Moreover, I argued, how could he say Li lacked initiative and enterprise? On the contrary, he had them, but put them at the service of feudalism and capitalism. In conclusion, I pointed out that whoever said that Li's problem was just one of slackening his ideological remolding was actually confusing the contradiction between ourselves and the enemy with the contradiction among the people.

Nee Mo-yen immediately put up another big-character poster alongside mine. In a tone of teaching people morals, he wrote that a Party member with such a muddled idea was a serious problem deserving to be squarely faced. In other words, my criticism was correct. I, a rightist, was praised for having taught a Party member a lesson. From then on, I stood at the battlefront with great confidence.

In those days on the battlefield of big-character posters, everybody strove to keep his or her way in the camp of good guys by making others fill bad roles. The prerequisite was writing big-character posters. Many people were willing but lacked the ability. They pulled a long face all day long and produced only a few words.

Having written a self-criticism every month for so many years was a kind of training in writing and enabled me to deal with the current situation without difficulty. I could easily produce a wall poster with hundreds or even thousands of characters each day.

There were several principles which I did not forsake in writing big-character posters. First, I absolutely acknowledged myself a sinful rightist and never voiced grievances by saying that since those who had labeled me a rightist were now revisionists, I should be rehabilitated. A lot of other rightists were making such complaints and demanding rehabilitation. I stated explicitly that I had been labeled a rightist by the great Communist Party, not by those bad guys. I also said that I wished to be delabeled, not through redress, but through remolding myself under the supervision of the great Party and the masses. The reason that I acted differently from the other rightists was that they had illusions about the Communists while I entertained none.

I was never accused of slandering anyone in my wall posters, because none of the facts listed on my big-character posters were refutable. Although, as my conscience told me, the conclusions I had reached might be controversial. By that time, I was already versed in criticizing myself and others from the high plane of Mao's two-line struggle theory. No matter what you said, once you became the target of mass criticism, your words could be considered to be malicious attacks against the Party and our great leader. I knew how to do that.

I was proud of myself, because whenever I, a veteran rightist, put a piece of large-size paper on my desk and dipped my writing brush into the inkpot, the entire staff of the editing department, which was housed in a huge room of the original theater of the former Chun-Hwa Academic Society, got nervous, and I could sense that the entire attention was being directed to my desk. Some of the older intellectuals became so fidgety that they could not help rising from their chairs, pretending to pass by my desk and taking a glance at what I was writing. They felt relieved when they saw I was not writing their names on my big-character poster.

In addition to Li Chun-min, Chen Hsiang-ping and Ch'i Min-ch'u were also ferreted out as counterrevolutionary revisionists. Almost the entire staff of the editing department, with the exception of only one or two persons, were uncovered as "monsters and demons." I should be credited for many of these "monsters and demons" being uncovered. Very often my posters condemning someone would turn out to be the first heavy bomb which instantly sent him to the "cowshed."

I never regretted, nor will I ever regret, denouncing them. They got what they deserved. I would not have written one single line of a big-character poster, had I not been labeled a rightist. Now, I was obliged to write it in response to the call of the movement on the one hand, and on the other hand, out of my desire for "being delabelized through making my contributions." During the previous movement, the Anti-Rightist Movement, they had made their contributions by making me a rightist. At least one of them had avoided the fate of being labeled a rightist because I became his surrogate. I would have forgiven them for their basic desire for survival, if they had stopped at that point. What I could never condone was that after I had been labeled a rightist and they were free of apprehension, they not only did not show any gratitude or mercy to me but continued dropping stones on me as one who had fallen into the well. They did everything possible to keep the rightist hat on my head. So my active participation in writing wall posters was encouraged by two urges: to have my hat taken off, and to have these people taste the flavor of being condemned.

Moreover, I never accused them of unwarranted charges. Take Chu Chin-chen for instance. He escaped being labeled a rightist and got a promotion solely because he had trumped up some charges against me. Now, it was time to get even for the wrong done to me. As a matter of fact, I did not need to search and make new discoveries. In a certain brief, relaxed period before the Anti-Rightist Movement, Chu Chin-chen had once talked about the former romances of Madame Mao. During the Anti-Rightist Movement, in retaliation for his unwarranted charges against me, I exposed his gossip about Madame Mao. It was bad timing.

First of all, the fact that I did not unmask him until he had attacked me gave others the obvious impression that I was taking my revenge on him, although it was required that every rightist denounce the crimes of others as well as his own. Secondly, in the 1950s, Madame Mao's position in the Chinese Communist Party was not as unchallenged as in the late 1960s. Therefore, at that time Chu Chin-chen could be protected by Vice President Chen Hsiang-ping, who declared in his concluding remarks at the general meeting: "We have to make a distinction between ourselves, our friends, and the enemies. Some comrades like Chu Chin-chen have made mistakes and even quite serious ones, but harbor no malicious intention toward our Party. They should acknowledge their shortcomings and overcome them but need not be weighed down with worries. We should aim at our targets, the rightists."

Now the Anti-Culture Movement offered a good chance, because any gossip about Madame Mao, especially about her notorious affairs in Shanghai in the 1930s, would be a criminal offense. When I brought up Chu Chin-chen's old "crime," he was instantly labeled a counterrevolutionary, and one more crime of "shielding evildoers" was added to the so-called capitalist roader Chen Hsiang-ping.

After that, whenever Chu Chin-chen met me, he would stare at me angrily and gnash his teeth. I was amused by his fierce look.

The tangled warfare of the big-character posters made targets palpitate with anxiety and fear, but as there was no authority at that time, they were not given any punishment for the moment. A couple of months later, a "working group" was dispatched into the publishing house to fill the leading positions left vacant by the downfall of the "capitalist roaders," as all the leaders had fallen from power. Nee Mo-yen, of course, was one of the new leaders handpicked by the working group.

A general meeting was held in honor of the so-called working group. The slogans chanted at the meeting were "Resolutely carry the Cultural Revolution through to the end," "Down with the capitalist roaders," "Down with the reactionary academic authorities," "Welcome the working group," and "The working group members are dispatched by Chairman Mao." In truth, Mao might have known nothing about our publishing house except some of our publications. Sent by the Municipal Party Committee, these several members of the working group had no connection whatsoever with Mao. However, it was a disgusting practice at that time to address anyone sent by the higher level as a comrade "dispatched by Chairman Mao" or "coming from Chairman Mao's side."

After the arrival of the working group, the "cowshed" was set up as a concrete measure for carrying out Chairman Mao's policy of "distinguishing the contradictions among the people from those between ourselves and the enemy." All those who were deemed enemies should be driven into the "cowshed," because all enemies were "cow monsters and snake demons." The "cowshed" was a figure of speech employed to humiliate enemies rather than to refer to a certain place. Our "cowshed," for example, was first located at the corner of the former theater hall which was now occupied by our editing department. There was no such tangible shed, only an area of piles of desks surrounded by big-character posters hanging from strings. This was a place allotted to those considered to be "monsters and demons" including, but not necessarily limited to, the three "capitalist roaders," Li, Chen, and Ch'i, two so-called delabeled rightists, Chien and Fu, a rightist of long-standing—that was me—and several "historical" and "active" counterrevolutionaries. According to the "Sixteen Regulations Regarding the Cultural Revolution Movement" issued by the Central Committee of the Chinese Communist Party on August 8, 1966, the cowshed was not the final treatment given to monsters and demons; therefore, this would be suspended at the end of the movement. This was only a theory, for the day would never come when it would be formally announced that the Cultural Revolution had come to an end.

If one could disregard the name, which sounded rather insulting, the "cowshed" was really not a bad place. I enjoyed it and used it to learn English. As we were supposed to sit in silence all day long ruminating over our crimes and reading Mao's works, I placed an official English version of a volume of *Mao's Selected Works* on my desk and a dictionary by its side. It looked as if I was studying the English edition of *Mao's Selected Works* with the help of a dictionary, but as a matter of fact, I was trying to learn new English words by heart, one by one. I turned the pages of *Mao's Selected Works* from time to time so that I was not suspected.

Needless to say, we "monsters" did not have the bliss of sitting and reading all day. We were frequently ordered to do the physical job of cleaning restrooms, which, it was said, would help remold our world outlook. It was regrettable that there were not enough restrooms to go around, for there were only three of them. "The gruel was meager but the monks were many," as the Chinese saying goes. We had to break up into several small teams and did the work in turns. President Li and I formed a team and were responsible for cleaning two toilets and a tub and sweeping the floor around them, several square meters in area. I proposed to President Li that I do this cleaning job and he take a rest. To my disappointment and even indignation, this old official did not appreciate my goodwill and resolutely declined my offer. He kept saying, "This is an opportunity to remold my ideology, and the remolding can never be done by somebody else."

Advanced in age and slow of movement as he was, he was terribly conscientious in doing physical labor. He mopped the floor and wiped the walls. Not satisfied with simply flushing the toilets, he washed them with a rag, and flushed them with a bucket of water. Then he mopped up the water spilled on the floor and washed the mop. On a job I could easily finish within a quarter of an hour, I had to spend at least two hours when he kept me company. I was somewhat irritated, but managed to control myself, because I had a principle to the effect that I had to respect these veteran officials in private even though I had attacked them in my wall posters. This principle was formed through studying Ssu-ma Kuang's *Tzu-chih-t'ung-chien*, which taught me how to survive in a totalitarian society, where the ups and downs of officials were frequent and unpredictable. Of course, it could only be implemented through an exchange of personal feeling, never by words, for words could be used as evidence of my opposition to the so-called Cultural Revolution.

Other "monsters" were far less happy and relaxed than I was. The veteran officials were incessantly pressed to write about their former comrades-in-arms, who had been leaders in other places and were now also "capitalist roaders." Those old intellectuals who had friends in the art and literary circles suffered as much as the officials. All of them had much less time for reading than I did. When they did have some free time, I could perceive that they were unable to concentrate on reading, but anxiously pulled long faces as if their doomsday was imminent.

Toward the end of 1966, a new nationwide movement, "The Great Contacting," was launched. As a matter of fact, it was not a movement in its usual sense, nor was it intended to enable people to establish ties with one another. It was only a ridiculous practice, which would send millions of students and youths—the so-called revolutionary young militants—riding on trains across the country. They could have a free ride on board the train to any destination they wanted, and all the institutions nationwide prepared piles of straw as makeshift sleeping mats for waves upon waves of young militants. For several months in a row, all the youths in China had good times when they made free trips across the country. Our publishing house was not an attractive scenic place, but among the swarms of young visitors a few dropped in to read our "interesting" big-character posters—outstanding both in quality and quantity.

One day a group of youngsters arrived. When they got tired of reading the big-character posters extending all the way from the gate to the upper floors, they caught sight of a group of people sitting in the corner of the hall, silent and timid, just like cows lined up in the slaughterhouse awaiting their fate. Though still green, these young revolutionaries had "faced the world and braved the storm" according to Mao's teaching, and could tell at once that these downcast people were "monsters and demons." As if dutybound, they went up to lecture them on morals. Suddenly, they found that among the "monsters" there was a person who looked quite pleased with himself, and that was I. They seemed a little puzzled by the sight and did not treat me as arrogantly as the other "monsters and demons." "Hi! We are going to give an admonitory talk to these old fellows; what the hell are you mixed with them for?"

"Well, I, too, am a 'monster and demon,'" I replied with a carefree air.

Some of them laughed while some shouted to me, "What a damnable joke! You just get out of here!"

"Why? This has to do with one's political life." I thought I might as well assume a joking attitude while speaking seriously. "How can you conclude someone is not a 'monster and a demon' while he himself says he is?"

Half convinced and half suspicious, they looked at one another without knowing what to do and left in disappointment. The other "monsters and demons" must have felt indebted to me for warding off a round of being struggled against.

While "monsters and demons" could only reconcile themselves to

their fate by taking shelter in the "cowshed," the so-called revolutionary masses also had a hard time, for they had to be subjected to screen-
ing by the "working group." The doorless "cowshed" could have new
members put in, with multifarious labels, at any time.

Hwa Shou-yi, a Party member and the leader of my group in the editing department, who had been in charge of me for several years, was
now a target of attack. He had been an underground Party member at
some textile factory in Shanghai before the liberation. The fact that he
had seen the world had made him more human than the average Party
member. He had been quite kind to me in his capacity as my political
supervisor. As he had little knowledge of Chinese classics, he, as the
leader of the editing group, gave me a free hand in my editing. He was
supposed to supervise my ideology remolding, yet he was very lenient.
He was smart enough to know the limit. He managed to make things
easy for me while avoiding suspicion of shielding me. It was through
him that I had submitted my manuscript of *Chi-ku lu*. For this, to this
date, I have always felt indebted to him. The impression I got from the
big-character posters exposing him was that he seemed to have committed no serious crime except that he had helped to collect fixed interest* for his father-in-law. Before the Anti-Culture Movement, nobody
had ever questioned the appropriateness or legitimacy of collecting
fixed interest paid by the government. However, by now the Anti-Culture Movement was in full swing, and nobody dared to challenge the
allegation that collecting fixed interest was a crime. One alleged crime
could lead to another, and a person could eventually be found guilty
and convicted by using a minor alleged crime as a breach. While Hwa
was writing a self-criticism, I was ordered by the hatchet men to expose
him. Apparently, they were not satisfied with charging Hwa with such
an alleged crime as collecting fixed interest. They needed allegations of
more serious crimes before they could further harass him; therefore,
they sought my assistance. They could not understand that since I had
already ferreted out so many "enemies" in the editing department, my

---

*Fixed interest was an annual rate of interest paid by the state to the national
bourgeoisie on the money value of their assets for a given period of time, after
the 1956 conversion of capitalist industry and commerce into joint state-
private enterprises.

goal of having my revenge on them had been achieved. I decided to wash my hands of this dirty deal for good.

I was summoned by a handsome young Party member by the name of Fong to a "provisional court," which was housed in a corner just opposite the "cowshed." An ex-policeman, Fong had been sent by his organization to the university to study as a professional student and then assigned to work in our editing department after his graduation on the eve of the Anti-Culture Movement. As a new arrival, he was clean-handed, having committed no "crimes" of ever editing any books. Therefore, he was the right person to play the role of hatchet man. Now, he was cast as a temporary prosecutor.

With an air of importance, he began to interrogate me. "Do you acknowledge yourself a rightist?"

"Yes, I do," I answered.

"Do you want to have your hat taken off?"

"Yes, I do."

"What do you think of Hwa Shou-yi?" he asked.

His intention was clear enough. Instead of playing hide-and-seek with him, I came straight to the point.

"Over the past few years, Hwa has, on behalf of the Party, supervised my ideological remolding and given me criticisms and education regularly. For this, I am grateful to the Party and him. It is true, as some wall posters have exposed, that Hwa trusted me with the editing work and helped me to overcome financial difficulties by giving me some extra work to do. I always considered these kinds of lenient treatment as favors shown to me not by any individual but by the great Communist Party. It is also correct, as some wall posters pointed out, that Hwa gave me the biggest editing workload in our group, but I must admit that it was due to my earnest request. I thought that I ought to perform well in my work, so that I could have my hat taken off as soon as possible. Before the Cultural Revolution, I didn't realize that all the classics were feudalistic, poisonous weeds, and that the more classics we published the more crimes we committed. Therefore, I strove to accomplish the tasks assigned to me as fast as I could. Hwa, as my supervisor and group leader, never allowed me much free time. As soon as I finished one task, he gave me another, which I also tried to fulfill in as short a time as possible. In this case, if my hard work is considered a crime, it is I who should take responsibility. As to the accusation that almost all the publications of this publishing house are poisonous weeds and have exerted a very bad influence, I fully agree to it and assume full responsibility for the works I edited. I would not put the blame on any leaders, including Hwa Shou-yi."

"You are stubborn. Very stubborn." His face turned from pale to red and to pale again. "Apparently, you are unwilling to cooperate with us. Do you think your reluctance can help to have your hat taken off?"

"I am eager to have my 'hat' taken off, but this can only be achieved through honesty and sincerity," I retorted, looking him in the eye. "I appreciate your offering me an opportunity today to perform meritorious service to atone for my crimes. What I have said is from the bottom of my heart. I cannot cheat you. To cheat you is to cheat our great Party."

He seemed to be somewhat moved, but did not want to be considered in the wrong. "You are stubborn. We'll wait and see." With that, he left.

Not long after that, the internecine struggle characteristic of the Anti-Culture Movement caused the leadership to be in a state of flux. With the downfall of the Shanghai Municipal Party Committee, the working group quietly disappeared. Everybody claimed he or she was a revolutionary rebel, a phrase coined by Mao Tse-tung. These revolutionary rebels formed different factions, each claiming to be "the true and loyal followers" of Chairman Mao's political line. Hwa Shou-yi became the leader of a short-lived rebel faction, and Fong, who had been Hwa's friend before the Anti-Culture Movement and foe after the start of the movement, was now on good terms with him once again. This was not unique, because all the revolutionaries were as broad-minded as a Confucian gentleman, who always "forgives an old wrong." Fong, after he was on good terms with Hwa again, must have told Hwa about my remarks about him, because Hwa was now more kindly toward me.

The downfall of the Shanghai Municipal Party Committee on January 1, 1967, sent a misleading signal to many people who overlooked the basic fact that this was only a dog-eat-dog type of struggle within the Party. They were very happy that the working groups across the country, especially in Peking, were being driven away amid the shouting of the slogan, "Down with the reactionary Liu-Teng line," and thought this was a real change of power. By that time, several "monsters" not only refused to stay in the "cowshed" any longer, but posted a *ta tzu pao* (big-character poster) to proclaim their "self-liberation" as encouraged by Mao. Since they thought they were no longer "monsters and demons," they proudly joined the ranks of revolutionary rebels and formed a faction, headed by Hwa Shou-yi, which tried to seek power from another faction headed by Nee Mo-yen. For a time, the former outnumbered and overpowered the latter.

After the withdrawl of the working group, which had been Nee Mo-yen's firm backing, Nee fell into disgrace and was even thrown into the "cowshed" for a few days. At this period, even Chin Hsin-yao and Mei Lin, who were labeled counterrevolutionaries, took advantage of the situation and semiretired from the "cowshed." They did not make any proclamation to "liberate" themselves and join the ranks of the rebels, as others had done, but stopped observing the regulations imposed on them. For example, they no longer posted their ideological report in the form of a wall poster each week. I not only remained in the "cowshed" and continued posting my weekly ideological report, but also clearly stated that I would never quit the "cowshed" on my own and that I was determined to make efforts to expiate my crime by good deeds, so that I could get a pardon from the Party and the people.

As long as the two rebel factions were locked in a tug-of-war, it made no difference whether one stayed in the "cowshed" or not. Self-liberation from the cowshed would meet no hindrance, while staying in the cowshed did not entail any hardship. Liberty inside the cowshed was no less than outside.

As the two self-styled "genuine rebel" factions accused each other of being "royalist," each held its own meeting "struggling against capitalist roaders" to show it was really revolutionary. These struggle meetings had a common formality. After a self-appointed leader sitting on the rostrum declared the meeting open, he would shout awe-inspiringly: "Now, bring the capitalist roaders So-and-so, So-and-so, and all the 'monsters and demons' onto the stage." Then all the "criminals," that is those who still acknowledged themselves "monsters and demons," such as I, and former leading revolutionaries, would step onto the stage in a single line, each flanked by one or two Red Guards. Some of the Red Guards escorted the victims with a military bearing, while others grabbed the victims' hair or held their hands behind their backs, a so-called jet aircraft treatment.

Li Chun-min, president of our publishing house, was always the major target at the struggle meetings. For example, when one faction, which was formed by those persecuted over the past few months, presided over a meeting against the other faction, who had been their persecutors, they ordered Li Chun-min to stand on the stage as the chief criminal, despite the fact that Li had been subjected to persecution along with them. The logic was that Mao's political line was always and absolutely correct. Mistakes, if any, came from Liu Shao-chi and Teng Hsiao-ping's reactionary line, and all capitalist roaders together with monsters and demons had been and should be supporters of Liu and Teng whether they had been persecuted by Liu and Teng or not. The real motive behind these formalities was to struggle against the other rebel faction.

I played the supporting negative role, and always stood by the side of Li Chun-min, Chen Hsiang-ping, and Ch'i Min-ch'u, who had labeled me a rightist. On most of these occasions, the majestic-looking Red Guards forgot to signal me to step onto the platform. Maybe I was such a small potato that they did not care at all. However, I would voluntarily go and keep company with the lovable "capitalist roaders." Sometimes, I would say to the person who chaired the meeting, "I would like to accompany the 'criminals' onto the platform, so that I can benefit from being struggled against." In fact, in most cases I just walked silently up to the stage, stood there silently with my head hung, and silently walked away after the meeting was over. Although my ears were full of noise, my mind was quiet.

Only once was I called by name, and I had to rack my brains to answer questions. This happened at the meeting held to struggle against Nee Mo-yen. After Li Chun-min, Chen Hsiang-ping and Ch'i min-ch'u, who were capitalist roaders, and I, who was a rightist, had been ordered to stand on the stage with our heads hung, and after the typical slogans had been shouted, the rebel leaders who presided over the meeting pointed their fingers at the real target, Nee Mo-yen. Nee had been ordered to stand as a "criminal" on the same platform where he had frequently sat before as chairman. The masses angrily struggled against him for having implemented Liu and Teng's line for the past several months and victimized so many people. He slyly but categorically rejected all the charges. On the one hand, he apologized "to those comrades who have been hurt in the past months," and on the other he insisted, "I always cherish a deep affection for Chairman Mao and his line." Of course, he had to acknowledge that he had been taken in by Liu and Teng's line, as most people had. Therefore, he could not be considered an enemy.

Then the masses called my name. They first reprimanded me for the large number of big-character posters I had written. I answered explicitly, "I should acknowledge that some analysis on my big-character posters is wrong because my way of thinking was wrong. I apologize for the mistake I made. However, the instances I cited are 100 percent true. I did not fabricate any stories or distort facts, although I may have drawn wrong conclusions."

My statement was, of course, unacceptable to those whom I had exposed. Then the masses began to shout slogans against me, amid which Chu Chin-chen jumped onto the rostrum in an attempt to hit me. Hwa Shou-yi immediately stopped him, saying, "What we need now is his confession. We don't want to beat him." Then he, in the capacity of chairman, shouted at me, "Wong, you have to confess honestly how Nee Mo-yen managed to make you work for him." Hwa had hit the point, but he could not draw me out.

"I have no idea. He never asked me to work for him," I said flatly.

At that moment, I was thinking of freeing myself from the predicament by telling them about the conversation that took place between Nee Mo-yen and me in his dormitory. The rebels would have been very satisfied if I had made a confession, for it could be used as evidence for Nee's pursuit of Liu and Teng's line and his plot to conspire with a "monster" to persecute the revolutionary masses. However, I refrained from doing so. I just kept silent.

For my stubbornness, I had to pay a high price. The masses shouted like mad. Some demanded that I kneel down, but I took no note of it. Then some intellectuals, following suit with Chu Chin-chen, jumped onto the platform. These were people who had just "liberated" themselves from the "cowshed" by taking advantage of the downfall of the Shanghai Municipal Party Committee. They kicked my knees and pushed my head, trying to make me kneel down, but I stood still.

That day, the person who escorted me was Hsiao Fan, a young man who had entered this publishing house just one or two years before the Anti-Culture Movement. While in his junior high school, he had been in Jane's class. During a chat after he entered the publishing house, we discovered this relationship. After that we became very close, and used to walk together when we met on our way to work. He was that type of young man who had "good" class origin—with a worker's family background and himself a "revolutionary militant" whom each rebel faction liked to rope in. When Nee Mo-yen was in power, Hsiao Fan was one of his warriors. When the other faction exercised control, Fan was also recruited, with the same status. This was due to Mao's very logical theories: "Masses are true heroes," "Masses in any reactionary factions have only been hoodwinked by their leaders and, hence, should not be held guilty." With these famous directives of Mao, people like Fan could everlastingly play the role of innocent heroes. He could have joined these old fellows in beating me, but he did not. At last, he said to them, "Get out of here, all of you."

As these old fellows were always docile and submissive to the young militants, they obeyed his order instantly.

Hsiao Fan had to defend his prestige as a young militant. After the old fellows had left the platform, Fan began to pull my hair and forced my head up. He looked me in the eye, yelling, "Wong, now that the masses want you to kneel down, why don't you just kneel down?"

His yell was meant to be heard by the audience, as well as to show his revolutionary militancy, but the expression in his eyes gave the unequivocal message, "You'd better be sensible and kneel." He expected me to comply, so that he could win respect from those old fellows who had failed to make me kneel. He did not understand my philosophy. My firm belief in Chinese tradition forbade me to kneel down, because one's knees are only bent in front of either an emperor or parents.

As I kept on standing, Fan tried to force me to kneel down, but was not strong enough to move me. He seemed to be humiliated by my steadfastness. Either because of embarrassment or because he tried to save face, he pulled my hair with one hand to force my head up, and struck my face with the other hand, cursing between his teeth, "You are such a stubborn fellow!"

Under this circumstance, Hwa Shou-yi immediately stepped to his side, and said to both Hsiao Fan and all the audience, "We have to obey our Party's policy. We must defeat the reactionaries through reasoning, not through using our fists." Fan took this chance to extricate himself from the awkward position, loosened his grip on my hair and pressed on my back, shouting, "Okay, if you don't want to kneel, then bend your waist." This I obeyed without reluctance.

Most of the "monsters and demons" preferred kneeling to bowing. As bowing for a long time was physically unbearable, they would often beg permission to kneel down. I would rather endure the physical pain of bowing than kneeling. Although Chu Chin-chen stepped to the front of the platform and pulled my head all the way below my waist, almost to the level of my knees, I remained unmoved. The longer I maintained this posture, the more sore my waist became. Then numerous sparks began to appear before my eyes, and I almost reached the limit of my physical endurance. Other "monsters and demons" who had been forced to maintain this posture would raise their bodies a little from time to time until the escorts discovered it, swore, and made them resume their original posture. But they had already stolen a break. I could have chosen to invite such an insult in exchange for a short break, but I did not. I recalled an ancient aphorism, "A real man should be able to suffer the unsufferable," and kept this posture unchanged. No matter how painful this posture was, I regarded it as something that could temper me both physically and spiritually. I perspired profusely. As my head was kept below the level of my knees, perspiration ran from my face into my eyes and caused much pain. I had to close my eyes. While I could see nothing, my sense of hearing became more acute.

I heard the following dialogue:

"This guy is very well-behaved while bending his waist. Just look at him bowing motionless."

"This also reflects his stubbornness."

This further proved Mao's maxim that people's eyes are discerning.

Soon after this assembly, another strange incident occurred. Hsiao Fan came to the "cowshed" with another young revolutionary militant to fetch me for interrogation. Being fetched for interrogation was the common fate of the members of the "cowshed," especially the former leaders, as the whole country was resonant with slogans like "Down with this," and "Down with that." Interrogators in search of materials with which to denounce their adversaries had the pleasure of traveling everywhere. The more comrades-in-arms a person had, the more opportunities for interrogation he would have. I seldom had any. To my astonishment, I was honored with one that day. Also to my astonishment, I was not brought to a room or a place with desks and chairs so that the interrogators could take notes. Instead I was taken to a corner at the foot of the stairway. Although they did not carry with them the regular paraphernalia needed for an interrogation, they gave the whole process the appearance of a trial.

"You practice *tai-chi*?" they asked.

"Yes," I replied, thinking that they were asking while knowing what would be the answer.

"Whom did you learn it from?" They knew the answer because I had already told Hsiao Fan about Master Yue while we were walking together to our office.

"Master Yue, Yue Huan-chi," I answered politely.

"It is widely said that Master Yue could strike people down from a distance or from another room or place. Was that true?" Evidently they were serious.

"Yes, I also heard about it," I said.

"Be honest. We are not asking about what has been said. We are asking you whether it was true or not."

"Well, Master Yue himself always denied it and resented this rumor. However, while teaching his pupils, he sometimes demonstrated this kind of *kung-fu*. I used to witness and even experienced his long-distance hitting." I purposely turned simple things into mysteries.

"Ah, Wong, be honest now. Don't talk about irrelevant matters. We don't want to hear you talking at random. Now, answer me directly: Do you have this kind of *kung-fu*, too?"

So that's how it was! Despite their severe tone, they did not make a show of their strength as they had done before. Their last question instantly revealed the intention of this interrogation. While I was groping for an answer, Hsiao Fan, unable to restrain himself, asked impatiently, "You have to confess if you have ever beaten people."

"No," I replied flatly, because that was the truth.

"Did you ever hurt people without beating and hitting them?" Hsiao Fan's question revealed his fear.

I suddenly realized the whole purpose of this interrogation. I recalled that before the Anti-Culture Movement, when Fan met me on the way to the publishing house, we had often walked the rest of way together and that during one chat about *kung-fu*, I had told him how one could use *tai-chi* to hurt people without raising his fist or finger. He must have remembered my words after he pushed my back and struck my face. He had come to interrogate me with the purpose of removing his doubts.

Hsiao Fan, as a young militant, had the habit of showing his strength and bullying honest people. Therefore, it would benefit us, the oppressed, to let him keep this doubt. Honestly, I did not have this kind of *kung-fu*, but why should I let him know? I never lied and boasted of myself. If he liked making a hypothesis, it was his problem, which I was under no obligation to solve.

When my mind was made up, I stopped talking anymore. I continued to assume the attitude that a "monster and demon" was supposed to adopt, that of hanging my head.

"I want you to answer yes or no," he demanded.

I kept silent. He raised his voice, "Confess honestly. Do you have this kind of *kung-fu*?"

I remained silent and said nothing, testing his patience. He then softened his voice and attitude. "Don't be obstinate. You will only bring things to a deadlock. It will do you no good. All you have to do now is answer yes or no. All we need is to clarify a thing. We don't want to make things difficult for you. Just answer us, and you will be free of any trouble."

I held my tongue, regardless of their soft or hard attitude. They asked the same question over and over again. They finally got angry, and shouted, "What the hell are you thinking today? You used to maintain a posture of hanging your head, confessing your crimes, and obeying our commands. Why are you so stubborn today? Do you really want to incur some severe punishment?"

Aha, here they are! I considered their intimidation as a test of my will and theirs. I just wanted to see what they would do with me if I refused to cooperate with them. If I persevered and they did not dare to hit me or beat me, it would indicate they were really afraid of me. In order to prove this, I used the same will power to keep my mouth shut that I had used to bend my waist at the struggle meeting. In the end, although they were furious with me, they let me go and sent me back to the "cowshed" without touching a single hair of mine. I was relieved to know that these young militants were worried about my *kung-fu.*

However, their lack of will to hurt me physically provided no reason for relaxation of my vigilance, for I knew the nature of the proletariat only too well. I did not in the least envy those who had been "self-liberated" from the "cowshed." I was sure that they would soon pay for their rashness. Therefore, I continued to beg those revolutionary militants to exercise a proletarian dictatorship over me.

Following is one example. My eldest son, who had just entered junior high, took advantage of the "Great Contacting Campaign" and walked from Shanghai to Changshu to visit his maternal grandfather. On his arrival there, he contracted epidemic encephalitis and was hospitalized. As I got a call from my parents-in-law and had to go there, I went to ask for leave. I approached Hwa Shou-yi, the leader of the rebel faction which had just seized power, and told him about my need for several days' leave. At first, he expressed his concern about my son's illness, then he said, "I can't make any decision on this question. You'd better talk with whoever is in charge of the 'cowshed.'"

I thought, "Have you really seized power as you claimed? Then why do you let the power of supervising me remain in the hands of your rivals?" While keeping these questions to myself, I followed his advice and approached my former supervisor. Hearing about my son's illness and my request for several days' leave, he expressed his sympathy, but replied, "Well, we are no longer in power now. Why don't you ask the others to make a decision regarding your leave?"

Thinking that an argument was inevitable, I resolved to challenge him. "Whether you are in power or not is an internal affair between you two rebel factions. As an object of dictatorship, I should not be interested in which of you is in power. All I should do is accept proletariat dictatorship. I request that I be supervised by both of you. I would like to obey orders from both of you. Now, the other rebel faction refused to make a decision on my request for a leave, and you refuse, too. Then who should make the decision? Who should be my supervisor? I don't want to act without permission from either of you."

He was dumbfounded for a while and looked straight at me. During this period, there were plenty of "self-liberators," but it was very rare for someone to seek desperately to have proletarian dictatorship exercised over himself. He was so unprepared for my challenge that he could not but approve my request by saying, "Since they don't object to your leaving, just go."

I insisted on getting to the bottom of the matter. "They neither objected to nor approved my request. They simply said they were not in charge of this kind of thing and told me to ask you."

"Why ask me?" He glowered at me. "I'm no longer in power. Why ask me? I'll tell you what. I won't say yes or no, but I will acknowledge I have been informed of your request. Whether you leave or not, that's your business, not mine." Before completing the sentence, he had already turned around and started walking away.

Then I began to realize that both rebel factions had hinted that I could go. However, neither of them wanted to take responsibility, because they were accusing each other of being "royalists" and "conspiring with monsters and demons." Each of them refused to grant me approval for fear of giving the other a handle. Once I understood this situation, I felt at ease and went to Changshu. My son, though in critical condition, was recovering fast. I did not have to stay in the hospital all day long. I visited the nearby Yu Mountain several times to listen to birds singing and smell the fragrance of its beautiful flowers. I enjoyed the mountain very much, although some famous ancient cultural relics on the hill had been reduced to rubble.

Carefree as I was, I was still constantly haunted by the proletarian dictatorship. I stayed in Changshu for two weeks. On the weekend I mailed my weekly ideological report to the publishing house. After the setting up of the "cowshed" on the order of the revolutionary rebels, all the monsters and demons had to post their ideological reports on the wall every week. In the first couple of weeks, all members in the cowshed observed the order, and had quite a few readers. As time went by, the reports became a mere formality and fewer and fewer people cared to read them. After most of the monsters and demons had left the cowshed and refused to post their weekly reports anymore—even the capitalist roaders had stopped posting them regularly—I was the only one who remained faithful to the formality. I did not care if there were no readers, neither did I mind if the other monsters and demons no longer wrote any weekly reports. I decided to follow all the formalities laid down by the rebels. Even while I was on leave in Changshu, I still sent them my ideological report by mail. I used carbon paper for writing my reports, so that each time I could mail two copies of my report, one for each rebel faction. Each report was a brief restatement to the effect that I had decided to accept proletarian dictatorship and obey the orders of both rebel factions.

When I reported to the publishing house after an absence of two weeks, the two rebel factions had entered into a cease-fire. During this period, a new term came into vogue, "carefree nonfaction," referring to those who had grown tired of the fighting among various rebel factions in almost every institution across the country and refused to take sides with any group. They seldom came to work or had to observe office hours. When and if they came to the office, they just did personal things. If they were male employees, they washed clothes or cleaned bicycles or installed semiconductor receivers. If they were female employees, they knitted or sewed or whatever. They did no work, but received full pay. They were the happiest people in the whole world. I envied them. This was the period in which I hated the rightist label most intensely. If I had not had such a damned label, I thought, I would certainly have been a thoroughly carefree nonfactionist, and the struggle between rebel factions would have had nothing to do with me. What a pity it was that I was still a rightist and had to come to the office every day!

Although there was no editing to do, since the publishing house had stopped publication, I enjoyed little free time the moment I came to the office. I was busy during office hours every day. The two rebel factions were formed by gentlemen who never fought by fists but by words. Each faction attacked the other with the weapon of the wall posters. The two factions shared, free of charge, a "mercenary"—me. In a certain section of the downtown area, two street blocks of walls had been alloted to this publishing house for use as bulletin boards for "special columns for mass criticism." Since the majority of the employees in our work unit were carefree nonfactionists who took no interest in criticizing capitalist roaders, the privilege of using the spaces for "special columns" automatically belonged to the two antagonistic rebel factions. As I mentioned earlier, the members of these factions were gentlemen and never exchanged blows in order to get these spaces. Indeed, they did not need to come to blows, for each of them had already been given one street block. Each space could be covered with ten or more big-character posters, which usually were the size of one issue of a special column. The contents were invariably attacks on or exposures of the rival faction, which allegedly had followed Liu and Teng's line, shielded monsters and demons, and opposed Mao's line. Both factions used the same jargon and, most interestingly, the same calligraphy style. I always wondered how the pedestrians could tell the difference between them if they ever stopped to read these big-character posters. Funny enough, they usually drafted the contents, but it was I who copied them onto the big-character posters with a writing brush.

I was not only the sole copier, but also the sole person to paste the big-character posters on the walls. It was no easy job. To tear down old posters and put up new ones required energy and time. As the street walls for special columns were very far from the publishing house, rolls of big-character posters and baskets of paste had to be transported by pedicab. There were few rebels who could pedal a pedicab, and I was the only "monster" capable of doing so. Therefore, both of the rebel factions made me responsible for pasting their special columns. To be responsible meant that I had the right to summon other monsters and demons to assist me in this work. Each time the revolutionaries handed their manuscripts to me, they would say, "You can judge yourself. If you need help, you may select someone in the cowshed who has nothing to do to go with you." It seemed that I had been promoted to the untitled position of manager of the cowshed, but I never took any other monster and demon with me, but preferred to do the job myself. There were several reasons. First, all the members in the cowshed were old and weak, and I could not expect to get any real help from them. Second, the addition of a person would increase the weight of the pedicab and consume more of my energy. Third, as no time limit was set for the job, I could spend a whole day doing it and enjoy some quiet moments by myself. I did not want to run the risk of having a potential informer with me.

Both of the rebel factions were reasonable. Either intentionally or unintentionally, they staggered the publishing dates of their special columns. Faction A would have its issue pasted this week, then it would be faction B's turn next week, so that they could always keep me busy while never overwhelming me with work. In this period, I struck a balance between work and rest. Most of the time, I copied big-character posters in the work unit and took the opportunity to practice calligraphy. Only one day a week I pedaled the pedicab to paste big-character posters on the street walls, and took this as an open-air activity which would do good for my health. I did not really enjoy this kind of life, but had no complaint.

One thing was most interesting. Among the crimes of which each rebel faction accused the other was "collusion with monsters and demons." The evidence both sides produced to sustain their charges against each other was that I was working for both of them. Faction A said, "The big-character posters of Faction B's last special column frenziedly attacked us. They were not only copied but also pasted by Wong." Faction B protested, "Faction A has deviated from the proletarian revolutionary line so much that they even employed the rightist Wong to copy and paste the special column to attack the revolutionary masses." According to the prevailing practice at that time, wherever the characters of my name appeared, they had three red crosses on them, and this meant that this fellow was a criminal. In ancient China the feudal bureaucrats did this in the announcements of execution. The revolutionary rebels always put three red crosses on my name in their original manuscripts. I followed suit when I copied them and put red crosses on my own name. When one faction attacked the other, that faction pretended to have done nothing it was accusing the other faction of. When I copied the manuscripts, I pretended that that Wong was not me. Maybe I had already attained the Buddhist goal of "nonexistence of self."

Another thing reflected the same spiritual state. In the autumn of 1967, the bulk of the staff of the publishing house, except the capitalist roaders, who had to write materials about their former comrades-in-arms, went to the suburbs for two weeks to help with the "three autumn jobs," namely, harvesting, plowing, and sowing. The motive behind this activity I never knew. Maybe many people had begun to feel guilty because they had been idle for a long time. Anyway, both rebel factions went together with carefree nonfactionists. So did I. The living conditions in the village were poor. Over ten people shared one room. At that time I was the only person who had been formally labeled "monster" by the Party committee. The rest, who had been ferreted out and subjected to harassment in the current movement, had not yet been officially labeled "monsters and demons," and since "selfliberation" had claimed to be members of the revolutionary masses.

Among the people living in the same room, there were rebels of different factions, carefree nonfactionists, and I. By that time, Peking had already tried very hard to urge rebels of all factions to unite. In reality, the attempt was to no avail. Rebels of different factions were still conspiring against one another. Even some carefree nonfactionists were beginning to have different orientations and sided secretly with this or that faction. As a monster and demon, I was not supposed to chat with anyone. In the evening, when I had nothing else to do, I used to go to bed. My bed was canopied with a mosquito net, in which I enjoyed staying, for it separated me from the rest of the world. Staying inside the mosquito net in the evening was delightful to me, not necessarily to others. Many preferred to devote the evening to socializing. In order to avoid disturbing each other, the two rebel factions tacitly reached a gentleman's agreement. If rebels of Faction A who were chatting in this room happened to be in the majority, then those of Faction B would voluntarily retreat to another room. When rebels of Faction B became the majority in that room after their fellow rebels came in, those of Faction A who were there would rise and come into this room. All in all, in the evening each room was always packed with rebels of a faction. Then they could talk without restraint, either sneering at or planning a conspiracy against the other faction. Strangely enough, whichever faction occupied this room, it never showed any misgivings because I was in the room. Although I was quiet inside the mosquito net, I did not think they believed I was asleep at such an early hour. Maybe both factions had confidence in me, or maybe neither of them regarded me as the same kind of human being as they. I did not care what they thought of me.

I shall never forget another incident. The village in which we stayed and helped with the three autumn jobs was in a typical southern region of rivers and lakes. The local transportation relied heavily on boats, which were not motorboats, but had to be sculled. This aroused my interest. While I was at St. John's University, I used to go boating at a river formerly known as Rio Rita, close to the campus. One day, when I

followed the revolutionaries to work and passed by a boat, I unwitting-
ly blurted out, "Oh, that's fun! I like rowing." One of my colleagues
asked me, "You know how to row?" "Yes, I do," I let slip. Suddenly he
yelled to others, "Come on, let's get on the boat. Wong knows how to
row!"

The whole team to which I belonged seemed to be tired of walking
and was glad to have someone row them to their destination. As I was
known to be good at handling various kinds of transportation, like
pedaling a pedicab or pulling a flatbed cart, they believed I was skillful
at rowing too. Since I was an object of dictatorship, they did not bother to seek my consent. They just stepped aboard the boat and took it
for granted that I had to row. In reality, the boat with which I used to
have so much fun at Rio Rita had oars, which was totally different
from sculling. I had never tried to scull before. I pulled myself together
and tried. After I untied the mooring rope and moved the boat off the
bank into the river, the scull slipped again and again, and the boat
turned round and round in the middle of the river. My face was drip-
ping with sweat, and I was all in a muddle. The revolutionary rebels
were so panic-stricken that there was an uproar and some of them began to blame me. "Wong, you don't know how to row, do you? Why
did you boast you can?"

"Damn you, how dare you make fun of us," others shouted in
despair.

I had neither time nor wit to reply. Fortunately, someone stamped
his feet with fury, shaking the boat violently. Then someone yelled,
"Don't rock the boat. We'd better stay calm and let Wong row us back.
I tell you, Wong, if you fail to row us back, you can be sure you'll soon
find yourself on the spot."

Thus, the passengers gradually calmed down. Although Mao's slogan "Fear neither hardship nor death" was always on their lips, these
revolutionary rebels were frightened out of their wits in face of the imminent danger that the boat would capsize.

At that moment, pressure on me was beyond description. I was facing a struggle of life and death. If the boat capsized, anything could
happen to me. In the era of class struggle, the fact that a rightist over-
turned a boat and sent a team of revolutionaries into the river, even if
no one was drowned, was a towering crime never to be pardoned. Oh,

how outrageous! I ground my teeth. No matter how difficult it was to control the boat, I was determined to tame it. I compelled myself to make the impossible possible. I tried and failed, then tried again and failed again. At last, I managed to cool down and recollected how the local people sculled. I tried to imitate their posture. Bit by bit, the boat began to move and drifted toward the bank. After the revolutionaries landed safely, they neither gave me credit nor blamed me.

From then on, I spent my leisure learning to scull. I learned it from the local people, and kept practicing it until I had a full mastery of the technique. Years later, when I went to do physical labor in the suburbs again, I could scull like a professional.

In 1967, several veteran bureaucrats and generals in the Central Committee of the Chinese Communist Party were embroiled in the so-called Adverse Current of February. After that, institutions across the country began to struggle against those class enemies who had tried to reverse the verdict, with "Never allow rightists to wreak vengeance" as their chief slogan. By that time, not only self-liberators began to reenter the cowshed, but those who had never checked into the cowshed became new members. The original cowshed in the corner of the hall was not spacious enough to accommodate the increasing number of monsters and demons; therefore, it was moved downstairs to the backyard. The original desks did not come with us. Each person was given a small stool and a small teapot and stayed under a canopy. Now it looked like a real cowshed.

Factional struggles came to an end, at least outwardly, when Mao Tse-tung, astonished at the nationwide tumult, sent soldiers and workers to the cultural and educational institutions to control the chaotic situation. The publishing house was also provided with new leaders with red collar badges. The first "good" thing they did was to enlarge the cowshed. As the result of their hard work, the population of monsters and demons amounted to two or three dozen at the cowshed's pinnacle of prosperity, approximately half of the publishing house. Except for one or two individuals, the entire staff of the editing department became monsters and demons. At the struggle meetings, the accusers said to the former officials while pointing to the beleaguered editors, "Look, all these intellectuals you recruited as editors are monsters and demons.

They show that you are true capitalist roaders." Then they would say to the editor intellectuals, while pointing to the downfallen old officials, "Look at the men who shielded you and put you in important positions. They are capitalist roaders. This proves you are out-and-out bad guys." The logic had been carefully thought out.

Then something new emerged. Each institution picked some special targets and isolated them for interrogation. These poor fellows were not allowed to return home and stayed in a single small cell, serving an endless term of imprisonment. They were people with "complicated personal histories" or with "important questionable social relations." In our publishing house, there were several such objects, among them Hu Tao-ching. As our work unit did not have its own cafeteria, we all ate in the canteen of the Bureau of Publications, which was our next-door neighbor on our right. The objects "isolated for interrogation" were forbidden to meet anybody or go into the streets. The authorities assigned me the job of bringing food from the canteen for Hu. Apparently, they were confident that I would not play tricks like smuggling or poisoning. They were correct, but failed to comprehend that Hu was the scholar I admired most. As far as my personal feelings were concerned, I did not think of Hu Tao-ching as a prisoner, but as a respectable teacher. I took as good care of him as possible under this situation. For example, my respectful and submissive attitude toward him must have been a great consolation to him in view of his plight. I did not bring him food just as a routine, but asked him what he liked to eat and tried my best to give him what he preferred. My attitude toward him might have been felt by him to be a wordless message of goodwill which could not be discerned by others. Unfortunately, this period did not last long, for he was soon arrested.

Mao Tse-tung began to sell his so-called model experiences of struggle-criticism-reform to the whole nation. One of his new inventions was to hold "meetings of leniency and severity." Every institution in the country held this kind of meeting to follow the notorious slogan, "Leniency to those who confess their crimes and severity to those who refuse to." At one meeting, held in our publishing house, Hu Tao-ching was arrested along with Yang Yu-jen, Chu Chin-chen and Ch'u Tui-chih, who was not our regular employee but a contract consultant. They were handcuffed and taken away by the police. Before the masses had recovered from the shock, Nee Mo-yen, who had been reinstated as leader and acted as chairman of the meeting, called my name and set me up as an opposite example. He praised me for being willing to remold my ideology and promised to have my hat taken off during the late period of the movement.

Also during this period, a very interesting farce was played on a nationwide scale. It was a kind of ritual at which the masses, including the monsters and demons, were required to "ask for instructions in the mornings and submit reports in the evenings" under the portrait or statue of Chairman Mao. Our publishing house went even further. It played the farce three times a day, at the start of office hours in the morning, before lunch at noon, and before leaving the office in the evening. Revolutionary masses and monsters and demons observed the ritual separately. The latter were not allowed to "ask for instructions in the mornings and submit reports in the evenings"; they could only "apologize to Chairman Mao."

The monsters and demons had to wait in the cowshed for the revolutionary masses to observe the ritual first. The revolutionary masses first lined up in front of Mao's portrait and then shouted, "A long, long life to our most respected leader, the reddest and reddest red sun in our hearts, the great Chairman Mao," followed by a repetition of "a long life" three times, and "Everlasting health to our deputy commander-in-chief, vice chairman Lin P'iao," then a repetition of "everlasting health" two times. Finally they wound up their incantation by reciting one or two quotations from Chairman Mao.

After the revolutionary masses dispersed, it was our turn to line up under the expressionless Mao. We shouted slogans just as the revolutionary masses had done, but the revolutionaries warned me, the untitled manager of monsters and demons, "You monsters should not use the phrase 'the reddest and reddest red sun,' because you monsters and demons don't have a red sun in your hearts." So much the better. They also gave me an order: "Just call vice-chairman Lin P'iao, and omit the phrase 'our deputy commander-in-chief,' because you are not qualified to address him this way." Again, so much the better. I never questioned why we were qualified to look at Mao as our leader but not at Lin as our deputy commander. Talking about logic with these fellows was just like talking about ice with summer insects.

After the prelude of "a long life" and "everlasting health" came the main body of our ritual, which was much more tedious and time-consuming than that of the revolutionary masses. Instead of just reciting Mao's quotations, we had to recite Mao's two essays "A Letter Pressing Tu Yu-min to Surrender" and "Where Is the Nanking Government Heading?" These two essays, especially the latter, were quite long. In this area, I fully demonstrated my recitation ability. As leader of monsters and demons, I recited loudly and fluently without looking at the text for a moment. To be fair, these two essays were among the best of Mao's writings from the technical point of view and, therefore, not difficult to recite.

My performance in recitation may have helped improve my image in the eyes of the revolutionaries. Gradually, they began to look upon me as their "comrade." They stopped looking at me with fierce hatred as they did at other monsters and demons, but began to order me to do this and that in a cool tone. They trusted me to such a degree that they even used me for the transportation of personal belongings confiscated from the houses they had searched, although house searching was then deemed a genuine revolutionary action. This may have been due partly to my youthfulness and strength and partly to my ability in pedaling a pedicab.

I always thought I was a lucky monster and demon as compared with the others, especially those in the neighbor institution on our left, the Shanghai Peking Opera Troupe. Though our work units were separated by a wattled wall, I often saw from the window upstairs or through the bamboo fence the monsters and demons there, all of them first-rate actors or actresses, assembled on the sports ground while being reprimanded or beaten by the revolutionary rebels. Most of the time they were doing physical labor either under the hot sun or in the rain. Once, our publishing house joined with the Peking Opera Troupe in reconstructing the bamboo fence separating the two institutions. Both of them had a surplus workforce, as each had a huge contingent of monsters and demons. Thus, the two armies of monsters and demons, on the order of their respective revolutionary bosses, started a joint venture. We mended the fence face-to-face, silently, and not very adroitly. I could hardly imagine that these shabbily-dressed and ghastly-pale laborers before my eyes were formerly famous actors and actresses. Every day after work, I walked home and passed the Shanghai Traditional Opera School on my way. I often saw Yu Cheng-fei, the principal of that school and the best-known *kung ch'u* actor,* dressed in rags painting the gate or doing some other manual job at the entrance to the school. I felt awfully sorry for people like him, but at the same time I was amused by the fact that the Anti-Rightist Movement had made it possible for me to rank with some outstanding scholars and scientists while this great Anti-Culture Movement had put me on a par with big stars. I wondered whether I had been promoted day by day or whether the person who had promoted me had degenerated with each passing day.

My luck may have been due to the fact that those revolutionary militants and I were almost the same age. Before the Anti-Culture Movement, we had gotten along quite well. I used to chat with them and listen to their lewd conversations. The old intellectuals suffered in the Anti-Culture Movement not mainly because of political heterodoxy, but because of the generation gap. Lu Chen-pai was an example.

This senior scholar, who intentionally bent his back to make himself look old, knew very little about politics, let alone Maoism. However, he had been very much petted by the former leaders, because he was as shrew as a *shi ye*. The *shi ye* used to be a special kind of professional in feudal China specializing in legal, fiscal, and secretarial matters and working as private consultants to the officials in local administrations called *ya men*. They were acquainted with all the tricks of feudal bureaucracy and were the key link between the high officials and the rank and file. In dealing with the former leaders of our publishing house, Lu used the same techniques that the *shi ye* had used and adopted the same attitude and protocol that high officials had shown to the emperor. All three of our former leaders—Li, Chen, and Ch'i—had been very comfortable with Lu, and had always praised him for his "loyalty to the Party." They addressed him respectfully as "Lu Lao." In Chinese, *lao* means old. Following the surname with *lao* is a respectful way of addressing people. These former leaders used to say, "Although Lu Lao does not talk much, he has a red heart and loves our new society and our Party." Before liberation, Lu had for years been secretary to Wu

---

*Kung ch'u is the oldest style of classical drama in China.

Mei-sun, an entrepreneur and a real authority in Chinese classics. Thus Lu knew many people in literary circles, and was considered to be a petty authority on Chinese classics after liberation. Now, in the Anti-Culture Movement, he was placed in the category of "reactionary academic authorities." As such, he could have suffered less if he had known how to deal with the young militants properly.

Lu's old bureaucratic manner, which might cater to the taste of old officials, was worse than playing the lute to a cow when used before these young and semiliterate militants; it had only a negative effect. For example, old officials might enjoy his habit of bowing and scraping, as well as cringing and smiling obsequiously, but the young militants found them funny and sickening. In front of leaders, he was not accustomed to turn his back and leave right away. He used to take a few steps backward while facing them before he turned round. This behavior, in the eyes of young militants, was suggestive of a clown. Therefore, it was fun to struggle against him.

In dealing with these revolutionary militants, one did not have to be very logical or clear-minded. If one reasoned with them seriously, one would either be enraged or forced to commit suicide. However, one should not be too senseless and thoughtless either, or he would be at the end of his tether. Lu Chen-pai was never a major target to be struggled against, but always a supporting target. This role was very easy to play. All one had to do was just take a submissive attitude and not overtax himself. Alas, Lu Chen-pai was too submissive. Once he was seen shaking, and the rebels, to make a mountain out of a molehill, ordered him to step out of the line of supporting targets. "Damn you! Lu, come here, come! Don't put on a pitiable look. Why are you shaking?"

Lu shook even more violently, and instantly replied in his old way, "Ya, ya, ya!"

The young militants were upset. "What do you mean by 'ya, ya, ya'? We didn't ask you anything, so why did you reply 'yes'? Yes for what? We are telling you not to tremble."

To these unreasonable revolutionaries, one should not or need not give an answer. If I had been Lu, I would have kept my mouth shut and tried my best not to shake. If I could have managed to do so, so much the better; if not, then I would have let them reprimand me. That's all. At least I would not have had to utter a word. Unfortunately, Lu stammered out an answer in his habitual way, "I deserve to die! I—I—I—I deserve—deserve to—to die!"

Then the young militants raised their voices, "Why do you deserve to die? What crimes did you commit? Make a confession now!"

Terrified, Lu trembled fiercely and was about to collapse to the floor. The young militants could not help laughing and ordered Lu to step back into the line of other targets. As is the case with most people, once you have developed a habit, it will become instinctive. Lu Chen-pai must never have walked naturally in the awe-inspiring court. As he always took quick, short steps backward when he took leave of his superiors, he took a few quick, short steps backward before he returned to the line of monsters and demons. People who had some knowledge of court etiquette could certainly tell that this manner of walking was meant to show his respect to the superiors before him. It was regrettable that the people who knew this kind of thing were all in the cowshed and those who were issuing orders on the stage were too provincial to know anything about old etiquette.

These young militants shouted again, "Lu Chen-pai, don't play possum. Don't you know how to walk? You are not abreast of others in the line. Dress to the right and left."

Poor Lu Chen-pai had never had military drill, and did not know how to dress to the right or left. All he knew was to take quick, short steps forward or backward. After he had tried for some time, he still could never keep abreast of the others in the line. This made the young militants furious. They shouted again, "Don't play possum!"

At the end of the assembly, the supporting targets were driven away from the stage on the order, "Monsters and demons, go away!" The Chinese equivalent of "go away" is "roll down." But everybody just stepped down. Lu was so frightened that he was unable to walk in a normal way. Maybe he was intending to follow the order to the letter, thinking how to "roll down" from the stage. He hesitated for a while, and then took a few steps backward. While doing so, he was not aware that the rebels who had acted as escorts had not yet "rolled down" with monsters and demons and were still there. He hit a militant, who in turn gave him a heavy push, "Damn you! You are playing possum and stepping on my toes?" The push drove him to the middle of the stage and he became more frightened. He retreated to the other side, only to step on another militant's toes. Again that militant scolded him severely and pushed him away. He had probably never undergone an experience like this since he was born. He seemed not to know how to step down the several steps from the stage and looked as though he were really going to "roll down." As the young revolutionary militants in the publishing house were a little more civilized than those of other institutions, and afraid that an accident might happen, they commanded me, "Wong, you take him down." I was glad to. Because he was an elderly person, it was proper that I should give him a hand.

In 1968, as the entire country was locked in internecine warfare, the carefree nonfactionists were able to excuse themselves from work, but I had to go to the office every day. I envied them so much that I again resorted to my magic weapon of stealing sputum of the others and got several months' sick leave. With leisure at home, I felt eager to do some reading, but all the readable books had either been taken away by the Red Guards or thrown away or burned by me. During that period, anything I could borrow from my friends or relatives, whether it was social science or politics or history or literature, was as precious as gold. Fortunately, the ruling machine was now not as efficient as before, and large numbers of "materials for internal circulation only" began to be smuggled into the hands of the public and even of a person like me, who was at the lowest rung of the social ladder. Chinese translations of Fairbank's *The United States & China*, Nixon's *Six Crises*, and Harriman's *Memoir* found their way to my home. Most of them had to be returned the next day, but I never failed to keep my promise. Sometimes in order to finish reading a book on time, I skipped meals and cut down on hours of sleep. Moreover, I took good care of these books, never damaging a corner of the page. Therefore, my friends were glad to lend me books. I also paid for reading these books, by volunteering to translate for some friends works they had been assigned to translate in their work units. Thus I had access to some originals such as Margaret Thatcher, Indira Gandhi, and King Hussein.

Later, something happened that was like sending charcoal in snowy weather. Someone did me a favor by informing me that her brother was a Red Guard in the publication system and had been my escort and also a supervisor for all the monsters and demons of this system. He had asked us monsters and demons to tell him briefly our names, crimes, and labels before giving us an admonitory talk. My oral report on my identification and my unique attitude of acknowledging crimes had impressed him very much, she said. My friend's words reminded me of a special scene of which I had a vague recollection. Sometimes when I was escorted as a supporting target to a general meeting of the entire publication system, the escort had not been a rebel from our publishing house. There had been too many escorts to remember. He must have been from some other publishing house, because I could in no way remember him. Now my friend told me that her brother possessed some English books which had been confiscated from the houses they had searched and the contents of which he did not know, as he could not read English. Therefore, he was willing to lend them to me on condition that I not show them to anybody else. This condition I readily accepted. He gave me the opportunity of reading some 1940s or 1930s copies of *National Geographic*, all of which were so dear to me that I read them from cover to cover, even the ads. Among the books he lent me, there was a copy of Ellery Queen's *Greek Coffin Mystery*, which captivated me so much that I set myself the task of rendering it into Chinese. Almost everyone who knew me thought I was crazy, for at that time across the country there was not a single institution working on any publication other than Mao's *Little Red Book*. What was the good of translating an American novel? The work might not only be a waste of energy, but might cause trouble for me if it was known to someone who liked to poke his nose into other people's business. However, I firmly believed that human beings, especially civilized people like the Chinese, could not endure a period of spiritual hunger for too long, and my effort at this translation would surely not be a waste. Several years later, when a reorganized publishing house was desperately in need of materials for publication, my ready-made translation satisfied its need just in time and turned out to be the first American novel published in China after the Anti-Culture Movement.

CHAPTER 9

"The Cultural Revolution is Very Good"

"THE CULTURAL REVOLUTION IS GOOD!"

"The Cultural Revolution is very good!"

"The Cultural Revolution is really good!"

These slogans were heard every minute across the nation between 1966 and 1977. These official slogans sounded ridiculous, but they portended the approach of the end of the regime, which was what I had always wished for, because, as the proverb goes, "When God wants one to die, He first makes him mad."

I had no aversion at all to my role as a monster and demon in the Anti-Culture Movement. Bearing in mind Confucius' words, "Under a sensible and enlightened administration, it is shameful to stay in poverty and in straits; while under a brutal and ruthless rule, it would be a shame to be rich and honored." I deemed it an honor to be classified as a "monster and demon" by the Communist regime.

However, I was in great pain at times during the Anti-Culture Movement. It was not just because the movement had hurt or insulted me greatly, but because I could not take care of those I loved. I was tortured by helplessness to offer any protection to my family. I could protect neither my parents nor my children.

The month of August 1966 witnessed a nationwide house-searching campaign. Almost every household was subject to search, and it seemed that almost anyone who had joined a rebel faction was eligible to search any resident's house. There was no need for approval from the authorities.

Bang! Bang! Bang! Bang! There was a series of loud, hurried knocks at the door of our house late one night. We were startled, but no one in the neighborhood bothered to rush out to inquire what was happening, as they normally would have done, because in those days house-searching had become a daily occurrence. It was not something to be astonished by.

What surprised me was that the first group to search our house was not from my organization, the publishing house. In theory, monsters and demons should have had the "privilege" of their homes being searched first. As it turned out, this group came from my mother's organization, the Shanghai Traditional Opera School, where she had been a teacher of literature for many years. At the outset, the Shanghai Traditional Opera School had been dedicated solely to the training of *kung ch'u* actors and later developed into a school for nearly all local operas. As a devotee of *kung ch'u* opera, my mother loved her job because the students she was teaching would become famous actors and actresses in the future. She used the highly polished and sophisticated *kung ch'u* drama scripts as textbooks for her class. This way, she endeavored to help students both understand the scripts and acquire a thorough knowledge of classic literature. This endeavor was later to be considered a crime during the Anti-Culture Movement—the spreading of feudalistic poison. Now, as the entire society had been called on to rebel against the cultural heritage, the students who had been taught to be proud of our civilization became very savage. The first group who came to search our house included my mother's students who had been exposed to quite a few classical drama scripts and who later became famous performing actors and actresses, but were at that time small rascals. It was not their fault. The criminal was the one who encouraged these youngsters to be thugs. They followed this helmsman blindly and thought of rascally revolutionary acts.

My mother's political status in her organization fell into the category of "revolutionary masses." According to Mao's theory, revolutionary masses should not be subject to proletarian dictatorship; hence there was a lack of legitimacy in the search of our house. Accordingly, the first sentence these youngsters uttered after having crowded into our house was, "We've come for Sweeping Four Olds." As the Central Committee of the Chinese Communist Party had just put forward the slogan, "Sweep old culture, old customs, old habits and old thoughts," everybody, regardless of his political status, was supposed to participate in the destruction of the above four olds. They considered their search of our house justifiable, although I have never really understood the difference between searching a resident's house and sweeping the four olds.

My whole family got up because of the sudden arrival of these ten or more young militants. At first, they inquired about gold, silver, and jewelry. To their great disappointment, we had none. Then they interrogated my parents about "preparation for restoration."* These were things totally alien to my parents, but the young militants refused to believe what they said and kept pressing them to surrender what they did not have. I was worried that my father might lose patience and say something offensive to those young rascals, thus inviting trouble. Then I got an idea to divert attention from my father by saying, "It's impossible to find any preparation for restoration here, because all members of this household except me are revolutionary masses closely following the Chinese Communist Party. I am a rightist, but also trying very hard to follow the Communist Party." Apparently, the word "rightist" had some magical power for them.

A boy, who is now a leading actor and has led a troupe giving performances overseas, was, at that time, short and skinny with two large eyes. He remarked in bewilderment, "What? You are a rightist? With a hat?"

I tried hard to refrain from laughing. How could he have expected a rightist to be without a hat? He must have thought that as I looked quite young, I could not be a rightist who had been given the label in 1957, but in the current movement numerous people were attacked as rightist by the big-character posters, and he thought I might be one of them. Then I gave full play to my expertise of making a confession

---

* "Preparation for restoration" is a special term concocted by the Communists denoting items such as the records of usurious loans and former land holdings kept secretly by members of the overthrown classes who, as ascertained by the Communists, were destined to dream of a comeback.

while hanging my head and lowering my tone, "Yes, I launched an attack on our great Party by taking advantage of the Campaign of Free Airing of Views in 1957 and thus was labeled a rightist. I was guilty. I apologize for my crime. Right now I am apologizing to Chairman Mao and you, the young revolutionary militants."

A woman student took a step toward me. "What kind of crime did you commit? Make a faithful confession." She had a lovely face, with two shining eyes and a long, fat queue hanging behind her back. She could have been quite graceful and attractive, if she had had some poise. At this moment she had none of the bearing characteristic of an elegant young lady, as she played the role of female prosecutor.

"Yes," I hung my head lower. As an amateur of *kung ch'u*, Peking Opera, and once a fan of Soochow and Yangchow storytelling, I was very familiar with how interrogation was conducted in court in ancient China. Making the past serve the present, I now used "young militant" and "the Party" as substitutes for "Your Honor" and "His Majesty" respectively, and acted as in an ancient drama. "You young militants are high above me. Please listen to my story. I regret having attacked unscrupulously our great Communist Party. By miscalculating the situation, I indulged in a vain attempt at staging a comeback of the capitalist system. Just like a mantis attempting to stop a chariot, I overrated myself and tried to hold back the overwhelmingly superior force of the advance of the wheel of history. I smeared the image of the Soviet Union, which has been the lighthouse of the Communist world. I also vilified the leadership of our great Communist Party."

In imitation of the way in which a clown recited a written plaint in the Peking opera *Fa Meng Temple*, I reported my crimes in one breath and this apparently amazed these young militants, all of whom listened with wide open eyes. Having only a hazy notion about my crimes, they did not know how to criticize me even if they wanted to. They made no response and just cut short my recitation. Then they started to rummage through drawers and cupboards, boxes and chests, while calling their action "destruction of the four olds." They also knocked on the walls and ceilings here and there, with the hope of discovering a hidden cell or inner room where some secret treasures might be concealed. Of course, they made no discovery of anything precious, but did succeed in finding some "preparation for restoration."

I was around to help them with their search, showing my willingness to cooperate. When they went through the drawers in my desk, they discovered a bunch of bills of various denominations issued by the Bank of Communications. I explained to them that these bills were my collection, issued when my grandfather was director of that bank, his English signature printed on them being originally written by my father. That was why I collected and treasured them. They had already been out of circulation for several decades, since long before the "liberation," and therefore had nothing to do with any intent to restore the old regime. The young militants refused to accept my explanation and insisted that what they had found was exactly the "preparation for restoration." The fact was that because they were so eager to discover the so-called preparation for restoration, they had no choice but to reject my explanation.

They harassed the whole family all night and left at dawn. Besides my memorable collection of unused or useless bills, they took away some jewels of little value, which, to them, were precious, and some Manchurian gowns and high-heeled shoes, of which they said, "All of them are the four olds. Look what a degenerating and dissipated life you are leading!"

The real treasure taken away by them was a scroll of calligraphy written by Chao Meng-fu, the famous calligrapher of the Sung and Yuan dynasties, some seven hundred years ago, for which my mother had traded some of her valuable jewels before "liberation" and which she had treasured ever since.

These poor rascals could not find too much cash. I felt sorry for them. It cost them a lot of energy to discover some bond certificates of over one thousand RMB (*renminbi*). However, before they attempted to take it away, they were blocked by Granny Liu, who, as my mother's nanny, had never left my mother and was very healthy though nearing ninety years of age. She, an illiterate woman, had never cared about things outside the household, let alone politics. She shouted desperately when she thought her life savings were being threatened, "What the hell do you covet my blood-and-sweat savings for? This is the money reserved for my coffin. Who dares take it away?"

The young militants, intent on removing them, said arrogantly, "All the riches accumulated through exploitation should be confiscated."

"Whom did I exploit?" Granny Liu was outraged. "I have been a

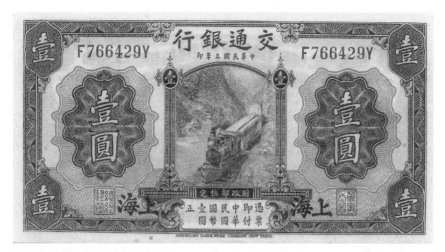

Bills issued by the Bank of Communications. My grandfather's signature, "T.S. Wong," was originally written by my father. My collection of these bills was taken during the Anti-Culture Movement as "preparation for restoration."

servant all my life. Whom did I exploit? Tell me whom I exploited? Tell me! Tell me!"

These young militants stared at her blankly and for a while remained speechless. Then I tried to ease the tension by telling them softly, "It's true she has been a servant all her life. She has been nothing else."

"What's her class origin?" they asked me after some hesitation. "What's her family background?"

Liu answered herself. "My family? I was born in a poor family. I suffered as a child bride in my native village. No property. Little food. That was why I moved to the city to be a servant. You guys just can't imagine how miserable a life I led in the past."

"She was a poor peasant by class origin." I said again, trying to alleviate the tension. "It is clearly shown in the census record. The policeman in charge of household registration of this area can verify it. You can check with him."

They were not too impervious to reasoning, and returned the bond certificates to Granny Liu.

In spite of the fact that I helped Granny Liu ward off the Red Guards' robbery by telling them her poor class background, I knew very well that the real person who had brought this luck to her was her darling son. Granny Liu was widowed without a child at an early age at the turn of this century. Having adopted a nephew as her son, she had left her native village for Peking and started her long term of service as a maid in my maternal grandfather's house. With free room and board and a good salary and her thrift, she saved a certain amount of money. Influenced by traditional ideas, she purchased some land in her village with all her savings. She did so in her son's name, as she conceived him as her rightful heir. What frustrated her, however, was the fact that her son was a typical idler who, instead of taking a decent job, goofed off by eating, drinking, whoring, and gambling and pawned it each time Granny Liu bought a piece of land. The more she purchased, the more he pawned. Nevertheless, Granny Liu used her new savings to make a last purchase, and admonished her son with great expectations, "Son, don't pawn it this time. Land is like the root of life to us farmers. You ought to work hard at it. If you do, you will become rich some day and glorify our family." However, just like what had happened before, her son squandered that piece of land. In utmost disappointment, Granny Liu severed all her relationships with her son, and started saving up again, but by that time liberation was approaching. Shortly after liberation, the Land Reform Movement was launched and everybody was classified into a class status according to the size of the land he owned. Given the total amount of the land which Granny Liu had once owned, had it not been gambled away by her "godsend" son, she would certainly have been labeled a landlord and compelled to go back to her native village. She would have undergone the ordeal of struggle and, if she could have survived the ordeal at all, she would have lived in humiliation for the rest of her life. She would never have had the audacity to argue with the Red Guards.

In spite of what the Reds did that night, I was indebted to these young militants for sparing my life. While they were ransacking the drawers one by one and about to go through the one containing my writings, I went up to them and said, "These are all my manuscripts for publication." They showed no interest in them and told me to submit them to my "organization" for review. "Disinfect them if they have poison or bacteria." With this they turned away. This incident was sufficient to remind me that I should heighten my vigilance.

As a matter of fact, that drawer contained my journals written over the past several decades. Numerous paragraphs of my diary were devoted to attacking the Chinese Communist Party, especially Mao Tse-tung, whom I hated so intensely. Had my diary been taken away or had the young militants scanned it on the spot and come across one of these paragraphs, it would have been a fatal disaster to me. I do not know if I would have been arrested right away if my diary had been found, but one or two years later, in the campaign of "purifying the class ranks," many people were persecuted or even executed simply for blaming the Chinese Communist Party or Mao Tse-tung in a diary or in personal correspondence.

I was lucky that I was promptly reminded of my diary by these young militants. After their departure, I destroyed all my journals and avoided a disaster.

The destruction of my diary was a huge job. In those days the wall posters reported from time to time that someone had been discovered burning something. In the course of the Anti-Culture Movement, whenever one was seen in such an activity he could be thought to be destroying evidence of his crimes and, therefore, could be arrested. If anyone had seen me burning paper or seen even the light or smoke of fire, I would have been informed against. Flushing my diary away in the toilet might cause the toilet to become clogged, and thus I would be exposed. What should I do then? For the safety of the entire family, I had to sacrifice myself. I shut the door and windows of the bathroom, tore dozens of my diaries to pieces, and then burned only two or three pages in the bathtub at a time, so that the fire was very weak and gave off no light. When ashes were accumulated to a certain amount, I flushed them down the toilet. To burn up dozens of diary books in this way took me a whole night. It was a hot summer. The smoke and heat in the tightly closed room and staying awake all night was really terrible, but I was happy that I had removed a hidden peril. Compared to the safety of my family, my personal suffering was nothing.

After that, house-searching grew in intensity. Under the slogans of "destroying the four olds" and "making a clean sweep of all monsters and demons," the Red Guards and rebel groups were given to beating, smashing, looting, and burning everything they could lay their hands on. Many responsible people were also burning their own things, for a single character they wrote on paper could be interpreted as anti-Party. It would be safer if one was left with no written words on paper. Of course, as there was nothing absolute, destroying possible evidence did not necessarily mean safety. There were instances in which those who had unintentionally left a fragment of Mao's picture among the heap of ashes were severly punished, because destruction of Mao's picture was a towering crime. Therefore, if one wanted to be absolutely safe, he might as well burn himself up. Not until then did I understand how lucky I was to have already submitted my manuscript of *Chi-ku lu* to the publishing house, and how fortunate that they were now lying in the safe, inaccessible to both the Red Guards and myself, and might remain intact throughout the movement. If these manuscripts had been in my house at that time, I would have burned them up with my diary, either before or after these young militants came to our house.

Several days later, the revolutionary practice of house-searching was further developed. Searchers became crazier. They paid less and less regard to ethics and protocol. The second search of our house was carried out by a rebel group from the banking system, to which no member of our family belonged. This gang consisted of approximately twenty persons, male and female, old and young, and looked much more rebellious than those young militants who had done the first search. This group of rebels were hedged in with no rules or regulations. All they cared about was money and jewelry. When they failed to find any, they started to make holes in the walls in the hope that some miracle would happen. But they just wasted the whole day.

Although they were interested only in valuables, they styled themselves "revolutionary rebels." They played the drama of class struggle to cover up their real motive. In this situation, the only way for me to protect my family was to step forward and draw enemy fire on myself. Just as in dealing with the young militants last time, I revealed my political status as a rightist. Unexpectedly, these searchers were less curious than those former young militants. Hearing I was a rightist, instead of bothering to inquire about my crimes, they pulled long faces and said, "As a rightist, how dare you not make a faithful confession of the whereabouts of the money and jewelry of your family?"

I told them that we had none of these things, but they would not take my word. All I could do was stand in front of them with my head hung. As there were many of them, they took turns interrogating me. When the first one became tired of questioning me, he or she would go away to search, leaving me to the next inquisitor, and so on, and when one got tired of searching, he or she would come to act as an interrogator. Although this was of little avail, they kept after me all the time. This process went on until late at night, when they finally seemed to be convinced that this was not a household containing what they wanted. They departed in disappointment.

Compared with those homes subjected to repeated searches, the inconvenience the two searches caused us was nothing. Some households were even more unfortunate because they were harassed by the notorious rebel organization called Pickets of the Western District, from Peking, which consisted solely of children of high officials and specialized in so-called destructive searching, that is, they did not take away anything but smashed every object which they thought was in their way, including kitchen utensils. They were thugs in the truest sense of this word. During that period, almost every household lived in constant fear of the arrival of Pickets of the Western District, which could occur at anytime. As nobody could foretell that my family would not be harassed for a third time, our hearts were in our mouths every day, awaiting the possible arrival of the next group of uninvited guests.

In my household, the only one unperturbed was Granny Liu. It was not because she had a good class origin so that she did not have to be afraid of those revolutionaries. No, not at all. To the best of my knowledge, since coming to our home she had regarded it as her own and always had our safety and well-being on her mind. Her detachment from the Red Guards and rebel groups came from the association these people brought up in her mind.

After the searchers had left our home, Granny Liu remarked casually, "Ah, these people must also be in the organization."

At first I misunderstood her and answered, "Who knows, and who cares if they are Party members or League members or if they are not?"

Then she said, "I'm pretty sure they know boxing."

"What!" I was surprised. "What are you talking about? What boxing?"

"Boxers were rebels. These Red Guards and Boxers are the same thing," Granny Liu said.

Then it occurred to me that she was talking about the Boxer Rebellion about seventy years before.

It seemed that past events were leaping vividly before her eyes. "At that time, almost all the males in my village were forced to join the Boxers."

"Were they immune from swords and bullets?" I asked with curiosity.

"Yes," Granny Liu seemed still convinced. "They practiced *kung-fu* every day."

"Were they honest and straightforward, or did they kill people and pillage the village?" I was still curious.

"Oh, they only killed foreigners, not villagers who were their relatives and friends." Granny Liu apparently still held them in respect, "The Boxers were very strict in discipline."

"Then, can you tell any differences between Boxers and those who came to search our house?" I asked.

"No, not much difference," answered Granny Liu. "Boxers also had red bands on their arms. But they were better, because they never attempted to rob poor people like me."

The red bands and the attempted confiscation of her bond certificates were carved deep into Granny Liu's memory.

"Did Boxers also search ordinary people's houses?" I asked.

"No," Granny Liu replied, "I never heard of Boxers ever searching their houses. However, I've seen a lot of houses searched. While your grandpa was staying in Peking, house-searching was part of daily life."

I called my maternal grandfather "Grandpa." He was one of the founding members of China's modern judiciary and had been principal of the first law school in modern China. He was also involved in politics. Once he was summoned by Yuan Shih-kai for consultation. When he stepped out of Yuan's drawing room and was asked about his impression of Yuan, he said, "He's a damned fool!" He was a dissident in Peking during the early period of the Republic.

"At that time," Granny Liu continued, "in Peking, house-searching was just a common occurrence. Sometimes the gate was sealed after the house was searched."

"Who searched whom?" I asked.

"I don't know," Granny Liu replied, "even your gandpa's house was once searched. I did not know why or how. Probably it was a misunderstanding. I saw a group of people come and search your grandpa's house, in which I was a servant at that time. Your grandpa was not home, so Chang Fu—one of your grandpa's male servants—hurriedly went to tell him about it. 'Sir, please don't come home right now, because there are people searching our house!' Your grandpa was outraged and hurried back angrily. He called someone on the phone. In the end, they said it was a misunderstanding, and apologized. But your grandpa didn't let them go. 'How dare you search my house!' He lost his temper. Actually it was nothing. At that time, people searched each other's houses. It was finally dismissed as a misunderstanding."

It seemed that Granny Liu took it for granted that one's house could be subjected to search without a warrant. Her narrative drove home to me that history repeats itself and that the Anti-Culture Movement and the Red Guards were actually phenomena passed down from the past and traceable to the same cause as both the Boxer Rebellion and the warlords who ran rampant for a time in Chinese history.

One day, amid the terror of house-searching, I met my cousin, the son of my second uncle. He told me that my third uncle, who once lived in Shanghai's most famous apartment building, popularly known as "Eighteen Stories," had committed suicide together with his wife by jumping out of the window. They were probably the first couple who had taken their own lives since the outbreak of the Anti-Culture Movement. Needless to say, I broke this terrible news to my parents as soon as I returned home. They were very sad and worried about how to break the news to my grandfather. They were also concerned that my grandfather's house might be searched someday.

My grandfather had had a quite modern and spacious residence since the 1930s. However, he was always of the opinion that children should stay separate once they got married. Therefore, my uncles and aunties moved out one after another after their marriage. By the time of "liberation," only my grandfather, my stepgrandmother, and one of my aunties, who was single, lived in this big house. We visited them occasionally. Now there was a regulation forbidding all monsters and demons to contact one another; therefore, we voluntarily stopped visiting him to avoid suspicion. Since all of us were known in that neighborhood, we did not dare to pass my grandfather's house for fear of being spotted by his neighbors.

I should therefore be grateful to Chu Cheng-jong, Jane's brother, an elementary school teacher, who had joined a rebel faction and wore a red band around his arm. He was loyal to his friends. He came to our home as usual even during the period of unbridled house-searching. When he understood that we were very much concerned about my grandfather but unable to visit him, he got on his bicycle and cycled there. He carefully read the big-character poster on the gate, observed the activity outside the house, and came back to tell us all about it. From what he said, we could infer that my grandfather was pretty safe. In a situation like this, property and everything else were nothing compared to one's life. However, our safety was at the mercy of others and we were totally helpless.

Jane used to enjoy great popularity with everybody, for she had always been on good terms with them. That is why she had never been a target in any previous political movement. This time she was not immune from harassment, not as a criminal but as an onlooker. The fierce torture of teachers by their students made her tremble. In spite of the fact that the firepower had never strafed her, she was under constant fear of being the next target. This was a situation in which I could neither help nor console her.

Both my father and my mother suffered terribly during the Anti-Culture Movement. My father had always been cautious about his words and deeds and had never transgressed against any regulations or acted inappropriately in his organization. His work performance provided no excuse for the revolutionary rebels to harass him. He knew the English, French, German, Russian, and Japanese languages, and had done a lot of translation of scientific and technological materials. Unable to find fault with him in these respects, the movement activists classified him as a capitalist. As a matter of fact, he had never operated any enterprise of his own. He did possess a certain number of shares of foreign companies, but the number was small. Who cared how many shares he had? They just labeled him a "capitalist," led him away, and put him to work in a plant—this was the way those revolutionary rebels dealt with people like my father. From then on, my father dressed in rags and worked as a coolie from morning to evening.

My mother's situation was even more deplorable. After the liberation, she sincerely believed in the revolution, because out of a sense of justice she had been deeply disappointed with the corruption under the previous regime. About all the official propaganda she did not have the least doubts. She thought she had finally found the truth by following the path pointed out by the great Communist Party. However, the Communist Party did not appreciate her faith. My mother, in the Communists' eyes, had a bad class origin, a reactionary family background. They made a secret remark on my mother's dossier, "This person should not be trusted," as they did with other people of such family background.

In this heavenly society, everybody had a mysterious file unknown and inaccessible to them. In the Anti-Culture Movement, these dossiers, formerly controlled only by the personnel departments, were leaked to different rebel factions, who used them as weapons to attack one another. In the tumult, the activists in my mother's organization, the Shanghai Traditional Opera School, relied on her dossier to struggle against her. However, my mother had no aversion to the way she was treated, because she had always considered herself to be lagging far behind the proletarian vanguard of workers and peasants. Since she had sincere wishes to remold her ideology, she took the so-called Cultural Revolution as a good opportunity to receive education and criticism from the masses. She willingly obeyed all the orders given to her. Ironically, the rebels and Red Guards did not buy this kind of attitude. They knew nothing about ideological remolding, nor dreamed of its existence. All they needed at that time was to press my mother to confess how she had opposed the Party, socialism, and Chairman Mao. Mother tried to explain to them that she had always been loyal to the Party and to Chairman Mao, only to evoke great fury from these activists, who said, "What! You love the Communist Party? How can you? How dare you! A person with a family background like yours is not qualified to love the Communist Party!"

My mother could in no way agree with their conclusions: She insisted that she had never lied to the Party which, to her, was just like God. She also said that she wanted to join the ranks of the revolutionary masses so that she could better follow the great leader Chairman Mao, whom she looked up to as a redeemer. Her attempt to plead innocence really sounded ironic, for it was the revolutionary masses whom she had aspired to identify herself with that tried to take away her faith in the Party. To me, this situation would have been very easy to deal with. You just chimed in with them and said whatever they liked to hear. Mother strongly opposed this attitude of mine, and did not take my advice. Only on one occasion did she accept my suggestion which, in hindsight, might not have been a good one.

During the nationwide internecine struggles, fighting between the two rebel factions in the Shanghai Traditional Opera School was quite fierce. My mother tried to treat everyone equally, as she wanted to follow the great Chairman's teaching of respecting the revolutionary initiative of the masses. However, to her great disappointment, the Red Guards and rebels were not only fake revolutionaries but real self-serving brigands. The fierce struggles between them were not conducted by debate but by fists. Mother was quite confused as to what course to take. I offered her my suggestion, "The safest place at this period is the cowshed. You just stay there and study Chairman Mao's works. Neither of the factions will annoy you and you won't have to join either of them." My mother thought this suggestion was not bad and was feasible. For the first time she took my suggestion. For a time, it really worked, because Mother did obtain peace in the cowshed, which was like an island isolated from the turmoil of the internecine struggles. Monsters and demons, according to Mao, were supposed to have no political rights, including the right to participate in struggles, and all they were allowed to do was study his works and do manual labor, to which Mother had no aversion at all.

Later on, my suggestion turned out bad. When Mao was worried about the nationwide chaos, he sent to each cultural or educational institution a "Mao Tse-tung Thought Propaganda Team" consisting of soldiers and workers to enforce the union among struggling factions. The team took over the leadership of each institution, and was authorized to carry out the campaign of "purifying the class ranks." All the members in the cowshed were regarded as suspects and were subject to investigation. They could be liberated only after being cleared. First of all, the team had to find out which rebel faction had put each monster and demon into the cowshed, and then check with that faction to see if the reasons for labeling were valid or not. In my mother's case, no rebel faction was responsible for putting her in the cowshed; she had gone on her own. Therefore, the team could find no one to work with for my mother's "liberation." The leader of the Mao Tse-tung Thought Team said to Mother, "Since you voluntarily came into the cowshed, there is no way we can set you free before we make a thorough investigation into your case." His words made my mother continue to play the role of monster and demon while waiting for the results of the investigation. As she always had faith in the social system and never adopted the cynical attitude I did, that period at which she was treated as a monster and demon by the Mao Tse-tung Thought Team was extremely painful and difficult for her.

The futility of my attitude toward that kind of social situation and my way of dealing with it was proved by the behavior of Uncle Yue, the younger brother of my tutor Master Yue. Although in his sixties at that time, Uncle Yue was still healthy and robust. He spoke with a marked accent of his Honan dialect. He started learning martial arts as early as his childhood, and for a time was a member of Hong Ch'iang Hui, the Red Spear Organization, which was a secret society in his native village. Later, his major interest switched to liberal arts and he became a disciple of a famous Chinese scholar called T'ang Wen-chih. He graduated from the Institute of Chinese Classics in Wuhsi, but he could not land a literature-related job after graduation, because of the chaotic situation of the War of Resistance against Japan. He became a tea merchant in Anhwei Province. During the war, Master Yue was a poor middle school teacher in Shanghai and unable to support his wife and children, and Uncle Yue volunteered to give them shelter and financial assistance. After the war, Master Yue's fame in the *tai-chi* boxing circles became such that it brought his family a quite comfortable life. Then Uncle Yue moved to Shanghai and lived with his elder brother, but did not take any job. All he did was read Chinese classics, study yoga, and compose poems. He did not like socializing, but was amicable. He was very friendly to some of Master Yue's pupils and liked to chat with them. I had the honor of being one of them. He was always very nice to me, and never cared that I was a rightist. After Master Yue passed away, I still visited him from time to time. One thing for which I shall always feel indebted to him, and which still remains vividly in my memory, is that when he learned from our casual conversation about my grandfather's melancholy over the damage and confiscation by the Red Guards of all his plants, which had been his only favorite pastime, Uncle Yue, who also dabbled with plants, instantly went to his small garden and picked some saplings of ivy and azalea and put them into pots and asked me to give them to my grandfather. What a nice and timely favor!

When the Anti-Culture Movement began, Uncle Yue, owing to his lack of any complicated political and social connections, managed to stay out of trouble, and continued to do so until the campaign of "Sweeping Four Olds" was launched. Given the fact that he had a large collection of sewn-bound books in his house, he inevitably became a target of search. But since search was at that time a common practice that affected almost every decent citizen, he should not have felt badly. Owing to my philosophy that one should not mind enduring some temporary hardships to stage a comeback, I earnestly advised Uncle Yue to avoid arguing or reasoning with the Red Guards or revolutionary rebels, just as I did my parents to enter the "cowshed" as a haven of refuge. However, Uncle Yue did not buy my words. When it came time for him to have the honor of a group of Red Guards' presence in his house to do away with his "four olds," which consisted chiefly of Chinese classics, Uncle Yue tried to reason with these heroic rascals, but to no avail, and in the end a dispute arose between them. Never accustomed to reasoning, the Red Guards became so outraged that they grabbed Uncle Yue by the collar and dragged him out of his house, with the intention of humiliating him in public. They put a tall chair in front of the gate of his house and ordered him to stand on it to receive mass criticism. Had I been in this position, I would certainly have obeyed their order without uttering a word. Whatever they would have said in criticizing me would not have bothered me at all. I would not have taken it as an insult, because in my mind these hooligans were not human beings. Uncle Yue apparently was not thinking that way. All of a sudden, he kicked the tall chair into the air and, before people recollected themselves from the stun, jumped up, grasped the chair, and broke one of its legs. With the leg as a weapon, he ran into his house and leapt up the staircase, which was so narrow as to allow only one person to pass. Standing in the middle of the staircase and holding the chair leg, he shouted, "Damn you! Whoever dares to come up can come up. Let's die together!"

Reared in the heroic spirit of "fear neither hardship nor death," a quotation from the Great Helmsman Mao, these young revolutionaries were really like "the sun at 8:00 A.M. or 9:00 A.M.," just as the Helmsman described them. They hid themselves at the foot of the staircase, shouting slogans vehemently, but none of these heroes dared to go up the staircase. After a little while, they retreated from the battlefield with courage, pride, and an air of triumph.

Later, Uncle Yue said to me, "In my early years, when I was a member of Hong Ch'iang Hui, I saw various kinds of people, ranging from real heroes to cowards. I know how to deal with those scoundrels who always bully the weak but fear the strong. Your bookish way of dealing with this kind of people will never work." It seems that he was right and I was wrong.

My children also suffered. My eldest son had just entered junior high when the Anti-Culture Movement began, and my second and youngest sons were in elementary school. For a while there were still classes, but youngsters had already been much influenced by the chaotic society. Those students with army, worker, or peasant family backgrounds were called "children of red categories," while those with bad class origins were called "children of black categories." Children of red categories had a sense of superiority and used to call their classmates of black categories "sons of bitches." It was a common practice in the classroom for some children of red categories to shout suddenly, "Sons of bitches, stand up!" and those with "bad" family backgrounds had to rise immediately and tolerate whatever humiliation or personal insults were heaped upon them. Sometimes children of red categories even beat those of black categories with a leather belt. Fortunately, my children were easygoing and went along very well with their classmates, and had no personal enemies in their classes; therefore, neither of them ever had his face bashed in. However, due to my status as a rightist, my sons' "bad" family background was known, and each time their names were called, they went up obediently and stood in the line of "sons of bitches." To my children, this practice was really a cruel, heart-rending torture. They were only teenagers, or even not as old as ten, but had already been repeatedly humiliated in this inhuman way, not for their own fault, but simply because they were my children. I, as their father, was in such a helpless situation as not to be able to protect them. This caused me great pain.

The humiliation brought on my children was insignificant compared to the waste of their youth. Only a few months after the outbreak of the Anti-Culture Movement, all classes stopped. Years later, when Mao put foward the ambiguous slogan of "Resume classes and carry out the revolution," nobody paid attention to it. Not a single school across the country was teaching anything to the students. Tests or exams were out of the question. However, students still graduated. A certain age and a certain number of years of registration in school became the sole requirements. The opinionated Mao Tse-tung said, "The junior high in our country can be equated with senior high." This ridiculous statement made all the junior high graduates qualified as senior high ones and gave them the same opportunity for jobs as the latter.

As the internal war between different rebel factions expanded on a nationwide scale like a raging fire, no arrangements could be made for high school graduates until 1969, the year when my eldest son graduated. This was the first year the government faced the problem of placing all the high school graduates. Altogether there were four years of graduates, namely the classes of 1969, 1968, 1967, and 1966, to be placed that year. According to the official plan, these graduates would be provided with several choices. The majority of them were to go and settle in the countryside, a few to go and work on state farms or enlist in the army, and a very few to go and work in the urban factories. An assignment was not based on one's grades or conduct. Apart from an assignment to work in an urban factory, service in the army was considered the best alternative. The reason was that after several years of service, one would be demobilized and in accordance with regulations would return to one's original place. That is to say that Shanghai youth could go back to Shanghai after being demobilized.

However, for children other than those of "red" categories, acceptance for enlistment in the army was something tantalizing. Even the "red" category kids were not necessarily accepted into the army, for the quota was limited and went only to children of high officials. Next came state farms. Although most of the state farms were located in the border areas, in either the extreme north or extreme south, this shortcoming was offset by the fact that they offered a monthly salary and seemed to be so organized as to help the growth of a youth.* However, the quota was also small, indeed so small that the children of "black" categories would in no way compete with "red" categories. In reality, the only way out for the black categories was to settle in the countryside with room and board at the homes of local farmers. The state was only responsible for their assignments, but not for wages or insurance. Usually the settlements were in remote and backward areas, characterized by barren land, poverty, and poor transportation. The children sent there had to be subsidized by their parents. Worst of all was the fact that they were supposed to spend their whole lives there, without hopes of being transferred to the cities where they were born.

Most ridiculous was the regulation that the oldest child of each family should without exception go and settle in the countryside. Only when the oldest child had done so could the younger ones be assigned to work in the city. In Shanghai alone, this regulation caused numerous family tragedies when some of the oldest children refused to make such a lifelong sacrifice for their younger brothers or sisters.

I felt lucky that my family was not troubled by such a problem. My oldest son, James, was destined to settle in the countryside. Except for Jane, his mother, who was weighted down with anxiety for quite a while, none in my family took this matter too much to heart. James himself was quite unaffected. On the day of his departure, as we feared

---

*At that time it was not yet known that a lot of shabby deals were going on on the state farms, because sexual abuse and bribery cases were not exposed until recent years.

that Jane could not control herself on parting, we managed to persuade her not to go to see him off at the railway station. I went there with her brother Chu Cheng-jong.

In those days, the Northern Railway Station of Shanghai was crowded with travelers. All the graduates of this year and the last three years assigned to settle in countrysides were to depart from this station. Those high school graduates, or "educated urban youth," as they were called at that time, and their families who were there to see them off made the station seethe with a sea of people. On the platform several ambulances were parked, with dozens of stretchers for emergencies. A large number of medical workers was also there, just as on a battlefield. In reality, many anticipated emergencies did happen when some family members, especially old grandmothers, fainted. When the train started to pull out with hooting whistles, cries both inside and outside the train grew so loud that the whole station seemed to be in tears. To my consolation, I found among the many faces inside the train that of James who was leaning out of the window and waving goodbye to us while wearing a bright smile. From his facial expression, it seemed that he was just starting on a short journey. Apparently he, like me, was not at all affected by the atmosphere around us. This was the first time I had felt really proud of my son, who was then only sixteen years old.

After James's departure, pressure on me became greater and greater. As they had no salaries, these educated urban youths could hardly support themselves. They had to be subsidized by their parents. Besides the economic burden I had to shoulder, the fact that my son's youth would be wasted was also on my mind. In fact, these young people, whom the local peasants regarded as unwelcome intruders, had really nothing to do in the country. Their residence registration in Shanghai had been cancelled and their domicile transferred to the village where they had been settled. Now, without the approval of the government, they could not return to Shanghai to reside permanently. In disappointment, some of these educated urban youths ganged together to commit crimes. Jane and I often heard stories to that effect and were deeply worried about James.

A "backdoor practice" began to flourish at that time. Some educated urban youths succeeded in having their domicile in the country changed through an illegal procedure. Jane and I tried in every possible way to find some back door, either in Shanghai or in the area where James had settled, but failed. It was not easy to find it. Many times I prayed in my heart, "Oh, back door, back door! Where art thou? How can I knock thee open?" No response. However, I firmly believed that no country could afford the loss of a whole generation of young people by denying them the opportunity to receive further education. The present situation could only yield one of the two following results: One, the Communist regime would make a drastic change in its obscurantist policy; two, the present government would collapse and be replaced by a new government which would attach great importance to education and human resources. Either way, people with knowledge would be in demand in the near future. With this belief, I encouraged James to prepare himself for this prospect. This meant that he had to study very hard even at this dark moment. It would be too late to start to study when talents were needed. I sent to him all the textbooks on physics, mathematics, et cetera which he needed and which I had obtained by every possible means. Thanks to his diligence, after almost ten years of suffering in the countryside, he passed the national college entrance examinations and was admitted into the Shanghai Mechanical Institute in 1978 and thus terminated his life in the countryside.

The Anti-Culture Movement could affect any aspect of one's life, whether or not it had anything to do with culture. Take housing for example. We resided in a big compound built exclusively for the employees of a former financial establishment where my father had served at the beginning of the 1940s. Since then we had lived in one of its apartments with a bedroom and a living room, both facing south, a small room facing north, which could be used either as a study or as a single bedroom, a bathroom, and a kitchen. After we moved in, my father hired some people to add two attic rooms to it. At the time when the Anti-Culture Movement started, eight of us lived in this apartment. My parents occupied the main bedroom, Jane and I the former living room next to my parents' after we returned from Peking, Granny Liu the small room, and our children the attic. Although no space was left unused, our living conditions were still much better than those of the average Chinese.

The Communist regime under Mao Tse-tung, who was fond of turning out a new policy almost every other day, had never done a single thing since "liberation" to improve the living conditions of the people.

With the growth of population, there was a rising rebellion against the housing shortage. Thus, in the wake of the house-searching occurred a wave of house-grabbing. At first, some rebel groups moved into the rooms of some big houses and used them as their headquarters. Then, the government stepped in and said "no." For instance, the Shanghai Municipality Party Committee issued an order to "stop the evil trend of grabbing houses." But to the great puzzlement of the people, in the end, the houses which had first been grabbed by either rebels or people having the backing of rebels became the property of the government. The municipal government had a real estate bureau, and each district government a district real estate bureau, and even each subdistrict office. This establishment must have been the biggest and the richest real estate enterprise in the world, because it owned all the land and houses in Shanghai. Although it had the ownership according to the policy made and pursued before the Anti-Culture Movement, the right to use a particular room, apartment, or house belonged to the current occupants, for one of the Communist principles was "Accept and honor the *fait accompli*." Now the Anti-Culture Movement offered the real estate officials an opportunity to do away with this restriction.

One day, Chu Hsi-yao, an official from the real estate group of the subdistrict where we lived, led a group of thug-like fellows and broke into our apartment. They neither searched our home nor interrogated any of us, but just gave us an order: "As you are monsters and demons, you are not qualified to live in any room facing south.* The whole family must move to the attic before such-and-such a day. Otherwise, we will take revolutionary action."† Having made this announcement, they swaggered out.

This announcement caused my family great anxiety. My parents had always been law-abiding and thought that this order, no less than an imperial edict, should be obeyed. However, my opinion was that this was beyond what we could comply with. How could all this family be squeezed into two small attic rooms? Under the circumstances in which

---

*In China, rooms facing south are considered the best living quarters.

†"Revolutionary action" was a phrase which came into vogue at that time, meaning violence or crude behavior.

a family's space could in no way be expanded, once you moved into a smaller room or apartment, it would be as hard to change the established fact as to climb to the sky. By that time, no private house was available for rent. Application for the expansion of space or change of residence was processed by the real estate bureau, which in fact never approved it.

Therefore, the only possible solution for us was to implore this official to countermand the order. As I was a rightist and my parents had been driven into the cowshed, Jane, who was a member of the revolutionary masses, was the only right person for this job. Although Chu Hsi-yao was a grassroots official, he was so arrogant and domineering that those who went to make a plea before him were often denied the door. He also arrogantly refused to receive Jane. However, once, after Jane had waited on the street outside of the real estate group for hours, she got hold of him when he stepped out for lunch. Jane implored him for magnanimity, but he replied, "There are only eight of you in your family. I have already done you a favor by letting you occupy the two attic rooms. In Shanghai the laboring people, on the average, do not have that much space. Don't complain anymore, or I'll give you only one of the attic rooms."

Fortunately, the back door practice was already flourishing at this period. We had a good friend by the name of Jennie Lin. She and her husband were basketball players. Among their acquaintances was one who belonged to the Shanghai Athletes Rebel Headquarters, an organization notorious for its fighting, smashing, and looting. It even held the real estate bureau in awe. Our friend made arrangements for Jane to meet an official in the district bureau of real estate, which was superior to the group. The result was that according to their policy—rebels had policies, too—Granny Liu was a laboring person, therefore, she did not need to move. Jane belonged to the revolutionary masses and, therefore, she could continue to live in the orginal room. But my parents could not stay in the room facing south; therefore, they had to move upstairs to one of the attic rooms. In other words, one room, the room where my parents had originally lived, was confiscated.

Always tame, my parents moved to the attic to stay with my children. Their original room was left empty. Thanks to the incessant nationwide internal struggles, to which the real estate system was not

immune, no new tenants moved into that room. Most of the employees in the real estate system were formerly rascals and scoundrels and
used to ride roughshod over others. During the Anti-Culture Movement, these people brought into full play their abilities, and the internal fighting in this system was notoriously fierce. Chu Hsi-yao, the
leader of the real estate group, fell from power and was replaced by a
person named Ke Chi-kun. These two fellows belonged to different
factions, yet, just as both of them shouted the same slogan of "loyalty
to Chairman Mao," their tyrannical lording it over ordinary residents
was exactly the same. Ke was even worse than Chu. Jane called him
several times, and each time his answer to her request was "no." No
matter what you said to him, he just refused to listen, let alone to be
reasonable.

Though the room in dispute remained vacant, our mental pressure
was not decreased with each passing day. It always seemed some family would move in the next day or the next week. As a matter of fact,
these officials, who were popularly known as "housing tigers," used
the vacant rooms under their control as bargaining chips in political
dealings, to rope in someone whom they needed to curry favor with.
However, for those in higher positions whom the housing tigers wanted to impress, there were lots of ways to secure housing. They did not
need to accept what they were offered. That was why our room was
left vacant for such a long time.

It became increasingly clear that this great Anti-Culture Movement
was actually a change of regime. The bureaucracy of the pre-movement
period no longer existed. Although house-grabbing was widespread in
Shanghai at that time, no formal directive had ever been issued to check
it, nor had any official expressed any objection to it. It was a kind of
pillage: he who struck first gained the upper hand. Under Communist
rule, the *fait accompli* was always acknowledged. We made inquiries
here and there, and were informed that some of the original tenants
who had moved out of their houses or rooms on the order of the real
estate bureau had moved in again and had caused no trouble for themselves, but some had failed to move in again after having had a quarrel
with the housing tigers. However, there were cases in which the quarrel
ended with the residents' triumph over the housing tigers. The situation
was totally different from that of the pre-Anti-Culture Movement

period, when nobody could win victory over the bureaucracy, which represented the Party and was not supposed to be challenged.

The housing problem remained. My parents flatly refused to move into the vacant room without permission. This state of affairs lasted almost a year, during which time there was a continuous stream of people coming to look at the room. Most of them expressed their dislike of the surroundings as soon as they stepped into the house, for living in a room surrounded by another family gave one no sense of privacy. We were glad that they disliked it. At last, two rascally-looking persons came, who, cigarettes in mouths, seemed satisfied with it. From their conversation, we gathered that they were likely to accept this offer. After they left, we thought that the situation had become such that if we let them move in, it would be no longer possible to make a claim for this room again. My parents still refused to challenge the authorities. Just as newborn calves are not afraid of tigers, my sons moved in. When the tenants-to-be came back again and found that we had already moved in, they gave way. It was evident that they thought that since they had the privilege of choosing a residence, they did not have to stick to such a room as would make them uncomfortable even if they succeeded in occupying it. Although they gave way, the housing tiger Ke Chi-kun did not. He truculently stepped into our house, making some punitive remarks. However, when he realized that my parents were still staying in the attic and that it was my sons who occupied the room and that they were prepared to fight with him, he went away and never came back. Later, my parents were both liberated from the cowshed and they decided to move back into their original room. Had it not been broken into by their grandchildren earlier, they would not have been able to move in again even if they had been liberated, because that arrangement could hardly have been changed.

My grandfather was also harassed by the housing problem. At the end of the 1930s, my grandfather built the residence in which he had stayed ever since. It was a typical piece of private property—he owned the land as well as the house, which was a large, attractive, single house with a beautiful garden. By the time of the Anti-Culture Movement only three people lived in this huge house—my grandfather, my stepgrandmother, and my aunt. Since Communist takeover of the mainland, the government had offered my grandfather the title of Standing

Director of the Bank of Communications, apparently for the purpose of carrying out the policy of the "unified front," and his private property had never been violated. During the early period of the Anti-Culture Movement, his house was subjected to search several times, and in the tumult of house-grabbing, my grandfather, his wife, and my aunt were ordered to leave this house and move into one large room on the third floor of an adjacent house, which was spacious enough to house the three of them. Grandfather always looked at things from a philosophical point of view, and did not take the change seriously. He was already well over eighty years of age, but was in good health. His gait was vigorous, his voice sonorous, and his hearing and eyesight still very good. His favorite pastime had been gardening and purchasing ancient Chinese paintings and calligraphy. Now, as the space had become much smaller, his garden was gone, his collection of ancient paintings and calligraphy had been confiscated, and he had nothing to do to while away his time. He began to go to the Hsiang-yang Public Park regularly to chat with some old and new friends.

This was a period of uninterrupted nationwide internecine struggles between rebels of different factions. Mao Tse-tung liked to call it "a period of surging forward with great momentum," but as a matter of fact the momentum was out of his control. In a period of comparatively relaxed control by the Communist Party, people could talk more freely. Grandfather was a person with a marvelous sense of humor. When people complained about the housing problem and discussed house-swapping, Grandfather used to say sarcastically, "I have changed twenty rooms for just one room." Roughly speaking, there were twenty rooms in his original house. Again, sometimes when people complained about the losses they had suffered during the previous years, Grandfather would chime in, "I haven't undergone too much change. I lost a son, only to be rewarded with a beard." The son referred to my third uncle, who had jumped from a high-rise with his wife, and the beard meant that my grandfather started to grow a beard after the outbreak of the Anti-Culture Movement.

It was a pattern under Communist rule that during a certain period people at first seemed to have the freedom to say anything they liked but later had to pay for what they had said. The same was true of the Anti-Culture Movement. In the wake of a period which alternated be-

數年以來沒有人要的骨灰空盒
今日能親身攝影留念為還值得
壬子年重陽 子祺九十一歲識華
（辛亥誤書壬子）

My grandfather in his new residence, after being evicted from his own house, posing with the casket he had prepared for his cinerary. His handwritten remarks on the back of the photo (at right) read, "For years the empty casket has been left alone. Today I pose with it as a consolation. T.S. [his name] brushed these words on the Double Ninth Festival [the ninth day of the ninth lunar month] in the year 1971, at age ninety-one.

tween internal struggles and a comparatively relaxed control over the ordinary people came the campaign of "purifying the class ranks," in which every work unit switched its struggle targets from bureaucrats to the masses. The banking system of Shanghai selected my grandfather as their chief struggle target. Assemblies attended by ten thousand people were convened at Shanghai Gymnasium, the former Shanghai Squash Court, to struggle against him. At first they denounced the above two cynical remarks he had made as his crimes. Grandfather immediately acknowledged they were what he had said, but claimed that he just told the truth and did not mean ill. Nevertheless, he said that he should not have made these remarks, which were nothing but nonsense. Then they sneered at his refusal to follow the Kuomintang to Taiwan and interpreted it as the trick of the Kuomintang, which had deliberately left him on the mainland as a pawn for staging a comeback. My grandfather had always been proud of his clear personal record, namely, his refusal to work with the enemy and the puppet regime during the War of Resistance against Japan, or to be involved in dirty politics during the period of the Kuomintang rule. He rejected all the accusations against him as reactionary.

By then, Grandfather was already eighty-nine years of age. My aunt was very devoted and begged to accompany him on the stage, but those rebels would not listen to her request. She could only stay and wait backstage. I, as a rightist, did not dare to show up, for fear that I would cause him more trouble. All I could do was promenade along Avenue Joffre or Rue Seymour during these assemblies. Although I could hear nothing but the slogans, I felt close to Grandfather. This actually did more good to me than to him.

At the first assembly, he was interrogated, "Why didn't you follow the Kuomintang to Taiwan in 1949?"

He replied with perfect assurance, "Because I felt it had utterly deteriorated. Before liberation, my friends often heard me reprimand the Kuomintang."

"What!" shouted these "heroes." "Did you say you had reprimanded the Kuomintang under the Kuomintang's rule? Did you mean the Kuomintang was quite enlightened?"

"This is your interpretation," my grandfather retorted, "I didn't mean that."

This kind of talking back caused an uproar of slogans, "Down with the Kuomintang," "Down with Wong Tzu-song."

Then another warrior came up to him. "You should make a clean breast of what task the Kuomintang entrusted you with before it retreated from the mainland."

"Nothing," Grandfather still replied with perfect assurance.

"Okay, then I ask you," the "hero" said mysteriously, "Chen Kuo-fu, head of the CC faction of the Kuomintang, held secret talks with you before he fled to Taiwan. Isn't that true?"

"We met each other before he fled mainland China," Gandfather answered honestly, "but we didn't hold secret talks. He came to my house on his own. He wanted to say goodbye to me. That's all."

"To say goodbye to you?" The "hero" seemed to be puzzled. "What kind of qualifications did you have so that Chen Kuo-fu had to come to say goodbye to you?"

"I was a good friend of his father-in-law," Grandfather replied. "Chen Kuo-fu's wife called me Uncle Wong."

"Okay, suppose that's the case. Then you must confess what you talked about."

"He did not talk much. During the whole meeting, I blamed Chiang Kai-shek and his administration, including Chen Kuo-fu himself. He did not refute me, but just listened."

"What," the proletarian heroes were startled, "the head of Organizational Ministry of the Kuomintang listened to you blaming the Kuomintang and Chiang Kai-shek? Nonsense!"

"Oh, I always blamed the Kuomintang," Grandfather retorted sarcastically, "I did it all the time, to everybody. You'd better go and make inquiries, and it's easy to verify."

Such an attitude was totally unacceptable to the rebels, who decided to struggle against him again.

After he returned home, all the family members gave him advice and begged him to soften his attitude. He flatly refused, saying, "I'm already eighty-nine years old. Even if I died right at this moment, it would not be considered a short life and I would not regret it. Why should I succumb to those unreasonable accusations?"

Now what Grandfather had said to me about two decades before came to my mind. I said to him, "Grandpa, I still remember you advised me to be realistic and face the reality of Communist control. You told me again and again that in dealing with Communists, we had to suspend our conscience temporarily and do whatever they ordered. You said that even if they wanted me to denounce you as a capitalist, exploiter, bloodsucker, robber, bandit, or whatever, I should go ahead and comply with their orders. You told me not to take the labeling seriously. You told me not to irritate them so as to get myself into trouble. You said it was not worthwhile to argue with them. I can never forget your brilliant and profound remark that if the Communists could be called human beings, then you would definitely refuse to acknowledge yourself a human being. You told me to be confident and flexible in dealing with devils. These words were what you told me over and over again more than twenty years ago. I still keep them in mind. Can you recall them?"

Grandfather acquiesced. He was paid back in his own coin. Finally, he agreed not to answer back to whatever blame or insult they would put on him. Furthermore, I suggested a strategy for him. At the next assembly he could take advantage of his advanced age and show himself senile and doddering instead of sharp and quick. He also agreed.

The next meeting turned out to be the last. Grandfather avoided answering any question directly. To whatever he was asked, he just replied, "It's my fault," or "I'm wrong," or "I'm sorry," or "I apologize." He repeated these words and thus passed the test.

After returning home, he told us, "What I answered at today's assembly was very sincere. I did think I had made a terrible mistake. I thought I had committed no bigger mistake in my whole life than when I refused to retreat to Hong Kong or Taiwan."

CHAPTER 10

"The Cultural Revolution Is Really Good!"

T HE SEA. NO SIGHT OF THE SEA. This was really the sea coast, but no beach. A vast stretch of saline-alkali soil. Not a blade of grass could be seen. Accurately speaking, the only sign of life was reeds and boundless marshes. In order to reach the sea, one had to pass through several miles of reed marshes. However, no one seemed to be in a mood to make such a trip.

This was Feng Hsian, a satellite county of Shanghai. There had been no sign of human habitation in this place until 1969, when several "May Seventh official schools" began to be set up here. Chairman Mao, the so-called Great Helmsman, had issued a directive on the seventh day of the month of May that all the officials should receive re-education from workers, peasants, and soldiers. Since his words were like edicts, the date on which he had issued such a directive became sacred, and May Seventh a sacred term.

Actually, the May Seventh official schools and regular schools had little in common. They were labor camps with only dormitories and a huge canteen hall. The May Seventh official school of Shanghai's publication system was in Feng Hsian, and so was that of Shanghai's cultural system, which was just next to us. As the land was barren and uninhabited, each official school was free to use it, and the personnel of the entire system were sent there as "students." The students of the May Seventh official schools were not called "students" but proudly termed themselves "May Seventh soldiers." However, people like me, that is, the monsters and demons, were not qualified for the term soldiers, our title being always "monsters and demons" no matter where we went, but I said to myself that we might as well be called "May Seventh captives."

I arrived at this place in October 1969 on an "emergency" order that all city dwellers, male and female, young and old, should go to the countryside. It was only several years later, when Lin P'iao died, that we realized that it was he who had issued such an order. According to the accusation made of him after he died, he had issued this order with the intention of strengthening his position and opposing Mao. Whether this accusation was true or not, only God knows. Anyway, the achievements that the Communist revolution had so far made had been none other than making the entire nation a barracks, and every citizen either a soldier or a captive. Whatever order the top issued could be implemented "with the power of a thunderbolt and the speed of lightning," as the Communist cliché goes. In our publishing house, only several days after the issue of the order all of us, me included, came to this barren location of the official school. The order was carried out more obediently than if it were gospel.

We came there standing all the way on big trucks, as this place was inaccessible on foot or by bicycle, by bus, or by train. It took about four or five hours from downtown Shanghai.

Before us, an advance party of May Seventh soldiers had already been dispatched here to build dwellings on this virgin land. Upon our arrival we could immediately check into our dormitory, which was a large, makeshift shelter built of bamboo, bricks, and mud, thatched with reeds and straw, and divided into several rooms. Each room was shared by more than ten persons and equipped with double-deck beds. Outdoors, there was an immense sky and an immense stretch of land, with nothing but fresh air. Indoors, each person's bed was his universe, in which he slept, sat, and ate. We had three meals a day prepared by the canteen, and ate from bowls with practically nothing but rice and some vegetables in them. The manager was Huang, tall and tough, formerly manager of the canteen of the Bureau of Publications. He was so resourceful and capable that the meals for hundreds of May Seventh students were arranged pretty methodically. For breakfast, we had porridge and pickles or fermented bean curd, and for lunch or supper we could make a choice between rice and steamed bun, complete with vegetables or sometimes a bit of meat. Judged by the standards of the place at that time, our food was quite satisfactory.

We lived a basically military life. We got up as soon as the reveille was sounded in the morning, and had to attend morning drill on time. Normally, as a "May Seventh captive," I should not have had the honor of attending such a drill along with the "May Seventh soldiers," but I did. This probably represented the People's Liberation Army's fine tradition of giving preferential treatment to captives.

The day was usually spent either attending struggle meetings or doing physical labor. The revolutionary masses were still busy ferreting out this or that bad element. Their continued revolutionary action was in conformity with the policy of "digging deeply and searching meticulously." Since Chairman Mao had ferreted out the "Khrushchev by his bed," as he called Liu Shao-chi, officials of every level followed suit by singling out their closest comrades-in-arms to struggle against, for if you failed to single out others, others would single you out. According to Mao's theory, the masses consisted of two kinds of people—good and bad. The former, he prescribed, constituted the 95 percent majority of the entire population, while the latter accounted for a minority of only 5 percent. In reality, the 95 percent always lived in fear of lapsing into the category of the 5 percent. However, I felt more secure than anyone else in the official school, for I had already reached the pit of the downtrodden and had no more to lose, either as a rightist or a monster and demon. Therefore, as an onlooker, I watched coldly their "building up a revolutionary momentum" or "blowing up a red storm," as they phrased it, to repress the innocent.

I spent most of the time doing manual labor, as I was not required to attend some of the meetings. So much the better, for I hated attending meetings and preferred doing physical labor. I enjoyed participating in the construction of a highway which, of course, was not a highway in the modern sense of this word, but just an earthen road built out of the wasteland. The official schools of both the publication and cultural systems shared the workload of building this earthen road and later using it. As a matter of fact, the mainstay of the workforce dispatched by both systems for this job were monsters and demons. Working shoulder to shoulder with me were famous actors such as Chao Tan and Chang Fa, who were also May Seventh captives.

I also built houses—not skyscrapers, of course, but makeshift shelters. Through this job, I acquired some interesting techniques of laying bricks and constructing bamboo frames. What I became most skillful at was transportation, like pedaling pedicabs, pulling handcarts, or shouldering heavy loads with a pole. I even participated in sculling a boat over a long distance. I found lots of fun in this slightly difficult and semitechnical work. Besides, doing these kinds of work exempted me from doing the manure spreading, which I disliked most and was so fortunate as never to be assigned. I did not mind using my strength, but hated to touch dung.

What I was most afraid of befell me eventually. The fellow occupying the bed below me was Chen Moon-hsiong, a native of Shanghai then in his early forties, who had been my acquaintance for quite a long time. At first, he had been a proofreader in the Chinese Classics Publishing House and later was promoted to editor as a reward for what he had done as a thug in the Anti-Rightist Movement. Little interested in classics, he specialized in Chinese literature of the 1930s and was very familiar with anecdotes of the literary circles of that period. His class origin and family background were flawless by Communist standards, and his political leanings were toward the Party. I did not know why all of a sudden, after we had arrived at the official school, he became the target of struggle. Big-character posters against him did not state what mistakes or crimes he had committed, but only urged him to confess. The logic seemed to be as follows: You are a criminal because you have committed crimes, and since you have committed crimes you are surely a criminal. However, there was something that did not need to be made clear and that everybody was expected to figure out for himself. During that period, none of the men of letters who had started their literary careers in the 1930s or anyone who was familiar with them could escape disaster. Whoever knew the ins and outs of Madame Mao and Chang Chun-ch'iao and their like would be a criminal, and would be struggled against for as long as he denied this.

One day, on my way to the dormitory during the lunch break, I noticed something extraordinary and chaotic had happened. When I approached closer, I was nauseated by an unbearable bad odor and saw someone posting a slogan on the wall of the dormitory which read, "Chen Moon-hsiong alienated himself from the people and was guilty of a crime for which he deserved to die ten thousand deaths." This was a typical slogan at that time, used for those who had committed suicide. I was astonished and stepped into my room. Chen was not on his bed, which was empty, but the stink seemed to permeate every cubic millimeter of the room. I thought Chen's body must already have been removed, but doubted how it happened that a person who had just died could smell so bad. Feeling perplexed, I walked over to the washstand by the double-deck bed I shared with Chen, with the intention of taking my basin. To my surprise, my basin gave out an extraordinarily stinky smell. Within the next few minutes, I gathered from the conversation of others that Chen had attempted suicide by jumping into the manure pit, but he had been rescued, and was now in the hospital.

Then I figured out that he must have been sent back to the dormitory immediately after being rescued, and this was why the dormitory became so stinky. I also figured out that those rescuers must have been in a great hurry and taken a basin at random to wash him, and that this lucky washbasin happened to have been mine; this was why my basin smelled so terrible. I could only throw it out, and I washed up by holding water with my palms. The problem of washing up was easy to solve, but sleeping in the dormitory was really an ordeal. I just could not understand why the room was even more stinky than the manure pit itself, and, worse than that, I was the one who suffered most, because as gas usually tends to rise, the smell from Chen's bed rose and surrounded my bed. The manure pit in the official school became increasingly impressive as the Anti-Culture Movement gained momentum. It was much larger than a "jacuzzi" pool in the United States, and without a cover. But I failed to comprehend why Mr. Chen should have jumped into the manure pit for an attempted suicide when there were so many rivers and lakes available, which, in my opinion, were surely much better places to die.

According to superstition, manure had the power to drive away evil spirits. Maybe the smell I had inhaled did help to get rid of my bad luck, but I really do not know. Soon after that, all the students of the official school returned to Shanghai for vacation—it was stipulated that we have four days off each month. As we never took a rest on weekends in the official school, the four Sundays of a month were used in a lump. This time we had five days off, but one of them had to be devoted to the general meeting of the entire publication system, which was not counted as part of the vacation. Good, very good. Even one more day in Shanghai was good enough. I had been told beforehand that on the day scheduled for the meeting I must arrive at the site of the meeting, the Shanghai Gymnasium, one hour early, and I gladly complied.

I did report there an hour early and was ordered to stay backstage with monsters and demons from various publishing houses. I knew none of them, although we all belonged to the official school of the publication system. After the general meeting was declared open, all the monsters and demons, including me as a rightist, were escorted to the stage on the order of the president. The stage turned out to be none other than a flat floor formerly used for playing squash, surrounded by a wall on one side and tiers of seats on the other three sides, crowded with people.

This general meeting was held for the purpose of "demonstrating leniency and severity," a much-propagated policy of Mao's. At the meeting, the leader of the publication system announced that some of the targets ferreted out during the campaign of "purifying the class ranks" should pay for their stubborn resistance to confession. While he was calling names, the police came to the stage, handcuffed the "criminals," and led them away. Then the leader called my name, announcing that, being a model of "hanging one's head and admitting one's crimes," I had been given leniency in order to reflect the matchless magnanimity of the great proletarian class. Thus, I was decapped as a rightist.

As a token of being allowed to return to the ranks of the people, I was instantly ordered to leave the stage and take one of the seats in the tiers by myself, without the "help" of an escort. I had been longing for my delabelization for nearly two decades, but when the time really came, I felt a bit nervous and awkward. Accustomed to being escorted, now I had to find my way from the stage into the stands on my own. I seated myself in a vacant seat in the last row by an aisle, with a feeling of unreality, as in a dream, and also a sense of helplessness, like a patient who has been sick for a long time and just released from the hospital. I could not concentrate on what was going on in the meeting, because my thoughts had been running on those unknown friends who were now just in a prisoners' van on their way to jail. I felt sorry for those wretched souls, although I felt happy for myself.

Did I really feel happy? No. I was actually aware of the true nature of this social system and the fact that a person with a label was constantly under surveillance. However, a person without a label was always subject to Mao's famous motto, "All members in the revolutionary ranks should be concerned with, take care of, and help one another." Whoever was so insensible as to refuse to be concerned with, taken care of, and helped would, eventually, be abandoned by the revolutionary ranks and caught in a counterrevolutionary trap and placed under surveillance. Which would be better, being constantly under surveillance, or being constantly helped? I did not know. The latter seemed to be preferable to the former in that it was a treatment which only the people could enjoy.

For the sake of safety, the best thing for a Chinese intellectual to do who had been labeled a rightist was to be voluntarily subject to examination by the Party and the masses. In spite of the fact that one's "hat" had been removed, the Great Leader Mao always hated to see intellectuals get cocky. I felt so indifferent to my delabelization that I did not even mention it to my family when I returned home that day. After I had gone back to the official school, some relatives informed my family of this good news, which had spread very fast since the meeting had been attended by thousands of people.

I led the same life after I returned to the official school in Feng Hsian and tried to maintain my "tradition" of submitting an "ideological report" each week, but was dissuaded from doing so. My group leader held a formal talk with me. "From now on, you need not hand in this kind of written report anymore. Undoubtedly, all of us have to further remold our ideology incessantly, and so do you. You should rely on the organization, and if you have any ideological problems, you may feel free to contact me anytime, but not in the form of written reports." I enjoyed this exemption.

Another benefit one could get from being delabelized was the privilege of subscribing to a small newspaper, *Ts'an Kao Hsiao Hsi* (*For*

Your Reference), which was a conglomeration of Chinese translations of the news releases of major Western media, edited by the Hsin Hua News Agency, China's official news agency. This paper was, of course, much more useful and interesting than other official newspapers. I enjoyed having this privilege.

The major benefit lay in the fact that in the month following my delabelization an opportunity occurred which I could not have taken advantage of if my hat had still been on my head. Feng Hsian, where the May Seventh official school was located, was such a saline-alkali area that whatever seeds were sowed, no harvest could be expected. Crops simply did not grow here. Now several thousands of souls were assembled in this area for the sake of "being tempered in the great revolutionary movement" and "supporting themselves by their own labor." As a matter of fact, while they may have been tempered, there was no possibility of supporting themselves. These wretched souls did not do any useful things, except to try to find fault with one another. This they called "bearing class struggle constantly in mind," as Mao had instructed. This place was certainly an ideal locale to launch political movements. The only troublesome thing was that the government had to transport truckloads of food from the city proper to this remote site every day to feed these official students, who were still receiving their original paychecks. In this sense, labor there was extremely expensive. Without having to use a computer, one could instantly tell that keeping so many people in such a barren land was an absolutely unprofitable venture. However, these people had come here in response to the sacred May Seventh instruction by the most brilliant leader, and it would be profane to retreat from the official school. It was now summer. Some wise men came up with the idea of launching a "campaign of fighting against high temperatures." Under this slogan, many May Seventh soldiers would be sent to factories in the city as seasonal labor support for industrial production. According to theory, this could be interpreted as a continuation of the May Seventh path, because the reeducation could be continued in factories. The real motive behind this was that people once sent to the factories would make, more or less, a contribution to production, much more than in the official school, where they did little except consume food and produce manure.

As soon as the call was issued, I jumped at it, for many of Shanghai's industrial plants were in the city proper and by "fighting against high temperatures" in a factory, I would be able to stay at home. To me, getting out of this official school was equivalent to getting out of the abyss of misery. It was true that the official school had a good environment, being surrounded by a vast extent of land and unpolluted by anything except the smell of manure. Doing physical labor there was not a burden to me at all. It was the collective life, especially the military life-style, that made me sick, for I felt as though I were living in jail. I began to contact leaders at every level to seek their approval of my application for "fighting against high temperatures." I behaved like an ancient warrior submitting a request to the emperor for a military assignment. Whether my attitude of volunteering for battle won their favor or I was already on their list of layoffs did not matter. I got the approval and was scheduled to leave the official school for Shanghai. I was filled with ecstasy.

I had another important secret motive behind my eagerness to leave this barrack-like school for home, and this motive was that I wanted to resume listening to the Voice of America. I had started listening to it during the Korean War. At first I listened at my grandfather's house, because he owned a good radio and also because his big house, with a garden fenced with thick, tall walls, gave a sense of security, since listening to the Voice of America was an act of high risk. As time went on, Communist rule became tougher and tougher, but I kept listening. In those darkest days, as in the Anti-Culture Movement, when listening to the Voice of America could be an act of treason, Grandfather and the other family members did not dare to listen to it anymore, and I had to take the small transistor receiver to my bed, put it close to my ear, and pull the blanket over my head to keep the Voice from being overheard by potential informants in the neighborhood. Though sometimes I almost suffocated, I felt some free air being blown from the broadcast. But confined in the official school, I could not breathe this air of freedom at all.

Having returned to Shanghai, I was at first assigned, along with Hwa Shou-yi, my former group leader, and other young officials, to work in a cold rolling-strip steel mill. We were asked to tend machines like real workers. It required strength to pick up or lay down every bundle of strip steel. I did not mind consuming my energy and was happy to be a worker, for I thought the conditions of the factory were much better than those of the official school.

Six months later, winter came again, but we were still "fighting against high temperatures." Some intellectuals started to complain that they had done physical labor for too long and that it was too much for them. They even went to the Municipal Party Committee to express their doubt about the legitimacy of the slogan of "fighting against high temperatures," since, they stated, it was below freezing now. I shared my dear Chairman Mao's disgust for intellectuals and declined to join their petition. To their chagrin, the Municipal Party Committee gave them a reply counter to their expectations.

In the first place, the Municipal Party Committee's directive pointed out that "fighting against high temperatures" was not an expediency, but a continuation of the implementation of the brilliant May Seventh instruction and, therefore, it should be followed for years, if not for one's whole lifetime. "Good, I agree," I thought.

Secondly, the document pointed out, for the implementation of the Party's Intellectuals Policy, those who worked in factories located too far away from home or requiring too much physical strength could apply for transfer to factories more suitable to them.

I said to myself that I did not want to be transferred, and that all I wanted was to be transferred to another country. Whenever I read in *For Your Reference* about the stories of some foreign people protesting to their governments when expelled from their home countries, I thought, "How stupid. Why protest? If I could be expelled from this country, I would kowtow to the government." In this mood, I did not have the least interest in seeking to change my factory.

However, Hwa Shou-yi was eager for a change of job that would require less physical strength, and he came to ask me to join him in making an application. In the years in which he was in charge of supervising me in the publishing house, he had been nice to me. I thought I had to comply with his request to express gratitude for his having protected me in previous years. On the other hand, I was suspicious that our "organization" might have arranged for us to "fight against high temperatures" in the same factory with the intention of using him to watch over me. I thought it would make no difference for me to work in any factory and thus told him that I had no objection to changing jobs and would follow him wherever he went.

After New Year's Day of 1971, Hwa and I reported to the Shanghai

Padlock Spare Parts Factory. This was a small factory located on a dirty, narrow street by the Soochow River. The noises of its machines were so loud that they could be heard when you were walking over the bridge. Around the factory were shack dwellers, who seemed unaware of the deafening noises which lasted all day and all year long.

Both Hwa and I were assigned to work in the workshop producing padlock cores. This was by the street. Through the windows we could see the kaleidoscopic scenes of slum-dwellers cooking, washing, chatting, and quarreling—all on the street.

There were two teams, responsible for two different working procedures. Hwa was assigned to the team for the first procedure of putting bronze sticks into the machine to be cut into pieces. As a bronze stick was much lighter than a bundle of steel strips, Hwa felt relaxed and was happy. I worked with the team for the second procedure, which was putting the bronze pieces into another machine to be processed into rudimentary padlock cores with notches in the middle. The small bronze pieces were even less heavy than sticks, but the trouble was that the specifications for the notches were strict and had to be satisfied with high precision; error could not exceed ten thousandths of a millimeter. The workers were required to check the notches on the products constantly with verniers and vernier calipers. Thanks to the art of seal engraving, which I had acquired in my youth and which had enabled me to detect an error of a micron with the naked eye, I was able to measure the products by eye after just a short period of adaptation, and felt quite comfortable with the job.

This factory had three shifts. The morning shift was from 6:00 A.M. to 3:00 P.M., the swing shift was from 3:00 P.M. to 11:00 P.M., and the night shift was from 11:00 P.M. to 6:00 A.M. The swing shift and night shift workers could each get a subsidy of twenty cents in *renminbi* per day. I loved to work in these two shifts, not merely for the money, which, though equivalent to less than a nickel in U.S. currency, was quite a help for me, but most importantly for saving time. The morning shift workers had to attend meetings after work, while workers of the swing shift attended meetings during their working time, and those of the night shift did not attend meetings at all. What a different treatment!

Nominally each worker had to take three shifts in turn, each for a week. In general, workers hated the night shift and almost all liked the morning shift. They did not haggle too often about the time spent on meetings after work, because for one thing meetings in the factory were far less demanding than those in the publishing house. Unlike in the publishing house, which was full of sanctimonious hypocrites, the workers openly and publicly acknowledged that meetings were good occasions for a chat for male workers, termed *ga san wu* in Shanghai dialect, and knitting for female workers, termed *ts'u sang wo*. Sometimes when the leader wanted to hold a temporary meeting, some female workers might complain openly, "Ah ya! Why didn't you tell us in advance, say, yesterday? I haven't taken my *sang wo* with me today!" The leader never criticized them for regarding knitting as a must for a meeting, and simply answered with a smile, "It took just a little while, a little while." For this reason, I could easily swap my morning shifts for swing or night shifts and was thanked for it. From then on, I always worked either swing shift or night shift.

In our workshop, each shift for one of the two working procedures was supposed to comprise two or three persons. However, as the factory had a high percentage of workers on sick leave, very often there were not enough workers for each shift, and one or two or three machines had to be stopped. The factory leadership was very concerned. At first they were reluctant to approve my swap of morning shifts for swing and night shifts. In order to achieve my goal, several times I asked for a sick leave of a whole week when it was my turn to work morning shift and never excused myself for the swing and night shifts. With this tactic, they eventually complied with my request and no longer interfered.

At that time, finding a pretext to take sick leave was very common. Many people came to the outpatient department not to see the doctor, but to ask for a sick-leave certificate. While working in the publishing house, I had seldom heard any intellectual say openly that his or her sole purpose of going to the hospital was to get a sick-leave certificate. The reason was twofold. Intellectuals were constantly under pressure to act upon Mao's instruction of "loving, helping, and taking care of one another," which was, in fact, a nicely worded directive to place each under surveillance of the other. Therefore, none of them would dare to make his hidden intentions known for fear he would be "helped, loved, and taken care of by others." Second, intellectuals had been already afflicted with various diseases in the course of almost incessant political movements and, therefore, did not need to feign sickness. The factory workers, on the contrary, had no scruples about acknowledging that all they expected from the hospital was a sick-leave certificate. The following statement could often be heard in the factory: "Oh, I have something to do tomorrow, I think I'd better ask for a sick leave." The leaders were so realistic that they sometimes even asked, "Is there anyone asking for a sick leave tomorrow?" Among the young workers especially, taking a chance to "ask for a sick leave" had become a catch phrase. Without any symptoms of illness, they would go to the hospital in threes and fours to see if anyone was lucky enough to get a sick leave from some Buddha-looking doctor. Even though none of them was given a sick-leave certificate in the end, they had already enjoyed several hours of free time in the hospital, because in the socialist paradise it was perfectly legitimate to call the clinics or hospitals during working hours. Clinics and hospitals were increasingly crowded by these healthy "patients," and became as crowded as marketplaces, which in turn attracted more patients.

Although doctors wielded the enormous power of issuing sick-leave certificates and were very arrogant, they had difficulties. If a doctor gave a certificate to A, but not to B, or if a patient failed to get a certificate from this doctor but succeeded in getting it from another, the doctor would be hated bitterly. Anyway, it was a common scene for a patient and a doctor to be bickering vehemently over a sick-leave certificate. Doctors were not afraid of the patients, but guarded against the organizations to which these patients belonged, for if they issued too many sick-leave certificates, the leadership of one of the organizations might come to complain to the clinic or hospital leadership, who would bring them to account.

For the sake of their own safety and convenience and to avoid bickering with the patients, doctors made lists of technical regulations they were supposed to observe. Symptoms described by the patients themselves, such as headache, dizziness, nausea, stomach ache, and sore back, were for reference only when doctors wrote out prescriptions. These symptoms could not be taken as the basis for a sick-leave certificate, which should be based upon strict scientific testable data, such as an X-ray negative, a laboratory test report, or an instrument-gauged result. The technical regulations were subject to change according to the political weather or production situation, somewhat like the market quotations at the stock exchange. During one certain period, for example, a person who had a temperature above thirty-nine degrees centigrade was entitled to have a sick leave of one or two days, and a person who had a temperature below thirty-eight degrees centigrade was not. For those whose sickness was based on a clinical thermometer only, but not on laboratory tests, the maximum sick leave would be three days. As far as I knew, in another period, a hypertensive patient could not get a sick-leave certificate if the mercury on the gauge did not reach 200. Even the criteria of the blood test for liver malfunction varied in different periods. When filling the sick-leave certificates, doctors used to be meticulously scientific. I often saw "one and a half days" or "half a day" or sometimes even "two hours" written on such forms.

In spite of these strict regulations, people still succeeded in getting sick-leave certificates from time to time. Very often there were stories of someone stealing blank sick-leave forms or someone with a real illness taking the patient's place with the other person's name in order to get a sick-leave certificate for that person, and so on.

Packs or bottles of free medicines were available everywhere, in the waiting area of the clinic or hospital, at the gate, and on the street. They were all discarded by the "patients" who had come to the hospital for the sole purpose of getting a sick-leave certificate. Doctors had to prescribe some medicines when issuing certificates. Though bearing the signature of the doctor, a prescription would not be valid until it had been sealed with the official chop, which was kept in the pharmacy of the hospital, and with which the pharmacist would stamp the certificate when the patient came to pick up the prescribed medicines. Although the socialist paradise provided free medicines, they were neither chocolate bars nor orange juice and not edible for these healthy patients. Hence, the litter.

The fact that I could obtain a sick-leave certificate at any time I wanted did cause some suspicion on the part of the factory's leadership, who then conducted an investigation. The hospital authorities said, "He is a really nice guy, never engaged in any bickering or bargaining with any of the doctors." As I had the perfectly safe, sure-fire method of raising my blood pressure through *ch'i-kung* without resorting to any observable fraud, no one could find fault with me, no matter how suspicious he or she might be.

The workers at this factory fell into two categories. One category was veteran workers over forty or fifty years of age, who had started working before or soon after the liberation and had tasted the bitterness of life in the old society. Normally they felt that they had persevered and were masters of their own fates. Most of them had had little schooling and some were even illiterate. They looked at Chairman Mao as their savior and benefactor. They exalted Mao as a Buddha or redeemer. Some of their pet phrases were "for the kindness of Chairman Mao" or "with the good fortune of Chairman Mao" or "blessed be Chairman Mao's name." Deep in their minds, they regarded intellectuals as untrustworthy, while envious of their knowledge and talents.

The other category was young workers who had been assigned to work in the factory when they left high school. Their ideology and educational levels were totally different from those of the old workers. About intellectuals they did not have a feeling of unfriendliness or jealousy, but a feeling of curiosity or admiration. For instance, while tending the machines, many workers used to chat or take a stroll, since the operation of the machines did not require eyes always to be fixed on them. I used to read my *For Your Reference*, in which all the young workers were interested and which they liked to come to my side to read without asking my permission. This I did not mind at all, but I really thought it ridiculous that *For Your Reference* was circulated internally and should not be accessible to workers, while, according to Mao's instructions, intellectuals should receive reeducation from them. How could the educated deny the educators the newspaper that the educated were reading? In face of this contradiction, I kept my eyes half-closed.

The old workers had different feelings about this matter. They frowned upon my reading papers by the machine, although they themselves often went away from the machines, they were not supposed to leave and chatted outside the factory. However, they never explicitly voiced their aversion, but tried to show their displeasure in other ways. For example, the old worker Yuan, who was head of the workshop and concurrently the quality examiner, used to come to my machine when I was reading and make spot checks. I took it easy, because I had 100 percent confidence in the quality of my products. After the checks he usually went away without making any comments, but his facial expression clearly revealed his aversion to my reading newspapers. However, I went my own way, reading my papers as usual. Once he could no longer take it and challenged me. "How come I've never seen you use a vernier or vernier caliper to measure the notch?"

"I did. Nothing abnormal," I retorted.

"Since you've never used a vernier or vernier caliper, how do you know there is nothing wrong?" His tone sounded as if he already had a handle against me.

Uttering no more words, I immediately picked up a newly processed piece from under the machine, took a swift glance at it with my naked eye, and handed it to him, saying, "I can tell by my naked eye that the notch of this padlock core is three-thousandths of a millimeter away from the center, and within the tolerance."

He remained speechless for a short while, and then checked it with his vernier and vernier caliper. The result was just as I had told him, so he went away without uttering another word.

It was a pity that I did not know when to stop and failed to control myself. I thought workers were straightforward and much less frightening than intellectuals, and I no longer appeared as humble as in the publishing house. The fact that I contradicted that old worker in a gentle way would never have happened while I worked in the publishing house. In a way, I had gone too far; therefore, I had to pay for it later.

Though the factory was small, it had bureaucrats at every level. Its party secretary acted concurrently as its director in order to strengthen the unified Party leadership. Under him there were two deputy directors in charge of production and one personnel manager/security commissar, who was enormously powerful since he was in charge of both the Party's day-to-day duties and the files of all employees. This man, Liu Kuo-tung, was in his thirties at that time, tall and robust and very smart, at least always playing smart. He had not received much education, but had the gift of gab. He had been brought up in a poor urban resident's family and had been a young vagabond and a small rascal before he became a worker. Because of this background, his language was vulgar and coarse. As he was considered a descendant of "Red class origin," he had easily become a Youth League member and later a Party member. The Anti-Culture Movement offered him the golden opportunity of first being a "rebel" and then soaring on the wings of a cyclone to the position of personnel manager. Unlike both the old and young workers, he was a typical Communist bureaucrat who took pleasure in punishing people and seeing them in difficulty. The first time he punished me was during Nixon's first visit to China.

Prior to President Nixon's arrival, Henry Kissinger had come to China in advance to make arrangements. At first he came in secret, but later the news of his trips was released before his arrival. My strong desire for freedom was aroused when the Chinese government for the first time publicly announced Henry Kissinger's visit. The official announcement contained just a few lines, but I read it dozens of times. Then, based on the time he was scheduled to arrive in Peking, I calculated the approximate hour at which his plane was to fly over the Shanghai area. An hour earlier, I climbed onto the roof of my house and began to stare into the sky, trying to have a look at his plane. I climbed down from the roof after two hours without having seen anything. The mere idea of Kissinger's airplane flying over my head gave me great consolation.

I became aware only later that I was lucky that Kissinger had not flown via Shanghai; otherwise I would not have been so free as to climb onto the roof to wait for his plane to appear. This was inferred from what was to happen to me later, during Nixon's first visit.

After having talks with Chinese leaders in Peking, Nixon arrived in Shanghai one afternoon and left China the next morning. On the day of Nixon's scheduled arrival, it was my turn to work the morning shift. One day earlier, the group head had consulted with me. "As tomorrow's swing shift will be short of hands, would you please work for an extra shift?" This meant that I should work both the morning shift and the swing shift the next day. This offer was not unusual. As a matter of fact, I was often asked to do so, and often accepted this kind of proposal with willingness, because by so doing I got subsidy pay.

The next day Nixon arrived in Shanghai, and I worked from 6:00 A.M. until 11:00 P.M. in the factory. Unexpectedly, in the evening Liu Kuo-tung came to my machine and said to me, "Wong, you have to work for another extra shift tomorrow." This was rare, as he was so important that he had never bothered about shift arrangements. Now he not only concerned himself with such a trivial matter but also talked seriously with me in a tone that suggested that he was representing the "organization." Since I had seldom objected to working overtime, I answered, "Okay."

Then he said with an even more authoritative attitude, "Okay, then you need not go back home tonight, because when you reach home after this shift it'll be midnight, and how can you get here early tomorrow morning? In my office I've got two beds. You can sleep in one of them after this shift, and Master Yuan in the other one." With this, he left. Yuan was head of this workshop, as mentioned above, and "master" was a respectful form of addressing a worker.

I was quite slow and even at that moment did not quite understand his real intention. This personnel manager had both adopted an authoritative attitude, which did not allow a negative answer to what he had requested, and shown his thoughtfulness by trying to save time needed to go back and forth between the factory and my home after I had worked for sixteen hours in a row. It sounded reasonable and considerate. But why did they want me to work the morning shift for two consecutive days? I could not understand, nor did I try to. Later on I occasionally heard someone reveal in a chat that during Nixon's first visit to China the police had detained a number of people several hours before Nixon's arrival and released them several hours after his departure. Then I suddenly realized why my leader had asked me to do extra shifts for two consecutive days and had not allowed me to go back home for one night. In other words, during the period from several hours before Nixon's arrival to several hours after his departure, I had been in the factory. How smart! It was custody in a disguised form! The extra shifts had nothing to do with production, but with the U.S. president. I had not had the least idea that the Chinese host had taken such great pains to take precautionary measures.

That was an episode none too pleasant, but not too unpleasant either. As a whole, life in the factory was much easier than in the publishing house. I enjoyed being with workers more than with intellectuals. My old group leader, Hwa Shou-yi, who had been "fighting high temperatures" along with me, treated me very well. Apart from the above episode related to the U.S. president, about which he could be of no help, whatever happened to me, he would deal with the factory administration on my behalf. As he was still in the Party, the Party organization in the factory showed some respect for him, and as he was easygoing and friendly, he enjoyed great popularity among the workers, who believed what he said. I owed him a lot, but I also did something nice for him. Although he had lost his position as a group leader, I still treated him as my superior. Not only did I take a respectful attitude toward him, just as in the old days when he was in power, but I also secretly protected him. Hwa was in his prime: tall, well built, handsome, and gentlemanly. In our workshop there was a female worker, who, though not very young, was still attractive with her graceful bearing. As a romantic woman, she did not conceal her admiration for Hwa. They seemed to be on very close terms. Almost everyone in the factory was pretty sure they were in love, and there was even gossip that they had been seen walking hand-in-hand. Anyway, people gossiped about their affair with such certainty that they gave the impression that they could produce irrefutable evidence.

In this factory, just as in the whole society, there was no such thing as privacy. Anything could be a topic for gossip. People tended to make unbridled assumptions and roundabout inquiries into a person's private life, and add some inflammatory details. At the time, the affair between Hwa and this female worker was the favorite topic in the factory, but whenever it was mentioned in my presence, I always dismissed it as nonsense, saying seriously, "Matters regarding a man and a woman are something that no third person can ever really know. Even a father cannot speak for his son, or brother for brother. Only God knows! However, I know Hwa very well. He is a man who gets along well with everybody, old and young, man and woman, and I know he is very devoted to his wife. I can be sure that he treats this woman in the way he does his other friends, and there's nothing unusual between them." No matter how people laughed at my remarks, I stuck to my view.

Actually, "fighting high temperatures" was an exaggerated slogan. First of all, as we were just lowly workers, there was little that needed our "fighting." Secondly, there had been no really high temperatures to fight, because we had worked for several summers and winters. I was content with my lot, but my former leader, Hwa, was not. After four or five years of "fighting high temperatures," the publishing house resumed business, and this Party member strove to return to the publishing house and succeeded. Although he did not return to his job as group leader, leaving behind physical labor and scandal must have been a great relief for him. He was happy. Putting himself in my position, he thought I must be disappointed at not being recalled by the publishing house. He was kind enough to have a heart-to-heart talk with me, and consoled me and asked me to be patient. As a matter of fact, I did not want to be recalled and would have been happy to stay put, because I had found it much easier to deal with workers than intellectuals. Yet, as the custom was, I had to congratulate him on the termination of his "fighting high temperatures." Then I revealed my desire that, since *Chi-ku lu* could not be published in the current social and political climate, I would appreciate having my manuscript back so that I could continue to polish it. He readily promised to help me. In this sort of matter there were no formal rules to observe; what we needed were connections. If he had a low opinion of me, he could have regarded my request as a serious problem and, by making a mountain out of a molehill, referred it to the higher leadership for decision. It could have taken a long or indefinite time and, in the meantime, new problems might have cropped up. But he was sincere in his attempt to help me. As though pushing a boat along the current, he just quietly talked to someone in charge of my manuscript and notified me to take it back. There was nothing wrong with them doing so, because I, as the author, had the right to recover my manuscript. Thus Hwa did me a great favor which cost him nothing. Years later, having the manuscript with me, I was able to get it published after I came to the free world.

With Hwa's departure from the factory, it seemed as if I had lost an umbrella. In case any problem arose, no one could intercede for me. Unfortunately, a problem did arise.

Wendy was a female worker who had entered the factory as a junior high school graduate in 1966. As both her parents were old workers, her family background was "Red," really up to the mark. However, she was a good-natured girl, modest and particularly nice to me. Twelve years younger than I, she liked to work the same shift with me and keep me company. Knowledge seemed mysterious to her, and she admired intellectuals. She had loved studying during her childhood, and thought that, given her class origin and as the only daughter of a working couple, she would easily make her way into a university, until the Anti-Culture Movement shattered her dream.

She was not alone in stopping by at my machine from time to time. Many young workers, male and female, used to stand around my machine chatting with me or among themselves. This kind of chatting was called *ga san wu* in Shanghainese. Since Wendy was on the same shift with me, it was more convenient for her. The noises made by the machines were so deafening that private conversations could hardly be heard by others. We trusted each other, but so far nothing called "love" was going on between us.

Understanding helps foster what is called love. When Wendy heard of my plan to take a trip alone on Labor Day, which falls on May 1 in all Communist countries and is a good time for traveling, she asked to go with me, as she had never traveled before. I readily agreed. We visited Hangchow together, and our love was born beside blue lakes in green hills.

We left the factory after the swing shift, got on a bus which took us directly to the Western Railway Station, and took a night train for Hangchow. Before leaving home for work that day, Wendy had told her parents that she was not returning that night because she was going to travel with a girlfriend for several days right after work. Her mother was suspicious about our recent closeness and took for granted that her daughter would take the train at the Northern Railway Station, which was just a couple of blocks away from their home as well as from our factory. She went there around 11:00 P.M. to investigate who would be traveling with her daughter. Of course, her efforts were to no avail. However, the next day she got in touch with the girl whom Wendy had said she would be traveling with and found herself deceived. When Wendy returned home after three days in Hangchow, she was instantly interrogated by her mother. She could not but admit having traveled with me, but flatly denied there was an affair between us.

Old workers like Wendy's mother were very conservative and very concerned about decency. As she was afraid that her daughter's premarital affair would become a galling shame and unbearable humiliation to the entire family once it was disclosed, she tended to accept her daughter's words and was reluctant to dig out the truth. However, she did not want to see us continue as lovers. She put Wendy under close surveillance and took strict precautions to prevent her going out with me. The major weakness in this strategy lay in her attempt to save face.

Unwilling to talk about this with the factory, she could not ask that arrangements be made to assign Wendy and me to work different shifts or in different workshops. Had she done so, the leaders of the factory would surely have complied. Since she did not do so, Wendy continued to chat with me while we were on the same shift.

Destiny plotted against us, and our happiness did not last long. We had taken some pictures on our trip to Hangchow, and I had them developed and printed. I took them to the factory and showed them to her. As she was afraid that her mother might see them, although they were all pictures of individuals, she asked me to keep them for her. Thus, I put these pictures back into my bag. That day we were on the swing shift. While I was at home in the morning, I wrote a letter to Chairman Mao. Knowing that common letters could never reach him, I had indulged in wild fantasy and written the letter in the style of ancient rhythmic prose characterized by parallelism, ornateness, and archaic words. This is what I had calculated: Only if Mao's secretaries failed to decipher my letter might there be a possibility that they would show it to Mao. The subject of my letter was simply imploring him to grant me permission to leave China. I contended frankly that my continued existence in mainland China would be a burden to them, while his permission to allow me to leave China would be proof of the magnanimity of the Chinese Communist Party as well as his own greatness. I kept my fingers crossed, thinking that if the letter should reach Mao, he might approve it, because he always did something unexpected by adopting an original approach. I wanted to take a chance anyway. Knowing that nobody would support me in this effort, I did not mention my letter to anyone, not even to Wendy, although I had the letter with me that day. I simply told her that after work I would go to the general post office, which was not far from her home. As I wanted to send the letter registered, I could not put it in a maildrop but had to go to a post office. Since no post office was open at midnight, I wanted to go to the general post office to see if it stayed open late.

"I don't think it is open at that hour," Wendy said.

"I want to try anyway," I said resolutely.

Although Wendy's home was close to the factory, it was in a quite secluded place and it was scary for a woman to go home alone at midnight. Therefore I walked her home every night after the swing shift.

Two of the pictures taken in Hangchow that caused a calamity to me.

That night, when we walked out of the factory, I asked her, "Shall I walk you home first?"

"No, let's go to the post office first," she answered.

When we arrived, we found it was closed. I felt disappointed, and Wendy was very annoyed. She reprimanded me for not having listened to her and having wasted time and energy in the wee hours. I did not answer back, and we walked to her home in silence.

Just when we reached the entrance to her lane and she started to enter it, a number of people suddenly emerged out of darkness, and we fell into an ambush. All the ambushers did not come from Wendy's family. But one was Wendy's mother, who had been waiting in the dark for quite a while. Worried that Wendy was unusually late, she had hidden herself somewhere outside the lane to wait for her daughter to return. When she caught sight of us, she rushed out of her hiding place and began to interrogate Wendy.

In the meantime, I was surrounded by the other ambushers, who apparently had been following us for some time. They claimed that they were members of "Civil Attack and Military Defense" and wanted to take me to their headquarters. I was deeply puzzled. I knew, as everybody else knew, that Civil Attack and Military Defense was a semiofficial organization which had branches all over the country. It had been established in accordance with an illogical instruction of Madame Mao's, "We should attack the enemy by civil means and defend ourselves with military means." This organization was a mixture of militia, police, and army, and was composed of scum and rascals. Besides being employed by the ultra-leftists as a tool for seizing power, the Civil Attack and Military Defense shouldered the responsibility of maintaining social order and dealing with gangsters. What did they have to do with me?

After we interrogated each other briefly, I found they had misunderstood me. It was a very hot summer. Whether at work or at home or on the street, I always wore a sleeveless sweater, a pair of shorts, and a pair of plastic sandals on my bare feet. Wendy, like other young women workers, was well dressed and always changed clothes before and after work. When we were walking to her home from the general post office, and these Civil Attack and Military Defense members saw us dressed totally differently and walking abreast without uttering a word, they became suspicious and thought that I must be tailing an unknown lady; therefore they wanted to arrest me.

I could not help laughing and said to them, "We are colleagues. I walked her home after the swing shift. I was not shadowing her."

By the time I dispelled the misunderstanding, Wendy and her mother seemed to have finished their conversation and had started to walk into their house. The Civil Attack and Military Defense warriors called Wendy back and asked her, pointing at me, "Do you know him?"

"Of course I do," Wendy sneered at them, "we are in the same workshop. How can I not know him?"

It seemed that all misunderstanding had disappeared like thawing ice, and I was ready to leave when, like a bolt from the blue, Wendy's mother turned round, came up, and shouted to the warriors, "Please arrest this man." She pointed at me, "He is a bad man, a very bad man." The Civil Attack and Military Defense warriors looked at her for a second, motionless and expressionless, and showed no intention to comply with her demand. It was very obvious that her words only proved that Wendy and I were acquaintances and totally dispelled their original suspicion. Then Wendy's mother shouted again, "I tell you, he is a rightist. He is a very, very bad man." With this crash of thunder, she took Wendy into their house.

The word "rightist" to these brave men was what a drop of blood is to mosquitoes or flies. They encircled me for the second time. "Aha! You are a rightist!"

"I was," I retorted, "But I have been delabeled."

"Then you are a delabeled rightist," they said. "A delabeled rightist is still a rightist."

"Okay, even if I am a rightist," I argued, "so what? At first you thought I was tailing her, and wanted to arrest me. Then you realized that it was misunderstanding, and decided not to arrest me. Now you know I was a rightist and want to arrest me again. Should all rightists be arrested?"

These heroic warriors had been riding roughshod over ordinary people and were not accustomed to being contradicted. Hearing what I said, they flew into a rage and became desperate to have their own way. "Whatever you said, we learned from the masses a while ago that you are a bad guy. This is sufficient to give us the right to look into your case. You must go with us to our office now."

Flanked by the Civil Attack and Military Defense warriors, I went to their office. It was a small room on a narrow street, and a worker-like man sitting inside seemed to be their leader. His warriors reported to him, "This is a rightist, not behaving well and doing bad things, so we arrested him."

"What were the bad things?" the leader asked.

There was silence for a while. These heroes may have been too embarrassed to say that they had first thought I was tailing a girl and then realized it had been a misunderstanding. However, they did not acknowledge there had been a misunderstanding; otherwise, why should they have arrested me?

One of the warriors was clever enough to skip the first part of the encounter with equivocation, and stressed another topic, "We followed him and a girl from the general post office to the lane where the girl lives. We found out that they work in the same factory and that he was walking her home after the swing shift. Their factory is on the bank of the Soochow River, but they were walking to the girl's home from the general post office, which is in the opposite direction. There must be something wrong with them. Furthermore, the girl's mother revealed that he is a rightist, a very bad guy."

Without waiting for their leader to interrogate me, I answered, "I walk her home every day after the swing shift. Today I intended to send a registered letter and thought the general post office might still be open. We went there together and, on finding it was closed, turned back and walked to her home."

One of the heroes said, "Lie! The post office is not open at night."

"You are correct," I said, "but I did not know that until tonight."

"So you didn't send the letter?" someone asked casually.

"No, I didn't," I answered.

"Where is it?" someone asked.

"In my bag." I tried to remain calm, but was very nervous at heart, because in my bag there were two "bombs:" a letter to Mao, and pictures taken in Hangchow. These two "bombs" would prove fatal to me if they were discovered.

Hearing my answer, the leader snapped open my bag, and I said to myself, "Damn it!" The first thing that met his eyes was the sealed letter with the striking characters of the addressee, "Chairman Mao, Peking," and my name and return address. It also bore two other characters: "Registered." At that time anything involving Mao was treated with extreme discretion. These pawns retreated to another room, taking the troublesome letter with them and leaving me alone in the room for a long, long while. When they came back, they gave the sealed letter back to me and asked me to open it. I did what I was told. Then they grabbed it back and began to read it immediately. The letter was passed silently from hand to hand and did not evoke any comments from the readers, who just looked at one another in blank dismay. After many "heroes" had touched this hot potato for at least a minute, they retreated from the room once again, leaving me alone for an even longer time. Then they came in with resolution and the leader stated, "Your case is very serious. We are transferring you to our headquarters." I did not utter a word. I knew that I was already in the tiger's mouth and had no choice but to submit to the mercy of these "heroes." The only thing I could do now was obey whatever they commanded me to do.

They put me into a car neither like a freight truck nor a prisoners' van. It might have been a special vehicle used by the Civil Attack and Military Defense thugs for their "special" activities. I was moved to a building on a street close to Nanking Road, which seemed to be the headquarters. It was an old-style middle-class house, but with quite weird construction, for it had a room which was particularly suitable for use as a jail. I was placed in this room as soon as we arrived there. Those who had escorted me there did not utter a word, except to tell me to hand over my handbag. They also searched my body, and took away my spectacles, my watch, and the waist string of my underpants. After that, they disappeared.

This high-ceilinged room had no windows. There was a little hole in the wall to let in light. It was almost as high as the ceiling, so that it would be out of the question to reach it by climbing. The room was literally empty, and so spacious that it could accommodate about a dozen people sleeping side by side on the ground. It was late at night or nearly dawn when I was taken there, and there was not a soul in the room. I was so tired that I thought I could get to sleep as soon as I lay on the ground. However, I was worried about my family, because I thought they must be missing me. I stayed awake for a long while, but could think of no way to notify my family from here. I was also worried about Wendy and the pictures in my handbag, which, I was sure, would cause us serious trouble. Then I fell asleep, without knowing at what exact time. It was noon the next day when I awoke. I found that the room was packed with temporary prisoners, some sitting and others lying down, and that newcomers were constantly arriving. It seemed that the Civil Attack and Military Defense was very effective in making arrests.

Some of the inmates were called by name and led away, and did not come back again. This meant that this place was a temporary house of detention. I waited and waited, and anxiously gazed at the door until my eyes became strained. Evening came and passed into night, but no one came to fetch me for interrogation. At noon and in the evening, someone had come in to give me a rice box but had said nothing. When spoken to, he had just glowered for a while and left. I wondered why I had been left alone for so long, and could not close my eyes during the night.

Another day. Strangers came in one after another at dawn. Again, they left one after another. During the whole day, each time the door opened, I would think, "It's my turn. They have come to fetch me now." To my disappointment, they came either to put someone in or call someone else out, not me! As my watch had already been taken away, I did not know the exact time. All I could do was watch the sun on the wall, but I became startled whenever it stopped moving. Had I been forgotten? Full of misgivings and apprehensions, I felt that each minute was passing like a year.

Three consecutive days elapsed like that. My nerves seemed to be breaking. Fortunately, the walls of this building were thin, its sound insulation poor, and my hearing very sharp. On the second day of my detention, I heard someone in the next room saying the words "padlock spare parts factory," "a person of fighting high temperatures" and "Chairman Mao." This clearly indicated that someone was talking about me on the phone and that my case had begun to receive attention. Now, on this third day, I heard several people quarreling in the next room. One of the voices was very familiar to me, and it was the voice of Liu Kuo-tung, the personnel manager of my factory. It was quite obvious that there was a difference of opinion and that they were arguing vehemently, both sides raising their voices. Liu was normally very loud, but now he was even louder. It was strange that although I had never been well disposed toward him, I was now somewhat touched by his voice and hoped that he would come to see me. To my disappointment, after the argument was over, he did not show up. Had he left? I was depressed.

Day four. Liu came again, and brought with him the old worker, Yuan, the quality examiner and leader of my workshop. I was summoned into the office, where they were sitting with the Civil Attack and

Military Defense man. Near the door was a stool. They had obviously placed it there for me, because as soon as I reached the door, they pointed to it, saying, "Sit there." So I did. Thus, by comparison, I looked only half as tall as they did. I really admired their wisdom in using this method for making their image look big and mine small.

It seemed that everyone in this society knew the ABCs of obtaining confessions by compulsion. So did these two people. They first gazed at me, their eyes flashing intimidation. I knew the trick they were playing, but did not want to offend them by making light of their threat. Therefore, instead of looking them in the eye, I just sat in silence, putting on a pose of awaiting their interrogation. At the same time, I sensed that the Civil Attack and Military Defense representative, who was acting either as host or assessor, did not join in gazing at me, but just looked on.

Anyway, after a long silence, Liu and Yuan started questioning me. "Do you want to get out of this place?" The personnel manager took the lead.

"Yes, I do," said I.

"Then, first of all, you must plead guilty," said Yuan.

I did not answer him right away. On the one hand, I needed time to consider my words, and on the other I was thinking of dealing with them in the same way they were dealing with me—that is, employing taciturnity as a weapon in this psychological warfare.

The old worker was less patient and first broke the silence. "Do you plead guilty? If you don't, then don't expect to leave here. Do you plead guilty or not?"

By this time I had decided to use attack as a means of defense. "I went to the post office to mail a registered letter to Chairman Mao. First of all, there is not a word in my letter attacking our great leader. Second, I put down my name and address, therefore, it is totally different from counterrevolutionary, anonymous letters. I just exercised my right of writing to our state leaders. I was open and aboveboard when writing this letter. I am not guilty. I demand my letter be returned to me, because I still want to mail it."

Before the factory men had a chance to reply, the Civil Attack and Military Defense man said, "We are not going to look into your writing Chairman Mao. Everybody has the right to write Chairman Mao. We have never said you are guilty because you wrote the letter. However, I want to tell you this: we have investigated your letter and found you want to leave this country. It's only wishful thinking. You'd better give up this idea altogether. We are not going to return your letter to you. You must not mail it. We'll place it on file." His remarks apparently represented Civil Attack and Military Defense's view of this matter.

Then Yuan began to speak. "We are not going to talk about this anymore. We just ask you a simple question. Do you want to get out of here? If you do, then you must make a clean breast of your relationship with Wendy."

I answered him firmly, "We have no other relationship than that of colleagues."

The personnel manager chipped in, "I want to let on to you that due to the influence of her colleagues and family, Wendy is now coming to her senses. She hates you and has exposed all your crimes, which are serious enough to put you in jail. We have obtained all the necessary evidence and need no more, but we still want to give you an opportunity to seek leniency through a thorough confession."

This technique of trapping me into a confession was too familiar to me. I kept silent.

Yuan wanted to break the silence, but had a slip of the tongue, "What kind of relationship do you really have?" Obviously, they had secured no confession from Wendy, and his words laid bare the personnel manager's lie.

"We have no other relationship than that of colleagues," I insisted.

"That simple?" Yuan asked.

"Yes, that simple." I held my ground.

The personnel manager staged a comeback. "Don't be so stubborn. I will show my hand. According to the Civil Attack and Military Defense regulations, those detained here can never get out unless their organizations come to fetch them. It is we who can take you out, but we will not as long as you refuse to confess your relations with Wendy."

I still kept silent.

Then he held up a piece of evidence. "What's this?"

It was the packet of pictures they had found in my handbag. However, it did not surprise me. "They are the pictures I took for her. I've just had them developed and printed, and haven't had a chance to give them to her."

The old worker said, "Why did she ask you, not others, to take pictures for her? Isn't this an indication that there exists some special relationship between you?"

"This is a normal relation between colleagues, not an affair between a man and a woman."

"Okay, since you are still so stubborn, you'd better continue to stay here. We will not take you back today. Without our consent, there's no way you can get out of here," he said haughtily.

Then the Civil Attack and Military Defense fellow spoke up, "We are not running a hotel. This is not a place for someone to stay forever. If your organization does not take you back, we'll send you somewhere where you deserve to be."

I was aware that his words had been said to my factory men as well as to me, but the old worker seemed to have missed the subtlety of his words and interpreted them in his own way. "See? Did you hear what he said? Either we will take you back to the factory or you will be sent to jail."

"I've committed no crime. I won't be sentenced to imprisonment," I said.

Liu banged his fist on the table. "How stubborn you are! Now we will go. See if we can't send you to jail." With this, he and Yuan stood up and assumed a pose of leaving. But the Civil Attack and Military Defense man was sitting motionless, wearing an embarrassed expression.

Now it came time for me to make a scene. I was so anxious to get out of that bandits' lair that I could not bear to stay there one more minute, and the very thought that I would wait for my organization to fetch me day after day drove me mad. I earnestly appealed to the old worker, "Oh, Master Yuan, I have devoted all my energy to your workshop. We are not at enmity with each other. Take me back today, and I promise to work hard under your leadership and will try my utmost to support you in promoting production."

Seeing that I was becoming compliant and was anxious to get out, they took their seats again. The personnel manager changed his tone. "Today we did come here with the intention of taking you back. Your family is very worried and anxious to have you back. The day after you disappeared, your family came to the factory to inquire about you. At

first we did not know where you were either, but later we were informed by the Civil Attack and Military Defense of your whereabouts.
Your family is expecting you. Do you want to be released like this? We,
the leadership of the factory, are very serious about this matter and
have held several meetings to discuss it. We were nice enough to you
that we did not look into such a serious problem as your attempt to
mail a letter to Chairman Mao. How do you return our kindness? You
even refused to make a clean breast of your relationship with Wendy.
How can you expect us to let you out? How shall we justify ourselves
if we take you back under these circumstances?"

"I really have no special relation with Wendy."

"If you don't, how come you took so many pictures of her?"

"Because it was the first time she had visited Hangchow," I unwit-
tingly let out the secret.

"What? You went to Hangchow together?" They cried out simultaneously. Their four wide eyes revealed their extreme astonishment and
excitement. They seemed on the point of saying something but refrained from uttering it. They looked as if they were frightened out of
their wits. After they had exchanged a few meaningful glances at each
other, the personnel manager said, "You might as well stay here today."
With this they got out in a great hurry, as though in fear I would run up
to stop them.

Having returned to the cell, I began to review everything that had
happened, and it suddenly dawned upon me that I had committed a terrible and fatal mistake. It was obvious that they had been totally unaware of our trip to Hangchow before. This meant that Wendy had revealed nothing about our relationship. I had mistakenly thought that
since Wendy's mother had already known about our Hangchow trip,
she would certainly have told the factory leadership about it. Now my
judgment seemed to have been wrong. I had also assumed that since all
the backgrounds of the pictures I had taken of Wendy were
Hangchow's famous scenic places, they would be so easily identified
that it must have been discovered that Wendy and I had made the trip
together. Now it appeared that these factory men were totally ignorant
of Hangchow, and I had miscalculated. My blunder involuntarily provided a weapon for them to exert pressure on Wendy. There is nothing
more painful than making such a mistake. It was really inexcusable. I

repented of my carelessness so that I could not sleep a wink during the whole night.

From the last sentence the personnel manager had uttered, it could be inferred that they were going to take me back the next day, but they did not come. Throughout that day I waited and waited, and felt that I would go insane at any minute. The only time I felt some consolation was when I heard someone in the next office speaking, probably on the phone. As the voice was not too loud, I could not catch any full sentences but only some short phrases, such as "the padlock spare parts factory," or some remarks which sounded like an ultimatum, such as "he is not allowed to stay here anymore," "not even one more day," "tomorrow will be the last day," and "be sure to send someone here." These fragments of his conversation on the phone convinced me that if no one came from the factory tomorrow, the Civil Attack and Military Defense would make its own decision and send me away. Where? Tomorrow would tell.

Another night came, and I still could not close my eyes. The next morning Yuan came, but alone. He did not interrogate me. When he sent for me, he seemed to have already gone through all the formalities needed for taking me back. I was asked to sign some forms to acknowledge receipt of my spectacles, my watch, the waist string of my underpants, and the handbag, from which, of course, the letter and pictures were missing.

I followed Yuan and walked back to the factory, which was just a short distance away and which seemed to have undergone certain changes in the past several days. As soon as we got to the factory, the personnel manager announced to me that a "study class" had been established for my sake. "Study class" was a fashionable term borrowed from Mao's quotation "Establishing a study class is a good method." By that time this quotation had so taken root in the hearts of the people that study classes were springing up across the country. What was a study class? It was actually a series of meetings with different attendees held to obtain confessions, and had nothing whatsoever to do with either "study" or "class."

When the personnel manager had made this announcement to me, he grinned hideously and triumphantly. "You should work in your workshop as usual, but are not allowed to work swing shift or night shift. You dislike the morning shift, don't you? Well, we simply want you to do the morning shift only. Moreover, you are not allowed to converse with Wendy when you are with her in the workshop."

Again I perceived the difference between the factory and the publishing house. The working class, after all, was not as resourceful as the intelligentsia, who always had with them a whole bag of tricks. Had this incident happened in the publishing house, it would surely have been dealt with in a different manner. First, they would not have let me off for writing to Mao and would have raised a great fuss about my application to leave China. Secondly, as to the investigation of my relationship with Wendy, if we had been in a cultural or educational unit, it would have been far more thoroughgoing and serious, and Wendy and I would have been prevented from working in the same shift or the same workshop. More likely, the leaders of a cultural or educational unit would not have been affected by any personal feelings and given such a light punishment as making me work the morning shift every day simply because I disliked it. Just making things difficult for someone without thinking of producing any substantial political effect was not the mentality of the intelligentsia. Compared to them, the leadership of the factory was really stupid, and the study class was of no avail, for they did not succeed in squeezing any confession from either me or Wendy.

Wendy and I still worked in the same workshop, although not always on the same shift as before, when I could change shifts easily, yet we sometimes still worked on the same shift. Even if we were not on the same shift for weeks, or even if we were forbidden to speak to each other, there were many ways we could pass information. For example, nearly every worker had a small locker made from some waste material, and used it to store his or her personal belongings such as cups, bowls, and working gloves. The brass padlock cores were piping hot when they came out of the machine, so we had to wear gloves. People were accustomed to pulling off their gloves during breaks and leaving them by the machines or in any handy place, but always stored them in their own small boxes at the end of the day. I had no locker of my own. After I became intimate with Wendy, she offered to share hers with me. When I got out of the Civil Attack and Military Defense and came back to the workshop, I still used that locker, and no one seemed to pay attention to it. Again, this was the difference between intellectuals and "uncouth fellows," as workers liked to call themselves. The former would have been much more sensitive and would definitely not have allowed this kind of thing to happen.

On the morning of the first day I was back at work, I picked up my gloves from the locker, and when I was going to put them on, I felt something like paper inside. I knew it must have been put there by Wendy. I worked as usual, not turning a hair. Not until nobody was around did I take it out and read it. It was in Wendy's handwriting, and covered with small and closely spaced characters. It informed me of what had happened to her in detail. As expected, she had withstood all pressure, denying any special relationship with me and covering up our trip to Hangchow. Even when they pointed out to her that I had confessed everything, including our trip and having sex with her, she did not believe that they had gotten this information from my confession, because she knew that I had the pictures in my handbag that night and concluded that they must have identified the backgrounds in the pictures. Therefore she flatly denied having had sex with me. Her message gave me reassurance and courage to withstand pressure. Every evening I had to attend the so-called study class, but no matter what the intimidations, I remained firm.

Had this happened in the publishing house, I first would have been isolated from my colleagues, and no one would have dared to come near me or greet me, let alone converse with me. In the factory, although Wendy was forbidden to speak to me and she deliberately kept at a distance to avoid suspicion, other young workers, Cindy being one of them, were not subject to this prohibition and came as close to me as usual. Cindy was a high school graduate of the same year as Wendy. She did not work in our workshop, but was on intimate terms with both Wendy and me and treasured our friendship. After I came back from the Civil Attack and Military Defense, she kept coming over to me for chats and became a messenger between Wendy and me. Thus, not only did the whole process of study class produce no effects, but the "mass criticism" to which I was subjected by the factory leadership became a farce. When the leaders called on the young workers, especially those who were thought to have been close to me, such as Wendy and Cindy, to hand in their big-character posters criticizing me and they did not know what to write, I secretly drafted the essays for them and they copied them on the paper. At one of the general meetings the leaders even praised Wendy and Cindy for their good big-character posters criticizing me.

Of course, criticisms were mere formalities which could not do me any substantial harm. The motive behind them was to cook up charges and secure a confession from me.

Through Cindy, who frequently passed Wendy's messages to me, and through Wendy, who kept leaving notes in my gloves, I had a rough picture of my whole situation.

On the morning following my detention, the Civil Attack and Military Defense contacted the factory by phone and asked them to send someone to pick me up. As this notorious organization had Madame Mao as its backer, all the units tried their best to comply with its demands and none of them dared to offend it. Whenever a person fell victim to the Civil Attack and Military Defense, his unit was supposed to take action concerted with it. The Civil Attack and Military Defense had a fundamental theory to the effect that, being a dictatorial arm of the so-called proletarian headquarters—that is, Mao's clique—it never arrested any innocent people and therefore needed the cooperation of the victim's unit in picking him up when it intended to release him. The fact that the victim had to be taken back by his unit gave the impression that he had not been wrongfully arrested, so that the Civil Attack and Military Defense could preserve its dignity. On the other hand, when a victim's unit was asked by the Civil Attack and Military Defense to cooperate with it, it meant that this unit had become politically important since the Civil Attack and Military Defense had stooped to enlist its cooperation. However, in my case the Civil Attack and Military Defense met with a rebuff from our factory leaders, who had an axe to grind. They took malicious pleasure in my arrest and believed that writing to Mao was a serious crime and that they were going to see some fun. During the first days of my detention, therefore, they did not touch Wendy, as if she were innocent. In the opinion of the factory leaders I should have been handed over to the police and brought to court or put in jail, while in the opinion of Civil Attack and Military Defense I should not, because my letter to Mao was not an anonymous one and just contained a personal request without making any reactionary remarks.

Anyway, knowing that they could in no way raise a fuss about my letter to Mao, the factory leadership had to be content with the second-best choice, that of capitalizing on the so-called abnormal relationship between a man and a woman. Thus they went all out to secure a confession from Wendy, who they thought was vulnerable to pressure. But they were wrong, because Wendy was as firm as a rock. This really created a knotty problem for them, because Wendy was descended from a lineage of three generations of pure workers, by Communist standards a typical Red family supposed to have suffered bitterly in the old society and to harbor deep hatred toward the Kuomintang. Besides, some of her aunts and uncles were ranking Party officials. In an era when one's class origin was considered the most important asset, the leaders hesitated to take action against her immediately. They selected Wendy's mother as both an ally and a point of penetration, and tried to exert pressure on Wendy through her. Good for them, for Wendy's mother hated me so intensely that she could not be happier with anything than my death; therefore, it was possible to persuade her to cooperate with them.

However, there was a hindrance. Unlike the factory leaders, who were trying as hard as possible to dig out our relationship, Wendy's mother regarded our affair as a disgrace to both their family and ancestors. Her only way of exerting pressure on Wendy was to force her to sever her relations with me and get married as quickly as possible. At the same time, she did not want her daughter to acknowledge any sexual relations with me. On this point, not only did she refuse to keep in step with the factory leaders, but protected her daughter against any pressure from the factory. As the factory leaders did not dare to offend the old worker, they turned to the Civil Attack and Military Defense, asking it to detain me for a few days more so that they would be able to use my release as a bargaining chip and secure a confession from me. Unexpectedly, they did not communicate with each other very well and greatly upset the Civil Attack and Military Defense, which was normally ever-ready to suppress the oppressed. This time the Civil Attack and Military Defense acted out of character and retorted, "Do you think this place is a hotel? You can't even solve a problem which is purely your own internal affair?" In the end, as was widely known in the factory, the factory leaders received an ultimatum from the Civil Attack and Military Defense, which threatened, "If you don't send someone here to take Wong away before such-and-such time tomorrow, we will release him in our way." If the Civil Attack and Military Defense released me unilaterally and let me walk back to the factory by myself, it would be a great humiliation to the factory leaders. That was why they hurriedly sent Yuan to pick me up.

At the moment the Civil Attack and Military Defense broke off with the factory, the leaders were making every effort to press Wendy for a confession, partly because they had no other means left and partly because Wendy's mother had changed her attitude. After the factory leaders discovered that the pictures had been taken at Hangchow, they showed them to Wendy's mother and sent her into a fury. Before that she had tried to cover up our trip to Hangchow, and though terribly angry at heart, she had never thought that we had taken pictures there. Now, when she was shown these pictures, she felt as if she were suffering a head-on blow and could not contain her anger. She cursed between her teeth that she would kill me, and actively took concerted action with the factory leaders to bring pressure on Wendy. Her only reservation was to allow Wendy to keep denying any sexual relations with me.

At this point the factory leaders became wiser and reached a tacit understanding with Wendy's mother. They no longer seriously looked into our sexual relations, but strove to achieve a much bigger goal. They intended, as a first step, to frame a case against me of "a bourgeois intellectual corrupting a worker." If they succeeded in getting Wendy to expose some of the reactionary remarks I had made to her in private, then they could easily cook up much more serious charges against me. Wendy's mother heartily endorsed this plan, which would, at least on the surface, save her daughter's reputation as a virgin. However, the prerequisite for the success of this excellent plan was Wendy's cooperation in exposing my crimes. To the surprise of both the factory leaders and Wendy's mother, Wendy made a bold and explicit statement: "It was not Wong who corrupted me, but I who took the initiative to approach him, and I'll continue to keep in touch with him."

They were annoyed to such an extent that they decided to hold a "study class" for Wendy too. Then Wendy began to have a very hard time. She had to attend meetings after her day shift, and after returning home had to face her mother's advice and reprimand. She was attacked both from within and without her family. In the end, Wendy said to her mother, "I would rather die than act on your words." She mentioned several times that she wanted to die, and meant what she said. Fully aware of her daughter's character and temperament, Wendy's mother was really concerned about the possibility of her committing suicide, and reported her worry to the factory. The factory leaders were afraid of being held responsible for hounding a young worker to death, and began to adopt a strategy of taking one step backward but two steps forward.

They made their purpose known to Wendy and tried to win her over. "We don't have the least intention of giving you a hard time. Our goal is very definite. We just want to aim our spearhead at Wong. Now, let's put aside the question of your relation with him. Nor shall we talk about his corruption of your mind anymore. We will leave you alone if you agree to help us with Wong's political problems. Right now, the whole society is being mobilized by the revolutionary situation to find out the sources of rumors about Comrade Chiang Chin, which have spread in the past several months, and other libelous slanders against the proletarian headquarters. In keeping with this situation, we must make a thorough investigation into Wong. A person like him must have said some reactionary things to you. We only need you to expose his counterrevolutionary words, and then we can put him in jail. You come from a Red family of workers for three generations, and you can rest assured that we'll guarantee your personal record will be clean, both politically and in private life."

When I learned about the situation Wendy was facing, I was extremely scared. I really had told Wendy something that would put me in danger if it were known to others. There were at least two situations in which I could be condemned to die ten thousand deaths if she exposed me. For many years, I had been following Mao's health on television, analyzing each of his movements and then inferring from it how healthy, or how unhealthy, he was. I had said to Wendy several times, "I can tell from Mao's appearance on television last night that he won't be living long, and I can predict that his death will give rise to an open split at the highest level of the hierarchy. We've got to be prepared for the oncoming tumult."

The other case had taken place in the summer of 1975. Then it was widely rumored that Mao was outraged at his wife, Chiang Ch'ing's, behavior and that just when Chiang Ch'ing was going to be consigned to limbo, Chou En-lai had come to her rescue. Public sentiment at that time was unfavorable to Madame Mao, whom people regarded as synonymous with evil, and people were happy to see her fall into disfavor. One day I said to Wendy, "It was Chou's mistake to patch up the quarrel between Mao and Chiang to go along with Mao. Chou might eat his own bitter fruit. From the historical point of view, people like Chiang Ch'ing will certainly come to no good end."

During that period, whoever was audacious enough to say something against Mao or Chiang Ch'ing would definitely be labeled an active counterrevolutionary and even condemned to death. Therefore, if Wendy exposed even one of the two cases, I would be done for. However, she did not utter a word. I felt grateful to her and ashamed of myself for having been weighed down with anxiety for quite a while.

After several months of our seemingly endless distress, one day Wendy met me briefly at Cindy's. Cindy did not live far from the factory either and, in typical conditions for poor workers, in a house located in a narrow lane which accommodated many residents, with people of two or three generations sharing a single small room. Wendy and I, of course, could not talk in Cindy's room. After we met there, we stepped out of the house and talked in the lane in spite of the piercing cold wind. We stood on the lee side facing the wall. Several months of misery had made her look thin and sallow. As she had slipped out of her home on the pretext of running an errand and had not had time to change her clothes, she looked ever more haggard and pallid. Nonetheless, at this moment we were not thinking of our outward appearance, but of something more important.

"I never thought I would have caused you to suffer so much." I tried to console her, but did not quite know how to start.

"There is no need to say that. What's the use of it?" Totally unlike what she had been, she seemed to be rather cool. "What I want to tell you today is that I am feeling relieved now. I've not let you down. After this storm, I became very calm. It changed my whole life and my philosophy. I am disillusioned with this world. Nothing in the world can either cheer me or bother me anymore. My mother has long been urging me to get married, and I have long resisted her pressure. Now I think, why not? That might be good for both of us and for everyone in the world. I won't be happy anymore for the rest of my life anyway. To be married or not to be married, or to marry this man or that man, won't make much difference to me. But I wish you happiness and a bright future. I haven't yet told anyone about my decision, not even my mother. You are the first one in the world who knows it. The reason that I asked you to come here today is that I wanted to inform you of it myself, so that you won't be surprised when you learn it from somebody else. That's all I wanted to say. Goodbye, now." She turned away, then suddenly turned back, saying, "One more thing. I know you want to fly far and high. I pray for you that the day will come soon when you'll be off to distant parts." She had started weeping in the middle of her speech, and choked with sobs.

Before I could say anything she had turned away, wiping her eyes. She did not even go into the house to say goodbye to Cindy. This was the first time we had met since the Civil Attack and Military defense incident.

Thanks to Wendy's stubborn resistance to the pressure from the factory leaders, I was finally exempted from punishment. After Wendy's announcement of her decision to marry, her mother would not allow the factory to disturb her daughter anymore. Under this circumstance, the leaders could not but drop the whole matter.

This incident, though devastating to both Wendy and me, had in no way shaken my determination to stay in the factory. First, I had never desired any favorable treatment from any organization as long as it was controlled by the Communist Party and, therefore, had never been upset or disappointed by any unfair or unfavorable treatment. That's the way of the Communist system. Secondly, this incident convinced me once more that the working class was less resourceful than intellectuals and easier to deal with.

The thing which made me feel utterly disappointed in the factory was actually a trifle in others' eyes. After Hwa Shou-yi helped me to get back my manuscript of *Chi-ku lu*, the publishing houses began to resume their business one after another, and the situation at that time had developed to such an extent that one of the editors in the publishing house hinted that even though *Chi-ku lu* itself was still unsuitable for publication, the publication of its academic thesis could be taken into consideration. Although during the Anti-Culture Movement my manuscript of this book had been preserved by the publishing house, an essay entitled "A Comparative Study of *Tzu-chih-t'ung-chien* and *Chi-ku lu*," which I had written while working on the punctuation and annotation of *Chi-ku lu*, was missing. Fortunately, this essay had been condensed into the preface of my book. Now, since the *Chi-ku lu* manuscript remained intact, I decided to take its preface as a basis to restore the essay. For this, I had to go to the Shanghai Municipal Library to do research.

As soon as the Anti-Culture Movement started, the Shanghai Municipal Library was closed for the purpose of weeding out and destroying "black materials," those materials that were related to the histories of Madame Mao and Chang Chun-ch'iao. Now, after several years of closure, it reopened, but readers faced many inconveniences. First, there were no open bookshelves, as in the libraries of the industrialized countries. Whatever the readers intended to borrow, they had to find the call number for in the catalog case and then go to the counter and ask the librarian to retrieve it for them. At the entrance to the library, every reader had to show not only his identification card, but also a letter of introduction from his organization. I could never forget my encounter with my factory leader when I requested such a letter.

I reverently stepped into the office of Liu Kuo-tung, the personnel manager, and said, "I need a letter of introduction from our organization, because I want to go to the Shanghai Municipal Library after work and read the back numbers of *People's Daily* published over the last several years."

Liu asked arrogantly, "You want to read *People's Daily*? What for?"

"To do some research," I said. "Also, I want to verify the actual words of one of Chairman Mao's best-known instructions, the general idea of which is that we are doing something that our predecessors have never done. To quote any of Chairman Mao's instructions is a serious matter and there should not be even one mistake; therefore, I need to find out the actual words of the instruction. I remember it was given by Chairman Mao in one of the sessions of the Political Consultative Conference, but this also needs to be checked."

"You'd better ask the person who assigned you to this task to issue this letter."

"No one gave this task. I set it for myself. I want to study a certain subject."

"Don't forget that you are now doing physical labor in the factory," said Liu. "This is a golden opportunity that the Party and the people have given you to cast off your old self and to begin your life anew. Now there's not enough time for you to thoroughly remold your ideology. How do you have time and energy for other things?"

"What I am trying to do is to verify one of Chairman Mao's instructions."

"We have many copies of *Chairman Mao's Selected Works* at hand. Have you studied all of them well enough? There are many documents of the Central Committee and special features in the newspapers every day. Have you grasped the essentials of all of them? Do you mean you have no more to study and have to search out materials for yourself?"

"I don't think reading is something evil." I was annoyed. "Besides, I have the right to read whatever I like."

"What? Are you talking about rights?" Liu became enraged. "Are you getting cocky now? Don't forget that Chairman Mao has instructed you intellectuals to tuck your tails between your legs. I'm not going to issue you any such letter. It's within my power to refuse."

Apparently the personnel manager did not understand the true meaning of words such as "right" and "power," nor comprehended why reading was a necessary nourishment for the mind. This left me with the desire to take up my old job as an editor. However, I hated to return to the Chinese Classics Publishing House, where the intellectuals were most disgusting. By luck, I got the information that there was a possibility of my participating in the compilation of an English-Chinese dictionary if I returned to the publication system. I decided to strive for this job. It could, at least, give me access to the library.

The office for the group compiling the *New English-Chinese Dictionary* was set up in what was formerly the Aurora Women's College, which was on Avenue Joffre not far from my home. Members of the compiling group came from different institutions, such as the English departments of various universities, with the Translation Publishing House providing the support personnel. Organizationally, each member still belonged to his original work unit, but worked in the temporary office. As the compilers were from different work units, their relationship was on the whole harmonious, and the political atmosphere in that temporary group mild. What appealed to me most was the work itself, which was to collect words, phrases, and illustrative sentences from the original British and American newspapers and journals and transfer them onto record cards. Although most of these newspapers and journals were back numbers, to me they were like precious gems. What other job could I enjoy more, as long as I was stranded in mainland China?

In order to join that compiling group, first I had to enter one of the work units sponsoring the publication of the dictionary. Among them, the Translation Publishing House was the unit with which I had been associated for the longest time because it had been formerly the New Literature Publishing House, the predecessor of the Chinese Classics Publishing House. By then, the Shanghai editing bureau of Chung Hwa Printing Company, which had changed its name from the Chinese Classics Publishing House and had, since its establishment, been the original organization that I belonged to, changed back to its old name—Chinese Classics Publishing House—again. I had to contact the Chinese Classics Publishing House first, because, in accordance with the prevailing policy, everyone who had taken part in "fighting high temperatures" was supposed to return to his original unit rather than go to work in other places. I made it clear that I wished to join the Translation Publishing House, and at the same time I told the Translation Publishing House that I had no intention of being an editor in its main office, but wanted to participate in the compilation of the *New English-Chinese Dictionary*.

Fortunately, both the publishing houses approved my application. Under this circumstance, I was allowed to leave the factory where I had been "fighting high temperatures" and return to my original work unit, the Chinese Classics Publishing House, which then transferred me to the Translation Publishing House, which in turn assigned me to work with the compiling group of the *New English-Chinese Dictionary*. Generally speaking, transfer in China was most time- and energy-consuming, because it usually involved a lot of departments, any of which could upset the whole plan. I was lucky that the personnel manager of the Chinese Classics Publishing House, Comrade Sun, was on very good terms with Hwa Shou-yi, who understood my intent and fully

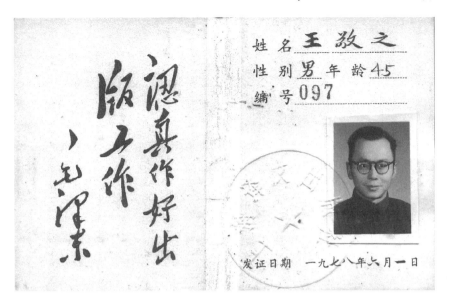

姓 名 王敬之
性 别 男 年 龄 45
编 号 097

发证日期 一九七八年六月一日

My last identification card in mainland China.

supported my application and put in a good word for me. Sun did not raise any obstacle to my transfer to the Translation Publishing House. The personnel manager of the Translation Publishing House, Ch'i T'e-p'an, was a nice person, very rare among officials of his rank. He was handsome, smart, scholarly, and professional-looking, and had nothing in common with the average personnel managers, who were just bureaucrats capable of nothing but putting on airs and playing for time. The director of the Translation Publishing House was a lady by the name of Chou Yi, who had received a good education and was amiable and easy to approach. Credit should be given to these people for my smooth transfer.

While I had the blessing of the publication system, I had to surmount the barriers of the factory and its leading unit—the Light Industry Bureau. The last incident had greatly jeopardized the relationship between the factory and me. Since their attempt to put me to death or at least to put me in jail had failed, my presence in the factory was an affront to them. This might explain why the factory did not make an objection to my application for discontinuing "fighting high temperatures." Neither did the Light Industry Bureau. However, the personnel officials in these two units were not different from those of other institutions across the country, for all of them were very efficient in making things complicated and counted time in months or years instead of in seconds or minutes. As a result, I was not able to leave the factory for good until the winter of 1977, when I started working with the compiling group of the *New English-Chinese Dictionary*.

The two years that I worked with that group were my last two years in the "freezer." The former classrooms of the Aurora Women's College were bright and clean, and the compilers from various institutions were polite to one another and totally different from people belonging to the same unit, who never trusted one another. Without intriguing against one another, it was possible to promote friendship in the truest sense of the word, and during the two years I developed several friendships which have lasted to the present.

One day in December of 1978, the anniversary of my association with the dictionary compiling group, while working in the office we were suddenly ordered to drop our work for a while and assemble in a room to listen to the radio. Just as I was wondering what was going to happen, the broadcast began to announce the Sino-U.S. Joint Communique of the normalization of relationships between the two countries. The communique was very brief, and we broke up right after the announcement. As far as I can remember, this was the first and only time in my life under Communist rule that no meeting had been held in the wake of a group listening to a broadcast. The phenomenon was as unusual as the announcement itself. Maybe just because of its uniqueness, we did not talk to one another but went back to our own desks and resumed our work right away. I sat at my desk, appearing cool, and concentrated on the newspapers in front of me, but I could not read even one word for the rest of the day. The papers before me had originally come from across the Atlantic or Pacific, and now associated my thoughts with the places they had come from. I tried to imagine what the world out there looked like, what kind of life people lived, and how they would feel if they lived under a mother-in-law-like regime. Though my eyes kept concentrating on the papers on my desk, I felt the sun outside the windows was extraordinarily bright, and this greatly excited me.

In the past several decades, whenever I had suffered, I had thought of Uncle Ramsey in the United States. Numerous times I had been so impetuous as to intend to write him requesting him to send me just an empty bottle full of air, because I was so thirsty for a breath of freedom. Through reading, I knew the United States of America also had the problem of pollution, but even polluted free air was much better than unpolluted nonfree air. While I was watching the news program on the television that very night and relistening to the Sino-U.S. Joint Communique, my nostrils almost touched the screen.

When I was released from the Civil Attack and Military Defense, which had detained me because I had intended to send Mao a letter asking to leave China, I had written another letter to Mao, and sent it by registered mail. Mao had never replied to me; he may have taken my letter with him to his mausoleum.

However, to dream the "American dream" in mainland China, especially to dream going there, made me very lonesome. I knew for sure that quite a number of people shared my ambition, but only secretly. Almost everyone, learning that I had brought my dream to the attention of officialdom, thought me crazy. I myself sometimes doubted I was really sane.

Luck finally turned in my favor. Uncle Ramsey's wife, Auntie Kay, now an American citizen, who had been very close to my mother and had cherished the desire to visit us for many years, had the opportunity to fulfill her wish after thirty years' absence. My whole family was excited. She arrived in Shanghai on January 1, 1979. While waiting in the lounge of Shanghai International Airport, we heard an official announcement from the loudspeakers that all U.S. passengers would be exempted from customs inspection, tariff, and other formalities that very day in celebration of the normalization of the Sino-U.S. relationship. As a matter of fact, it was only coincidence that Auntie Kay arrived in China that day, because both she and my family had not thought that she could benefit from that special occasion. Auntie Kay told us that before she boarded the airplane and arrived at the Shanghai airport, she had had no idea of the exemption which, as an unexpected favor, made her happy anyway. She said jokingly, "If I had gotten this information earlier, I would have brought more gifts for you."

However, this temporary measure of the customshouse straightened out my thinking. I did not care much about exemptions or gifts. What I was most concerned with was politics. This unusual way of celebrating the normalization of the Sino-U.S. relationship could not have been decided by the customshouse, but by the highest level of the hierarchy. It was a reflection of the highest leaders' sincerity about the open policy. If my analysis was correct, then to further remove suspicion both at home and abroad about their sincerity, the Chinese Communist Party would adopt a series of concrete measures to allow a number of people to leave China for the time being, but after a certain time it might tighten the issue of passports again. I could not afford to let this opportunity slip through my fingers.

The next day, while Auntie Kay and my mother continued pouring out their hearts to each other, I broke in. "Please stop shedding your tears for a moment. I have a very important matter to discuss with Auntie. I want Auntie to save my life." The whole room fell silent.

Then I said to Auntie Kay curtly, "I must leave China. I would rather die right away than stay on."

Since Auntie Kay had arrived in Shanghai, she had mentioned several times, "Ramsey and I have often thought of Yi-ling and Yi-ming." Yi-ming is my younger brother. Both Uncle Ramsey and Auntie Kay had really cared for me when I was a child. Seeing that I was in earnest, she asked in surprise, "What do you want me to do?"

"Very simple," I said, "I just need your verbal recognition of one thing."

"What is it?" Auntie asked.

"I just ask you to acknowledge that Uncle Ramsey is teaching Chinese history in a U.S. university and that now he is old and his eyesight is declining."

"Oh, no!" Auntie interrupted me. "The last thing your uncle would do is to acknowledge he is old. As a matter of fact, his eyesight is excellent and he doesn't even wear glasses now."

"I know," I continued, "I only need a pretext to apply for a passport. I want to tell them that my uncle is a professor in the U.S. and needs a young relative to help him do research in Chinese classics, but none of his children know any Chinese; therefore, he wants me to go to the U.S. to work as his assistant. I will use this pretext to apply for a passport. You can rest assured that I won't be your dependent when I get to the U.S. Besides, to tell the truth, I don't have to go to the U.S.A. I simply want to walk over Lo Wu Bridge. If I died without having ever done it, it would be my lifelong regret." I could not help shedding tears while saying these words.

Auntie Kay gave me a forthright answer, "Okay."

This was all I needed. I immediately went to the Translation Publishing House, to which I belonged organizationally. I did not have to go to work those several days, for I had secured a leave because of my auntie's visit to China. However, I made a special trip to the publishing house to talk to the personnel manager, Ch'i T'e-p'an.

I made a formal application for leaving China on grounds of helping my uncle with his academic work. At first, this personnel manager seemed a little puzzled, but was quite reasonable and sympathetic. He did not readily approve my application, nor did he show any intention to place obstacles. He said frankly that this was not a matter he could decide, but promised to report it to the leaders concerned. He told me that I had the right to apply directly to the Public Security Bureau. Again, I got what I needed. Then I went to the Public Security Bureau, got some application forms, and filled them out quickly.

The news about my application spread faster than the processing of it. In a closed society like China, serious business proceeded sloppily, but gossip about Tom, Dick, or Harry spread like wildfire. My application for leaving the country seemed to be known to the whole world within just a couple of days.

The several months during which my application was being processed proved very hard for me. Whatever forms needed to be completed had been filled out, whatever documents needed to be prepared had been finished, and whatever leaders needed to be contacted had been reached. What else needed to be taken care of? Nothing, but to wait for an answer. But when would the answer come? No one seemed able to tell me.

People around me took different attitudes. Some showed great concern for my application, while others secretly hoped it would be turned down. Most of the people thought that I was going to have great trouble, with the possibility of being labeled a monster and demon again.

One of my friends said to me, "You are really too rash in making such an application. Will they approve it? Absolutely not. Then what are you going to do? Did you ever think about that? Your application is like suicide."

What this friend said was true, but I did not mind. I said smilingly,

"Oh, I would commit suicide if I were sure I would never be able to leave this country."

What bothered me most was neither the gossip nor the terrible prospects my friend had described, but the fact that there was no way to know what was happening to my application. I was anxious to know whether it had been approved or not and when I could obtain the passport. Everything was up in the air, but I could do little. A certain man of letters once said that the most painful thing in life would be to awake from a dream only to find no place to go. In my case, my agony was that I had been to lots of places only to realize no dream.

During this period, my translation of Ellery Queen's *The Greek Coffin Mystery* was published by the Masses Publishing House in Peking, which also had just resumed business. As they needed materials and I had my Chinese translation of *The Greek Coffin Mystery* available, they accepted and published it immediately. To a society in which spiritual food had been in short supply for over a dozen of years, the book was like spring rain and became a best-seller as soon as it was published. This publishing house wanted to make a contract with me whereby I would translate Queen's other works for it. Other publishing houses in Shanghai also invited me to write or translate for them. For example, one of them invited me to translate into English the tourist guides for various scenic places in China. In this more relaxed political atmosphere, some people said that since life was getting easier and easier for me, I should not take the risk of going to live in an unknown country, and I had better withdraw my application. However, they could not shake my determination. I understood their kindness, but thought, "It doesn't matter how I am treated personally. I simply do not want to live under this system. Period."

I was greatly disturbed by the length of time it took to process my applications for both a passport and a visa. When Auntie Kay returned to the United States after a two-week visit in Shanghai, she told my plan to Uncle Ramsey, who immediately wrote several letters to dissuade me from coming to America, but it was too late, for I had already made the application.

Mail usually took about twenty days to make a round trip between China and the United States. Time and again I begged Uncle Ramsey to send me his Affidavit of Support, which was indispensable for securing a United States visa. I just could not get it, so I repeatedly had to make new explanations for my uncle's lack of support.

Six painful months elapsed. One day, the Public Security Bureau sent me a notice asking me to go to its office on a certain date. On that day I went and got my passport.

Again, news about the issue of my passport spread like wildfire. After that, life became harder for me. Whenever I encountered my acquaintances, either out of admiration or out of envy they would ask the same question, "When will you set out?" I did not know then. I was really in a dilemma.

Before I got my passport, Uncle Ramsey took a wait-and-see attitude. When I did receive it and told him that the only thing I needed now was his Affidavit of Support to get a United States visa, he flatly refused. His reason was perfectly correct. Under the United States law, anyone who was on a tourist visa is not allowed to work in the States, and in a country like the United States, which was founded on the rule of law, whoever signed an Affidavit of Support should take legal responsibility for the beneficiary. Since he did not want to take that responsibility, he refused to send me such a document.

Then I wrote him that I guaranteed that I would earn a living on my own and would not be his dependent. I also said that I myself was determined not to break the American laws, and in case I could not stay in the United States legally I would go to any desolate island and would not cause him any trouble. I even promised that if he did not feel comfortable with my stay in the States, I would be willing to stay in Hong Kong instead, and that all I wanted was to leave China. It did not matter whether I lived in America or Hong Kong.

In reply to my appeal, Uncle Ramsey reprimanded me for my insincerity. He said that as people all over the world sought to come over to the States, he was incredulous that a person who had got a United States visa would not come to the United States. He pointed out that I would have no promise of a future in the States and that under that circumstance he would have to take responsibility for all my expenses. He wrote in his letter, "It is not feasible that I should be encumbered with your dim prospects. No way. If you really want to come here, wait until you get an immigration visa." As we wrote back and forth a few times, another several months passed. I was at my wits' end.

Heaven never seals off all the exits—there's always a way out. Two of my mother's friends, who were sisters and had resided in the United States for years, had started to contact my mother by this time. Though both of them had known me when I was a child, I hesitated to request a favor of them, because they were not my relatives. It did not seem proper to ask them to be my sponsors. Besides, I had had no contact with either of them for three decades. However, since I was at the end of my tether, I was resolved to take a chance and took the liberty of writing both of them a letter to feel my way. I honestly told them the situation I was in, and asked if they could help me. Very soon, I was overjoyed at receiving their letters. Both of them expressed their willingness to help me out, then instantly took action and prepared their Affidavits of Support. As I did not need two documents, I accepted the one that arrived first and gratefully declined the other.

It was already the end of November 1979. I lost no time in going to the United States embassy in Peking, as there was no Consulate General of the United States in Shanghai. By that time, the issue of visas of the B-1 category had started to be tightly controlled and many applicants had been rejected. The consul in charge of this affair was Stephen Holder, well known for his severity to almost all the applicants or prospective applicants in China. I was quite nervous on my journey to Peking.

On the day I arrived in Peking, I immediately went to the embassy and watched what was going on from the outside, just like a general surveying the terrain before launching a big offensive. Early the next morning, before daybreak, I went there with the feeling of a soldier getting into position. I thought I would be the first to arrive there, but several people had already lined up in front of the gate. We stood and waited in the biting wind. Though it was extremely cold, I perspired.

The gate opened at long last, and they let us in and asked us to wait in the hall. I would have preferred to wait outside if I could have made a choice. The whole building was so warm that I almost suffocated. The intervening period between sitting down in the hall to wait my turn and being called into the interview room seemed to be several ages. My heart was in my mouth. I thought that I was lucky to have practiced *tai-chi* over the years and have a strong constitution and mind; otherwise I could not have stood the tension and would probably have fainted on the spot.

With my brother during a trip to Peking to get my U.S. visa.

Family photograph before I departed mainland China. Sitting in the
front are my parents and my daughter. On my mother's
side is my nephew. From left in the back: my brother,
his wife, me, Jane, and my three sons.

It was finally my turn. When I entered the interview room, I greeted
Mr. Holder by saying loudly, "Good morning, sir," to which he just
gave a polite nod. Mr. Holder did not ask the questions for which I had
prepared my answers in advance and which I had recited again and
again over the past several days. He glanced through the documents I
had submitted, saw the name of my sponsor, Professor Hans Frankel,
husband of the friend of my mother, and said, "Come back this afternoon to pick up your visa. Enjoy your trip to the United States." He did
not even take Dr. Frankel's Affidavit of Support and the letters from his
bank and his employer, Yale University, but handed them back to me.

The processing was so fast and brief that I did not have sufficient
time to relax my stiff facial expression. When I stepped out of the interview room and passed through the hall to the gate, those who were still
waiting their turn cast a sympathetic look at me, some of them sighing
softly, "Another rebuff!"

When I returned to Shanghai with an American visa, I did not have time to feel relieved, for I was very eager to leave the country. The train ticket to Canton was not easy to get. A friend of mine who had some backdoor connections helped me to get a hard-berth ticket. Meanwhile, I had to go through the formalities of my resignation and, most important of all, cancellation of my residence registration and, with it, my rations of rice, oil, cloth, and other necessities.

Saying goodbye to my family was not difficult at all. All of us had a feeling of relief. For decades, when I was downtrodden, my family suffered no less than me. Under the totalitarian regime, the categorization of anyone as a "bad element" would certainly affect all his or her relatives. As I could never compromise with Communist thought and always refused to accept my fate, there had always been a possibility that I might further offend authority. All members of my family had lived in uncertainty, in my father's words, "not even one day feeling safe." With my departure, a time-bomb was gotten rid of for them.

Epilogue

C HRISTMAS OF 1979 WAS AROUND THE CORNER when I boarded
the train bound for Canton. The Translation Publishing House
had sent a van to see me off to the railway station. This was the
first time that the regime I had served for several decades had let me use
its car. A belated favor was a favor neverthelesss, and never too late. In
fact, the approval of my departure from China by the regime was sufficient to make me feel grateful to it, and it could have given me nothing more benevolent than this approval.

I cannot recall now—as a matter of fact I did not even know then—
what I was thinking during the two days and one night on the train,
which was carrying me farther and farther away from my family in
Shanghai and closer and closer to a future totally unknown and unpredictable. Excited? Timid? Yearning for the past? Looking forward to
the future? I really did not know. All I knew was that I would not regret
it at all if I could not find an opportunity in the strange outside world
and died in an alien land, because at least I could enjoy breathing free
air there. I sat by the window all day, watching farms, villages, hills,
and rivers rush backward, and could not restrain my tears. I loved and
would forever love these familiar mountains and plains which, from
this time onward, would become very distant from me, while a foreign
land would be my permanent residence. Should I feel sorry for my
homeland, or should my homeland feel sorry for me?

In Canton, I was transferred to a train for Shan Chun which, at that time, was still a scene of desolation. I went through customs there, and finally left the territory of my beloved country, but was very happy that I could eventually wave goodbye to a system I hated so much.

Having crossed the border, I had to walk over Lo Wu Bridge before reaching the Kowloon railway station. I carried a heavy trunk and a large traveling bag in my hands and a knapsack on my shoulder. I wore a suit and heavy coat. Although it was winter, the shining sun made southern China very warm, and I perspired under the heavy coat. How I wished someone would lend me a hand! Only my dogged will kept me slogging on. At the end of Lo Wu Bridge, a peasant woman wearing a large bamboo hat with a conical crown and a broad brim came up to me. She spoke Cantonese, which I could not understand at all. From her gestures, and seeing the carrying pole in her hands, I realized she intended to carry my baggage for me. That was exactly what I wished for. But I did not know how or whether I needed to bargain a service charge with her. At this moment, I did not care about the cost. So what? The point was that I could not stand it anymore. As soon as I handed my baggage to her, she made gestures signaling me to go to someplace and said in Cantonese, *"Nei moi fei."* I could guess that the first character sounded somewhat like "you" in Mandarin, but did not understand what the last two characters meant. All of a sudden, the word "morphine" flashed through my mind.

What! She was asking me about the business of morphine! The propaganda with which I had been indoctrinated over the past decades—that the whole capitalist world was packed with thieves, whores, and scoundrels—began to act upon me at that moment.

I was alarmed. How could I meet a gang of drug traffickers when I had just arrived in this new world? I was so astonished that I felt my strength grow mysteriously. I grabbed all my baggage back and ran away as if fleeing some epidemic. I rushed to the booking office in one breath, and bought the train ticket to Hung Hom. When I got on the train bound for Kowloon, I was still shaking violently.

I did not recover from the fright until one day when some friends in the cultural circles of Hong Kong invited me to dim sum and were so amused by the scary experience I had had on my arrival in the free world that they laughed till they were unable to straighten their backs,

"In Cantonese, *moi* is equivalent to the word 'buy' and *fei* the word 'ticket.' What she was saying meant that you might go and buy your train ticket now. She meant well. What did it have to do with morphine?"

Actually, the "morphine" was conjured up out of the "thought-educating cabinet" in my former "heavenly freezer."

Adieu, the "freezer." *Adieu*, the "morphine."

I set foot on American soil on Christmas Eve of 1979. I had in my pocket only a $500 check and forty U.S. dollars cash. Forty dollars cash were the maximum amount of foreign currency allowed by the Chinese government, and the check represented the lump-sum payment for my service of more than twenty years. However, I could use the Chinese currency to purchase my air ticket from Shanghai to the final destination, which was supposed to be New York. When I arrived in San Francisco, I decided to travel to the East Coast by the Greyhound bus and save part of my flight coupon for refund, so as to get more cash, because I understood that as a visitor I would not be permitted to work in the United States, and I had to observe the American laws strictly.

Unexpectedly, I discontinued my continental bus trip at the very first stop, which was Los Angeles. There I met an executive of a big corporation who was a friend of my friend. This corporation had just begun doing business with Red China and he was in charge of that department, so he needed my special expertise and offered me a job as his aide. The company promised to hire a famous lawyer to change my visa status by legal procedures. I was only too willing to accept the offer and started working in this promised land. Ever since then, I have enjoyed my job very much and have been grateful to my boss for never having interfered with whatever I have written as a free-lance writer.

I have since been blessed by God. No more self-denunciation. No more humiliation in public. No more apprehension of being labeled as various "monsters and demons." My only regret is the problem with immigration procedures and lawyers' procrastination. Mired in the mud pit of red tapes and pettifoggery, I lost a tremendous amount of time in the legalization of my status. It took me more than a decade to obtain the pride of claiming myself a formal member of this "land of the free and home of the brave."

Postcript

W HILE I WAS WORKING ON THIS BOOK, my father devoted some time to reading the manuscript of its first several chapters. However, what saddens me is that he could not live to see its completion and publication.

In 1987 my parents came to the United States and stayed in this country for six months. During this period, they visited different places, and were very much impressed by the progress the United States had made over the past half-century, not only materially but also spiritually. Take the problem of racial discrimination. When my father obtained his doctoral degree at the Wharton School of the University of Pennsylvania in 1931, he had an opportunity to stay and work here. However, the American who offered him a job unintentionally upset him during the interview by saying, "You are really a nice and capable person. What a pity that such a talent is a Chinese!" The revelation of racial bias in his seemingly flattering remarks evoked all the memories of racial inequality that my father had been subject to during his study here, and gave him a rude awakening and hardened his resolve to return to China.

What is really a pity is that China has been a country constantly frustrating her own people. Just as a famous Chinese playwright said through the mouth of one of his characters, "You love your country, but does she love you?" In these several decades, the class discrimination prevailing in China has been much more serious than racial dis-

My first picture taken in the free world.

crimination or any kind of discrimination in any other place in the world. The ruling clique even put the concept of class struggle as the top priority of the whole nation. On the other hand, since World War II, the outside world, particularly the United States, has made tremendous advances in almost every respect.

During his last visit to the States, my father did not find the same racial discrimination which had prevailed in the first half of this century. After his return to China, he repeatedly expressed in his letters his nostalgia by hinting that he missed America very much. While I was trying to invite my parents return to the United States, my father fell ill and passed away in the summer of 1989, as did my mother five years later. This is a regret that will remain with me for the rest of my life.

With deep regret that my parents had not spent their remaining years in the United States, I readily complied with my mother's opinion

ABOVE: *My parents' grave in Westlake, California.*
REVERSE: *My calligraphy of the inscription on my parents' grave.*

that my father be buried in this country. After my father's cremation, my mother kept his cinerary casket in her bedroom for the rest of her life. She, however, had made arrangements to donate her own remains for clinical studies, and so after her funeral all I could collect was some of her hair. This I put in a casket as a mate to my father's casket, and I brought both to the United States.

But where would I find a proper location for their tombs? Traditionally, Chinese tombs are built in one's native place. For us that would have been Hangchow, and before the Cultural Revolution our ancestral

顯考妣遠葬異域志

維歲在乙亥二月十二壬寅錢唐王氏不孝子亦令與弟亦民各偕妻室率子
率孫謹奉
皇考府君諱允元
皇妣汪孺人諱一鶴之靈卜吉美國加州范卯拉郡之西湖村未問羅針算數
非經星象卦占純取其地譯意恰當故鄉之名也
府君生大清光緒三十一年歲次乙巳正月二十三日以西見乙巳之六月二
十一日壽終正寢於滬寓
孺人遲生
府君七年之正月初八遲殁五載痛於甲戌七月十七日
椿萱天年俱盡華夏奉安竟越重洋之番邦蓋有故也
府君弱冠卒業滬上高校即渡洋負笈獲博士位於賓夕凡尼大學之華頓書
院時為西曆本世紀三十年代初當有美企業擬聘業主措詞不慎直言憐君
高才惜為華人
府君怫然對曰吾以身為華人自豪也不勞憐惜遂不受邀返舊邦欲以所學
致國富強也孰料神州兵連禍結邪說紛行國既不國民漸非民空懷抱負報
國無門尋更山河巨變波瀾壯闊紅水深難測赤火熱非常鬥天鬥地人相鬥
無可樂之業無可安之居普天之下莫非公社率土之濱莫非螺釘並子若孫
咸作秦黎心力悉耗於苟全光陰盡付諸東流比及門戶乍開美置使館於燕
都亦令旋於是年之尾乘桴抵美八稔之後始得侍
親遊美
孺人固初臨斯土
府君則舊地重遊也睽違半世比境如新益惋故國之停滯逆進昔日同窗其
不返華而立足此境者皆事業成就兒孫茁長焉不能不慨歎當年忿於洋人
之乞言拂袖逕去視此地如敝屣今則欲合法久居竟比登天矣悲夫
椿萱守法唯謹旅遊簽證期滿即歸然自斯以後
府君殷望移民美國亦令亟辦手續而誤於貪庸之劣訟原庭以快速應付官
樣文章者也渠竟蓄意延宕以詐多金時不我待不幸
府君早於亦令擠身裔籍之前二年辭此塵世悲夫
孺人最諳齎憾之深也故火化後留
靈匣於原舍弗葬中華力主在美覓土永安蓋謂
府君衷心嚮往終餘年於此邦生未遂願死應得償也亦令敬遵而遷未行一
以每赴春申省侍
萱堂返美之際已自强忍唏噓若更奉
靈匣行恐益增
母悲也又因美國墓址多擇定殊難世之選墓總在家鄉
皇祖考子莊公曾於西湖畔桃源嶺下名小方井處依
祖宗墳塋所在購地闢築營佳園以為王氏墓道建園後嘗為
皇祖妣吳太夫人啟用越二紀而逢紅衛兵亂遍興刨墳之風惡德延及枯骨
先祖妣棺木被盜骨骸無存哀哉痛哉墓園全址被占至今莫可理論叵忍把
家鄉作異鄉異鄉從此是家鄉嗟乎美國固無掠墓之虞矣入土必安矣所難
者亦令在美亦如飄萍何處是佳城能得恰與故里之名合者堪稱上選焉爰
絕猶豫然仍有為難事蓋緣
孺人嘗與
府君約人死埋藏無用何若捐供醫學研究尚可利世唯人各僅一軀耳人亦
各有其志應有權各遂己志身後之事君若先我而去我必尊君之意我若早
死於君亦乞全我之志
孺人遂與醫學院簽訂約書百年後全軀捐捨由其時隨侍在中之不孝孫峻
充任遺囑執行人亦令在美聞訊素不以獻遺體為安擬從容諫阻旋遭
府君大故天崩地坼
孺人迄未釋哀不敢議此將俟稍緩而時又不我與前歲
孺人中風後雖稍痊而語言未復不便提及遷延至客歲甲戌亦令暑期赴申
孺人命奉
府君靈匣返美僅兩閱月忽報病危亦令急飛滬已陷彌留仍堅持呼吸似有
所待也迨峻自美趨抵榻前纔一覩面即止息矣從知獻軀志定必俟約書執
行人至始釋念撒手也
慈心堅決如此不孝子又何敢妄作別想遂恭剪遺髮權代骨殖以藏
靈匣與
府君合窆也嗚呼哀哉人間大痛莫過此矣既孤矣又哀矣昊天罔極欲報無
由大可痛也
府君壯懷愛國矢志桑梓豈期數紀淒風苦雨能令心寒心死無復葉落歸根
之想甘願埋骨異鄉又大可痛也
孺人高尚志願捨軀供醫仁慈濟世亦令固知人死燭滅之喻況魂魄離體古
有速朽之說其奈不孝子孫終難克盡入土為安之責是又大可痛也已矣天
乎痛哉天乎痛哉

tombs had been in the vicinity of West Lake, near that city. Thus I was very glad to learn that not far from Los Angeles there is a community called Westlake, and out of consideration for the namesake I had my parents' remains interred at the Valley Oaks Memorial Park in West-lake Village. I composed and brushed their epitaph, summarizing the vicissitudes of their lives, which was photoengraved onto the head-stone.

Index